"In *The Resilient Pastor* we discov
fainthearted in these turbulent tim‹
future of the church. This is a must-read for pastors and anyone
who loves the church."

Christine Caine, founder of A21 and Propel Women

"If there's anything pastors and church leaders need in these bewil-
dering days, it's resilience. In this volume, respected pastor Glenn
Packiam shows us the way to resilience in every aspect of life and
ministry. If you feel embattled or discouraged or exhausted, you
will find words of hope in this book."

Dr. Russell Moore, director of the Public Theology Project
at *Christianity Today*

"I rarely know what to do with religious statistics and trends,
as they typically spell doom and are incapable of capturing the
essential factor: God. However, Glenn Packiam, a faithful pastor
rooted in Scripture and Spirit, starts in the necessary place: who
we are before God and who God is long before us. With Glenn as
our trustworthy guide, we can discern how we are to live in this
anxious yet hopeful moment."

Winn Collier, pastor, founding director of The Eugene Peterson
Center for Christian Imagination at Western Theological Seminary,
and author of *Love Big, Be Well* and *A Burning in My Bones*

"It's not hyperbole to say that this moment in history is one of
the most difficult times to be a pastor. Ever. The convergence of
global crises, political animus, and worldly discipleship has caused
pastors to question their vocation. Yet, this moment has given us
the opportunity to reimagine pastoral ministry for a new generation, which is why I'm grateful for *The Resilient Pastor*. This book
could not have come at a better time. With theological precision
and robust sociological insight, Glenn Packiam offers pastors and
churches a road map toward a much-needed resilience. This is a
resource we all need to wrestle with together."

Rich Villodas, lead pastor of New Life Fellowship
and author of *The Deeply Formed Life*

"A savvy politician once said, 'A crisis is a terrible thing to waste.' By many accounts, pastors are in crisis today, and a frightening number are ready to abandon their calling. While Glenn Packiam offers solace and encouragement to his beleaguered colleagues, he also recognizes an opportunity in the present pastoral crisis. It's a moment to reconsider what ministry and the church are supposed to be and how popular models may have led us astray. Are we really exhausted because of God's calling, or because of what we've assumed about God's calling? Aided by the latest research from Barna and a spectrum of wise contributing voices, *The Resilient Pastor* should be required reading not just for those in ministry but for anyone considering a pastoral calling. Don't waste the opportunity the current crisis has created—read this book!"

Skye Jethani, cohost of *The Holy Post* podcast
and award-winning author of WithGodDaily.com

"In our generation, pastors are leading through a precarious combination of challenges. Consumerism, individualism, secularization, and polarization are a cocktail of complexity and spiritual drain. Right now, pastors like myself are as disoriented and depleted as ever, which is why I absolutely devoured this book. With wisdom, winsomeness, and brilliant expertise, Glenn answers many of the questions I have been asking and provides many of the insights I have been craving. This book is an incredible resource for pastors, and it has come to us not a minute too soon."

Sharon Hodde Miller, teaching pastor at Bright City Church
in Durham, North Carolina

"At peak moments of crisis, rays of light tend to come and break through the darkness. Now is such a moment of crisis for many pastors and ministers, and *The Resilient Pastor* is a ray of light, illuminating a healthier and more fruitful way forward for those called to lead and love in Jesus's name."

Mark Sayers, senior leader at Red Church, Melbourne, Australia,
and author of numerous books, including *Facing Leviathan*
and *Reappearing Church*

"One of the brightest and most thoughtful pastors in America turns his attention to one of the most pressing issues of our time, bringing seasoned wisdom to this cultural moment in which we find ourselves serving the Lord Jesus Christ and his people."

Pete Greig, founder of 24-7 Prayer International and author of *How to Pray: A Simple Guide for Normal People*

"All pastors need a trusted guide to lead us into an unknown future, and Glenn Packiam has earned the right to be that trusted guide. Glenn is a pastor, an academic, and an artist, and perhaps most importantly, Glenn has displayed phenomenal resilience in his own ministry. Because of Glenn's rare skill and experience, he has forged a helpful path for us in *The Resilient Pastor*. I commend this book to any pastor looking for a hopeful way forward."

Steve Cuss, pastor and author of *Managing Leadership Anxiety*

"For many of us pastors, the last few years we've grown profoundly weary in doing good. Dr. Glenn Packiam reframes the resiliency required to address the right challenges and seize the right opportunities so that we can prepare our hearts and minds for the redemptive potential before us."

Steve Carter, pastor, podcaster, and author of *The Thing Beneath the Thing*

"The high-profile falls of various Christian leaders in recent years have shown us something we should have already known—that ministry success should be measured not by the size of our churches but by the spiritual health of those leading them. I highly recommend Glenn Packiam's book. Leaders and lay people alike will find clarity, wisdom, and encouragement for navigating one of the most difficult moments in history to be a pastor."

Justin Brierley, host of *Unbelievable?* and *Ask NT Wright Anything*

the resilient pastor

Leading Your Church in a Rapidly Changing World

Glenn Packiam

BakerBooks
a division of Baker Publishing Group
www.BakerBooks.com

Text © 2022 by Glenn Packiam
Research © 2022 by Barna Group

Published by Baker Books
a division of Baker Publishing Group
PO Box 6287, Grand Rapids, MI 49516-6287
www.bakerbooks.com

Paper edition published 2022
ISBN 978-1-5409-0310-5

The Library of Congress has cataloged the original edition as follows:
Names: Packiam, Glenn, author.
Title: The resilient pastor : leading your church in a rapidly changing world / Glenn Packiam.
Description: Grand Rapids, MI : Baker Books, a division of Baker Publishing Group, [2022]
Identifiers: LCCN 2021029293 | ISBN 9780801018695 | ISBN 9781493415267 (ebook)
Subjects: LCSH: Pastoral theology. | Christian leadership.
Classification: LCC BV4011.3 .P33 2022 | DDC 253—dc23
LC record available at https://lccn.loc.gov/2021029293

The names and details of the people and situations described in this book have been changed or presented in composite form in order to ensure the privacy of those with whom the author has worked.

In all illustrations, data has been rounded to the nearest whole number, and therefore percentages may not total 100.

Published in association with The Bindery Agency, www.TheBinderyAgency.com, and The Denzel Agency, www.denzelagency.com.

Baker Publishing Group publications use paper produced from sustainable forestry practices and post-consumer waste whenever possible.

22   23   24   25   26   27   28   7   6   5   4   3   2   1

To *Sophia, Norah, Jonas, and Jane*,
who are growing up with pastors as parents:
You have embraced our challenges,
shared our burdens, and multiplied our joys.
May God make your light radiant and your faith resilient.

contents

foreword

t's hard to remember a time when being a pastor has been more challenging.

When we zoom in, we see that recent events—a global pandemic, digital worship, racial and social unrest, deep political polarization, and more—have greatly intensified the obstacles to forming human beings in the way of Christ. The disruptions of 2020 and beyond still ripple through the religious and social landscape. For pastors, things are unlikely to snap back to a sense of "ministry as usual."

And if we zoom out, we see the recent turmoil merely added to the massively shifted landscape that pastors already faced *before the pandemic*:

- Social norms and perspectives edging further toward secularism.
- A growing indifference toward Christianity, especially among Millennials and Gen Z.
- Increasing perceptions that orthodox Christian faith is extremist and wrong.
- The credibility gap facing pastors, in which they're viewed primarily as service providers for marrying and burying but not as leaders who have much more to offer.

- The promise and peril of ministry in the digital age, where attention spans are stymied and alternative sources of advice and authority grow like weeds. (The Gospel According to YouTube essentially is feeding those who seek whatever it is the algorithms can serve up.)
- The generational gaps that make ministry to Millennials and Gen Z equal parts vexing and more perplexing—and rewarding when it's done well.

All of these zoomed-in and zoomed-out trends—and many more—add up to a unique set of challenges facing pastors. Pastoring has never been easy, but it's much more difficult today. After one of the hardest, most bizarre years of ministry, Barna conducted our research for this book in the spring of 2021 and learned that 29 percent of pastors were giving serious thought to quitting.

Christian leaders need hope and a way forward, even those who haven't considered throwing in the towel. This incredible book, *The Resilient Pastor*, by my friend Glenn Packiam, helps pastors and future pastors consider the current landscape and issues a clarion vision of what the church must do to navigate eight major shifts swirling around us.

Because we wanted this Barna book to be *about* pastors and *for* pastors, we figured it was only natural to be *written by a pastor*. Glenn Packiam came immediately to mind, and he was our team's first choice. I met with Glenn over coffee in Colorado Springs at the beginning of 2020—just a few weeks before the coronavirus would massively alter the trajectory of church-based ministry—to ask him to consider writing the book you're now reading.

He prayerfully considered it and said yes!

I am grateful, and I hope you will be too, as you read his sparkling prose, fresh analysis, and hopeful vision for the future of pastoring.

As part of this book project and alongside Glenn's direction, Barna conducted brand-new research that explores the current state of pastors. I expect you'll be surprised, humbled, stirred, and inspired by the data among leaders who share the same heartbeat for the transforming message of Jesus.

At Barna, it's been a privilege to serve pastors since 1984, when George Barna began his pioneering work focusing on equipping church leaders. Barna Group has interviewed and listened to more pastors than any other research firm in the U.S. Through our research, we aim to be an accurate and helpful voice for pastors and leaders by allowing you to share your opinions and views, hopes and fears for the benefit of your fellow l eaders.

We care deeply about your health, well-being, effectiveness, and perseverance—you becoming and remaining a resilient pastor!

As you start this book, here are a couple of observations. First, in 2 Corinthians 11:28, Paul writes that he has the "daily stress" of the churches. As a church planter and apostle, he describes his concern and anger over the condition of the Jesus communities he's tending. Lots of things are going right, but he also says he is "furious" when someone is led astray. The context of the passage suggests that Paul considers the emotional strain of caring for the resilience of these churches to be at least equal to the strain of all of the life-threatening situations and conflicts he's endured.

This reminds me that being a resilient pastor does not mean we get to pack away our emotions or concerns. The church is worth our godly agitation, ambition, and urgent prayer and action. Resilient leaders, in other words, must be filled with realism about the actual, tangible, brutal reality of leading the church and forming people into Jesus's image.

The second perspective I'd like you to consider as you begin is this: in addition to realism, resilient pastors must be anchored to hope. Hope in the Lord's work in the world. Hope in a God who knows us and hears us. Hope in the reality of a resurrected Jesus. Hope that all this work and effort and toil really does amount to something both here and now and in eternity.

Resilient pastors hold realism and hope in beautiful tension.

I hope you discover both these themes, as I did, in *The Resilient Pastor*. For Glenn, for me, and for both our teams, our prayer is that this book refires your imagination and energy for a new, fresh, Spirit-driven season of ministry.

Come, Lord Jesus!

David Kinnaman
President, Barna Group
Ventura, California

prologue

Dear Pastor . . .

know you're tired. You've taken some hits, but you've kept on going. Perhaps you've been misunderstood and maligned and have made a few mistakes of your own.

But here you are. You've picked up this book. Weary as you might be, you are trying to grapple with the obvious fact that the pace of change in the world has accelerated. Maybe it sparks your own anxiety or insecurity, but you've got to face it. You want to last, to be faithful, to be *resilient*.

The last thing any of us needs is a condescending lecture about how unready we are for the new world. We don't need a futurist predicting trends and forecasting the demise of the church. We don't need a list of qualities we surely don't have or descriptions of a pastor we could never be. We don't need theories or hypothetical proposals drawn up in libraries or academic towers.

We need sages to guide us and mentors to speak to the moment. Pastors need a pastor too.

But there are times when a student might be better than their teacher. That's what C. S. Lewis wrote in the preface to his *Reflections on the Psalms*. "The fellow-pupil can help more than the master because he knows less. The difficulty we want him to explain is one he has recently met. The expert met it so long ago that he has forgotten. He sees the whole subject, by now, in such a different light that he cannot conceive what is really troubling the pupil; he sees a dozen other difficulties which ought to be troubling him but aren't."[1]

I write here as a schoolboy, not an expert. I write as a fellow student along the way. I write as your friend, your peer, your colleague and cheerleader. The pastoral vocation is holy—it is wholly other, a sacred calling that cannot be codified or copied. Pastors need a space for pastors to talk to one another, to question our assumptions and explore new perspectives. This book is an invitation to think out loud together.

This is not a manifesto. There are no prognostications about the future, no predictions about trends, and no easy steps to success. As we explore some research, mine the wisdom of church history, and let our roots go deeper in the soil of Scripture, we might gain some light for the journey. This book is a way to add my candle to yours as we step together into a world that is known and yet unknown, familiar and yet uncharted.

Above all, this book is written to give you hope. Hope is the spark of resilience. I have a framed quote from John Wesley that sits in my office, a gift from a dear friend and colleague at our church, Jason Jackson, that says, "Best of all, God is with us." That's what I want echoing in your heart as you read this book. *Best of all, God is with us.*

We're going to take a whirlwind tour in the first chapter of the shifting cultural trends. But be of good courage, Jesus is with us.

When we explore the challenges facing pastors and the churches we lead, remember that Jesus is the shepherd of your soul and the head of the church, and he is with us.

When we lift our heads in the epilogue to consider the reasons for hope, we remember that there are others who are traveling with us.

The church has been through the fire and the storm, walked through darkness and desolation, and has been renewed and purified through all of it. We have a great cloud of witnesses who have gone before us. Our calling is sure, our future secure. And best of all, God is with us.

That is why I believe by the grace of God we can be resilient pastors.

A Gradual Awakening

Maybe you don't see yourself as a pastor. I didn't always think of myself as one. In fact, my sense of calling as a pastor was a gradual awakening. For much of my adolescence and in young adulthood, I never imagined myself a pastor. I hardly expected to become one. Not because I did not esteem the profession. On the contrary, I held it in such high regard that I did not think myself worthy of it.

My parents were pastors. My mum has the gift of teaching, my dad of exhortation. Both of them were well-practiced in the care of souls. Our home was always buzzing with people, a motley collection of folks from church or work or the neighborhood—family, friends of a friend, friends we had not yet met. My mum was always ready to cook up a feast. My dad would sit with people who had been broken by the hardships of life and weep with them and pray for them. Sometimes he'd empty his pockets for them. Ministry life was personal and relational and sacrificial. I never thought I could care for people like they did. But then, somewhere in my midtwenties, I realized another way of looking at it: I had been preparing for pastoral ministry my entire life.

When I was eight years old, I sat on the floor of a retreat center in the highlands of Malaysia, listening to an American missionary lady tell a story about David Livingstone. In spite of what we now know about Livingstone and his weaknesses, in that moment, the hagiographical version was what God used to stir something in my soul. I responded to her altar call with tears streaming down my face, surrendering my life to be a missionary in Africa. That calling, though I didn't fully understand it then, was a symbolic calling. My yes was an act of yielding my life to God's service, whatever shape it would take.

When I moved to America for the second time, I was seventeen. We had lived in Portland, Oregon, for three years—for me, ages ten through thirteen—while my parents went to Bible college and my sister and I attended our church's Christian school. Having returned home to Malaysia, where I completed my high school through a kind of homeschool extension of the Christian school in Portland I had attended, it was now time to think about college. It made the most sense to think about colleges in America. I didn't know too many Christian colleges, and finances were a challenge. So when the doors opened for me to attend Oral Roberts University in Tulsa, Oklahoma, with some scholarship help, I took the opportunity. I knew I wanted to study theology, but I also wanted to be involved in music. And I was sure that I didn't want to be a pastor.

After graduation, I took a job at ORU for a year as the worship leader for chapel services. Then came invitations to work at various local churches. It seemed like the right next step, but I was unsure. My youthful idealism and vain ego had imagined being a touring artist or a traveling speaker. But to be planted in one local church . . . *Could I really do that?* New Life Church settled the question.

The first time I visited New Life, I wept during the entire worship time. There were flags from the nations hanging from the ceiling; the teal carpet and matching teal chairs faded to the background as the music transported me to a deep encounter with the Lord. I knew there was something special about this church. I remember saying to a friend shortly after that I wanted to live in Colorado Springs just so I could attend New Life. It would be a base of sorts for my itinerant music and teaching ministry. In hindsight, I realize that the Spirit was just setting the hook. Here I am, writing this over twenty years after my first day of work at New Life Church. I never thought I'd be a pastor, but God knew better.

I began my time at New Life as an apprentice to the worship pastor, Ross Parsley. Wherever he went, I went. If he was doing a hospital visit, I was doing one too. If he was singing at a funeral, I was the piano player. It was a great way to be a fly on the wall for the various meetings and moments that make up a pastor's day. He was and is a spectacular pastor, a true shepherd who cares for the flock.

My calling to pastoral ministry was a gradual awakening, but the final clarity came like the loud buzz of an angry alarm clock. In November of 2006, the founding senior pastor at New Life Church, Ted Haggard, had been caught buying drugs from a male prostitute. And while there are disputes about what else did or did not occur, the events led to his resignation and a remorseful letter of repentance to the church. I, a young twenty-eight-year-old staffer, was devastated. How could this be true? And yet, it became the catalyst for rethinking what pastoral ministry is actually about and what a church is meant to be. I had been so excited about our national influence and how I had benefited from it as a young worship leader and songwriter who was on a record label with his friends. But why did those things mean so much? How had I confused the American dream of success with the actual blessing of God? It spurred a spiritual awakening in my own heart.

In the months that followed, my focus became less on the failures of a leader and more on the condition of my heart. What pride and vanity were tainting my work? How had God become a means to my ends, the agent responsible for making my dreams and aspirations come true? I embraced the sobering and slow work of surrender. The eight or nine months between the founding pastor's departure and the arrival of a new senior pastor were difficult. Ross Parsley stepped up as the interim pastor in a remarkable way. He led with courage and compassion. He helped us lean into our roots of worship and prayer. The church survived by God's grace.

Our new senior pastor, Brady Boyd, arrived in the summer of 2007 and helped us heal. Then, one hundred days into his time, a gunman came onto our campus and opened fire in the parking lot, taking the lives of two teenage girls. As he entered the long hallway at the east end of our campus, he began shooting randomly. He was apprehended by a volunteer security team member before taking his own life. Tragedy reopened the wound of trauma. Yet with a steady hand and a gentle heart, Pastor Brady shepherded us through it. He kept us focused on Jesus, encouraged us to care for one another, and even brought in a team of counselors for our staff to get the help we needed.

Through scandal and shooting, my own calling as a shepherd came into focus. I didn't want to be a public figure or an itinerant speaker, holy as those vocations can be. *I wanted to be a pastor.*

When Pastor Brady came, he gave everyone who had been on staff seven years or more a sabbatical. Mine was six weeks. It was the longest consecutive time off I had ever received. While we were away, my wife, Holly, and I read a few books by Eugene Peterson on the pastoral vocation. The main one was *Under the Unpredictable Plant.* I'll share more about how reading Peterson deeply affected us later in this book, but for now I'll just say it woke us up. *This* was what God was calling us to be: pastors rooted in a particular place, paying attention and calling attention to God at work in that very soil. All my notions about being a missionary or a musician, a speaker or a teacher, coalesced in one clear vocation. *I am a pastor.*

How This Book Came to Be (and What It Aims to Be)

There are many books that deal with the vocational vision of pastoral ministry, what a pastor truly *is* or is called to be. And there are other books that forecast a future for the church, a prediction of the gathering storm. There are others still that seek to articulate a biblical theology of the church in fresh language for our day. Though this book will contain elements of each, none are descriptions of what this book is meant to be. Perhaps I should tell you the story of its genesis.

In February 2020, David Kinnaman, president of Barna Group, texted me to say he was coming to town and wanted to see if I had time for a chat over coffee. We caught up on life and the battle his dear wife, Jill, was fighting with brain cancer. Then he presented an idea to me. Would I like to partner with Barna on a book about the challenges facing pastors in the midst of a rapidly changing world. I was honored and intrigued. I knew of the many studies they had conducted and reports they had produced in the past few years on everything from racism to digital technology, from the state of pastors to the condition of relationships and community. This project would cull insights from each of those but would feature a brand-new study of pastors that I would help shape.

My love for the blend of situational analysis with theological reflection—a method I learned during my doctoral work at Durham University in the U.K.—led me to give David an enthusiastic response. Then COVID-19 happened. It didn't take long before I realized what a significant undertaking I had agreed to. I felt in over my head. But the team of researchers at Barna are world-class. We began regular Zoom calls; they took my chapter outline and the initial notes I had made cross-referencing their previous studies and added their own notes to it. As I began writing the chapters, I discovered gaps in the existing data and began to have a clearer picture of what our new study would need to uncover. They were brilliant about wording the questions and designing the survey. We were also able to include several questions about attitudes toward pastors and churches in a new study of the general population. Both studies were complete in late fall of 2020.[2] To retain focus, we had to restrict our study to the North American context, though I suspect those reading in other parts of the world will find places of resonance.

But this book is not really about data. This book is about you and me and the road ahead. It's about our stories and our struggles, our hopes and our longings. To move beyond statistics, I hosted three focus groups over Zoom with twenty-three pastors in the U.S., Canada, and the U.K., testing my hypothesis and listening to their perspectives on the key issues. These were faithful women and men of different ethnic backgrounds, lead pastors and associate pastors, church planters and church revitalizers in rural and urban contexts. I listened and learned as I reflected and wrote.

My goal in this book is to place ancient wisdom in dialogue with current challenges and opportunities. While Barna's researchers provide an analysis of the current situation and its trends, I try to provide theological reflection, drawing on the wisdom of Scripture and church history to guide us. There will be chapters where it seems we have a clearer picture of the problem than of the solution. Sometimes naming the complexity of the challenge is enough to get us started. I try to avoid cheap, easy, one-size-fits-all solutions. In short, this is an attempt at *pastoral theology*. Reading it will require wrestling with the Spirit in the context of a group of trusted friends and peers. Perhaps a pastors' book group is the perfect way to do that.

I am convinced that the darker the world gets, the brighter the church can shine. Amid all challenges, there are opportunities hidden for pastors and for the church. By the power of the Spirit, we can be faithful for the glory of God and for the good of the world.

The book is outlined in a fairly straightforward way. The first chapter is about how the crises we've experienced have exposed *and* accelerated the shifts and trends in our culture. We'll talk about seismic shifts, resulting storms, and the debris in the aftermath. The next eight chapters, parts 1 and 2, compose the core of the book. We will name eight challenges—four facing pastors and four facing the church—and grapple with how to live faithfully in the midst of them. These crises overlap and interlock, but they are artificially separated here to aid our reflection. The final section of the book, part 3, sketches the outlines of two characteristics of a kingdom community that will be critical in the season ahead: collaboration with one another and the presence and power of God.

This book is not only for those who are called "pastor" or "reverend." It is for all who call on the Lord and want to see Christ build his church. It is for the faithful women and men who pray and serve and give, who want to participate in the kingdom coming to the earth. It is for all who are burdened by the challenges facing the church, troubled by the turbulence of our times. It is for Christians everywhere. My wish for you as you read this, dear pastor, dear Christian, dear friend, is that you will know you are not alone. You will find in me another companion for the journey, a fellow student listening and learning and growing. Above all, my prayer for you is that you will be filled with hope. Jesus is the head of his church. The Holy Spirit is at work—in us and through us. God is making you faithful and helping you become a resilient pastor.

Take a deep breath. Close your eyes in silence and prayer. Our journey is about to begin.

the shift, the surge, and the aftermath

am writing in the middle of a pandemic. The situation changes nearly daily. We keep our eyes on a dashboard for our county that reports case counts, positivity rates, hospitalizations, and deaths. We monitor headlines for the latest restrictions from local government and the counterbattles in court. All these factors and more swirl in our brains as we try to prayerfully discern what being a good neighbor means. Do we close our doors and go fully online, or do we find a way to keep gathering in person? Do we weigh physical health more heavily than emotional, mental, or spiritual health?

One of the more interesting public conversations has been about whether churches are essential to a society. Are we dispensers of goods and services? Are we optional gatherings like concerts and sporting events? Are worship services leisure activities or sacred duties? In an attempt to justify its place in monetary terms, the National Churches Trust in the U.K. commissioned an independent study of all the food banks, alcohol support groups, mental health and counseling services, youth clubs, credit unions, and after-school care that were created and are supported by churches. Their conclusions, released in 2020 when all churches in the U.K. were forced to close their doors, was that the "market value of church-based projects" was about 12.4 billion pounds a year.[1] That's one way to make the case. And yet there is no ignoring it: Christianity's influence in society has been receding.

Did the pandemic cause that decline? In one sense, perhaps. The shift online for most churches created some bad habits in church-goers. It is, after all, so much more convenient to stroll downstairs in your pj's, prop up the iPad, and stream the service while making breakfast with friends or family. Engagement is optional. The restrictions certainly caused some churches to close their doors permanently because they could not survive financially. And for others, the pandemic became the occasion for people to go "church shopping" online and switch their place of worship. Worse yet, early on, Barna reported that "nearly half of churched adults—that is, those who say they have attended church in the past six months" say they "have not streamed an online service in the last month."[2] Even among "practicing Christians, who are typically characterized by at least monthly attendance, one in three (32%) admit they have not streamed an online service during this time."[3]

But in a wider sense, the pandemic accelerated changes. It's true that things change quickly in a crisis, but it's also true that a crisis makes changes already in progress occur more rapidly. The trends toward online everything—shopping, conferencing, working, connecting—experienced major jumps in 2020. Will it hold? Are these changes cemented? No one knows for sure, but it's hard to see things returning to pre-pandemic norms. Corporate offices are questioning the need for giant campuses. Business travel to connect with clients is now being reserved for only crucial situations. Even big shopping days like Black Friday have turned into weeks-long online deals, leaving brick-and-mortar stores to wonder if they will become nothing more than distribution centers for order pickups or item returns.

For the church world, some predict that online church is here to stay not as a peripheral ministry but as a central one. Notions of "digital discipleship" meet new vocations of "online pastor," as

Facebook groups become new "venues" for worship. Others have seized the moment to repeat a waning refrain that house churches are the future and mega-gatherings are over.

In still other ways, the pandemic—in fact, 2020 itself—has only revealed the state of affairs. When we think of the past couple years, we might be tempted to describe it as apocalyptic, meaning an end-of-the-world doomsday movie. But we'd be more accurate if we meant the term the way it's used in the last book of the Bible. St. John's Revelation is an *apocalypse*—a revelation not of end-times events but of the forces at work in the world.

When you consider the church's response—late or lackluster—to issues of racial inequality and justice, the Christian voice is to some like the drone of Charlie Brown's teacher. *We don't really know what you're saying or why it matters.* Worse, for many who have left the church, the evangelical response to the revelation of racism is seen as a reality-denying perpetuation of the status quo—one that looks suspiciously like it's trying to protect the structures that enshrine privilege and power for a White majority culture. Then there was the 2020 presidential election in America. White evangelicals and their support of Donald Trump became a topic of national conversation, with some assuming Christian nationalism as the cause and others pointing to abortion and religious liberties as the reason. To be a Republican was to be cast as a racist; to be a Democrat was to be assumed a socialist or a Marxist. Some tried to claim that the only Christlike way was to vote against Trump, hoping to reclaim their faith from the mire. The voices got louder and the divisions ran deeper. And the revelation became clearer.

Whether the pandemic has been the *instigator*, the *accelerator*, or the *revealer* of cultural shifts, the change has been tectonic: Christians are seen as irrelevant at best, dangerous at worst.

Shifting Tectonic Plates: Post-Christian?

The day after Christmas 2004, an earthquake registering at a magnitude of 9.1 shook the floor of the Indian Ocean. It propelled a massive column of water toward beaches in Thailand, Sri Lanka, and Indonesia. One Indonesian city, Banda Aceh, closest to the earthquake's epicenter, was completely engulfed by a one-hundred-foot mountain of water, which arrived a mere twenty minutes after the earthquake. One hundred thousand people were killed instantly. Buildings were leveled and cars and trees were swept off by the surging rapids. That bleak December day, over 230,000 people in several different countries were killed. It was the deadliest tsunami in recorded history.[4]

For decades now, cultural commentators and religion scholars have been talking about a shift in countries that were shaped by Christian impulses. Whether in Europe or in North America, the plates deep beneath the surface have been rattling and shaking, disrupting centuries-long norms. A few decades ago, many were referring to the dawn of "postmodernism."

Today, many are referring to a "secular age." The meaning is not necessarily clear. Canadian philosopher Charles Taylor sees a secular age not as one in which God has been removed from the equation. That would be a "subtraction story." No, ours is a secular age because faith is no longer the default position. God was first pushed to the margins—a supernatural being whom you dealt with only on issues related to the afterlife. Once God became irrelevant to daily life and the material world, belief in God became a kind of *providential deism*—trusting a distant god for general provisions and cosmic order but not much more.[5] That too could be dismantled by science and technology, or at least pushed further away from the field where life occurs. If life is compared to a football game, God is up in the sky, the retractable roof is closed, and he has no bearing on the game on the field.[6]

Meaning, then, is made by individuals and their experiences and expressions. It is all *existential. I need to do what is good for me, what makes me happy, what helps me reach my goals.* But the individual is "cross-pressured," with currents pushing from all sides.[7] Belief in a deity is not only not a "given"; it is contested.

This is why some people say we are living in a post-Christian world. But that phrase, *post-Christian*, may be misunderstood.

The term seems to imply that the world was once "Christian." That is certainly not true. Stories from the history of empires and exploits can testify to the falsehood of such an assumption. It can also sound as if Christianity and its influence are gone or have been erased. This too is untrue. Examples from daily life may be summoned as witnesses.

It may be more helpful to say *post-Christendom*. Christendom is a kind of mashup between *Christian* and *kingdom*. It speaks to the connectedness and symbiosis between Christianity and country that resulted in a prominent *presence*, pervasive *influence*, and at times even total *dominance* of Christianity in a culture. Ideals, morals, motivations, and more were shaped by Christian texts and traditions. To say we are "post" that is not to say Christian presence or even influence is gone, but its dominance certainly is. And the influence is tapering even while remnants of its presence remain. There is a fission between Christianity and culture, and still they move toward each other with a kind of residual magnetism. This push and pull creates its own friction. The tectonic plates on which many Western societies were built have shifted.

The Surge: Pluralism, Paganism, and Individualism

The oceanic waters have swelled and are surging toward the shores. It's taken years—not minutes and hours—but the effects are arriving. As you'll see in the chapters ahead, pastors are no longer perceived as a credible voice or a trustworthy source of wisdom on much. Churches don't have much of a role in a community unless they can provide tangible help or practical care. And people aren't likely to turn to a church for help when facing difficulties or crises. In fact, Christianity is just *one* way of making meaning of this world, and it isn't really even a respected way. For many, it is archaic and outmoded, prude and rude. *Sure, millions of people claim it as their identity, but how strange that is!* As David Kinnaman and Gabe Lyons demonstrate in *Good Faith*, Christians are seen as "*irrelevant* and *extreme*."[8] There are other ways of motivating yourself toward goodness and kindness and love.

And other ways of defining those words too that are less restrictive and far less judgmental of others. Spirituality and morality, vaguely defined, can be clear enough to provide you with a target and to mark you off from others but blurry enough to prevent you from pronouncing judgments. Post-Christendom is still not nearly specific enough as a descriptor for our age. There are other terms we can use, like lenses in the eye doctor's office, to bring the picture into focus. Here are three terms that help us identify the surging waters.

Pluralism

Some have compared the world in the West to the kind of religious pluralism found in Asia. There are resonances for sure. And the missionary mindset for the church—as Lesslie Newbigin notably advocated—is certainly on the mark. But today's pluralism is different. I grew up in a religiously pluralistic culture in Malaysia. The friends I rode the bus to school with every day were Hindus, Buddhists, and Muslims. And there might have been a Christian or two. The boundary markers between religions were well-defined. A Hindu friend might come to my house for a birthday party and even to a youth group function, but they could never actually go to church on a Sunday. And were a Buddhist or a Hindu to pray the sinner's prayer, they could certainly not get baptized. That would be a step too far and a great shame on the family and on their ancestors who were always watching somehow.

If you were to tell a Buddhist or a Hindu in Asia that their religions are essentially the same, they would laugh (if they were kind) and tell you that you don't understand these ancient religions. If you told a Muslim in Malaysia that they are not so different from a Christian, they might never speak to you again. Contrast this with Western Buddhism, which sounds like repackaged Hinduism, and is cloaked in Christian language. I once heard a prominent writer describe himself as a sort of Catholic-Buddhist and speak of his dark fiction works as a quest for redemption. Redemption, however, is not in the lexicon of Buddhist belief.

This new pluralism is the manifestation of Western arrogance. Empires from the West once moved slaves from one country to another to provide a labor force for their enterprises or an army for their exploits. These imperialistic impulses echo in the way the post-Christian West steals what it likes and marries it to what it wishes. We will take a little here, transplant it over there, mingle it with some of this—whatever suits our fancy and achieves our ends.

Today's pluralism is also different in its general attitude toward all religions. In the wake of 9/11, religious fundamentalism is singled out as a dangerous influence in the world. Rather than examine whether Islam is a particular seedbed for terrorism, *all religious fundamentalism* has become suspect for its potential to produce *fanaticism*. Thus, as Gene Edward Veith writes, "Before, all religions, in elite opinion, were considered to be equally good. Afterward, all religions were considered to be equally bad."[9] The antidote to fundamentalism is a kind of religious pluralism that more closely resembles *polytheism*. Where the old pluralism meant the view that "different beliefs and traditions were allowed to exist side by side," the new pluralism means that you "must accept all of these deities and religious traditions, but you are not allowed to believe in one of them only."[10] The new pluralism has no place for exclusivism.

In sum, the new pluralism is *imperialistic* and *polytheistic*.

Paganism

The eclectic approach to faith today—stitching various conflicting religious systems into one patchwork quilt of society—has led others to compare our cultural context to the paganism of ancient Rome. Religions in the ancient world were important for keeping the fabric of an empire together, but they were essentially private rituals that had little bearing on how one lived. Cultic practices in a local temple may have been strange, but that was all it was: an act or an event necessary to appease the gods and obtain favor for a harvest or a war or for the attempt to have children.

The key to the parallel, however, is not in the rituals but in the worldview. Paganism is about a sacred earth without a transcendent heaven. The gods are material and substantive, close at hand, and perhaps even shaped by our hands. In paganism, the rules are clear: offer these sacrifices for these outcomes. The gods become agents of human wishes.

The comparisons now become clear. Our society has the same pursuits of money, sex, and power. The gods that can deliver them to us are technology, commerce, and politics. Paganism is not simply about fragmented religiosity; it's about placing agency in human hands. The gods are not up there; they are down here. And you can make transactions with them.

The chief effect of the new paganism is therapeutic.[11] It gives us the veneer of a meaningful life—complete with rules and rituals—without the sting of a sovereign deity providing moral clarity or making claims of how we should live. Where the old paganism was about peace for the empire, the new paganism is about solace for the soul.

In sum, the new paganism is *transactional* and *therapeutic*.

Perhaps the main differences, however, between the new paganism and the old are that now the gods are not visible and the rituals are not public.[12] This leads us to the third and final lens.

Individualism

Charles Taylor describes the rise of "expressive individualism" in the "age of authenticity," where the definition of human flourishing is to be your truest and fullest self, and the highest good is the freedom to pursue becoming that. Andrew Root describes the progression as Taylor argues it: "The pursuits of flourishing had shifted from keeping the devil in the woods, to keeping the machines of urban America moral, to me being happy, flourishing in my own individual life project."[13]

Individualism is first about the exaltation of the self as the source and goal of "goodness." You are holy, divine, and sacred, and the freedom to unleash that being within, to express your truest self to the fullest, is the equivalent of eternal life. It works like a religious system except that it has no real interest in involving others.

And that is the second dimension of privatism—not simply the *exaltation of the self* but also the *exclusion of threats and dangers*, whether from the community or from the cosmos. Anyone or anything that stands in the way of your authentic self-expression is evil. They are either to be shrugged off ("Haters gonna hate") or defeated. Hence the "evil" of fundamentalism noted above. *How dare a religious system and institution try to tell you what is and is not off-limits in your sexuality! That is oppressive!* Earlier critiques of power structures, like those of Marx, are reformatted and re-aimed at *anything* that seeks to limit or restrain an individual's quest for self-actualization and fulfillment.

It's not just being self-boundaried from others; it is becoming a general way of seeing ourselves as what Charles Taylor calls "buffered": the "new sense of the self and its place in the cosmos" is "not open and porous and vulnerable to a world of spirits and powers."[14] Taylor tracks this as a development that came along with the disenchantment of the world. It isn't simply that the roof to the heavens has been closed; it's also that we have summoned a stronger "confidence in our own powers of moral ordering."[15] We can draw our own lines and dictate our own distances from the things that we don't like or that we perceive as dangers. Taylor draws out two facets of the contrast between an older "porous self" and the new "buffered self."

> First, the porous self is vulnerable, to spirits, demons, cosmic forces. And along with this go certain fears which can grip it in certain circumstances. The buffered self has been taken out of the world of this kind of fear. . . .
>
> The second facet is that the buffered self can form the ambition of disengaging from whatever is beyond the boundary, and of giving its own autonomous order to its life. The absence of fear can be not just enjoyed, but seen as an opportunity for self-control or self-direction.[16]

The stage is now set for the third dimension of what I'm calling individualism: the move toward an *exclusively interior spirituality*.

The effects of the buffered self are that our *spiritual choices* no longer have *social consequences*.[17] It also means that we become the author of our own story's meaning, the architect of our own structures of purpose. As James K. A. Smith, summarizing Taylor, puts it, we have developed a kind of "cultural Pelagianism," the "confidence that *we* can make *this* world meaningful."[18]

This meaning-making now is interior work. It does not come from a god or a spirit. It is not out there; it is in here. The focus on an interior life is found in many religions, including Christianity. But individualism locates the center in the internal, private world of the individual. In that sense, it is like a remixed version of the old first-century philosophy called gnosticism. Veith puts it nicely in saying that "secularists are not necessarily without religion," but "what makes them secular is that their religion has nothing to do with the world."[19] Their spirituality is interior, within themselves. This indeed is "the spirituality of Gnosticism."[20] N. T. Wright, in his book from his 2018 Gifford lectures, notes that the "Gnostic believes, not in 'redemption,' but in 'revelation,' the unveiling of the true self rather than its death and resurrection."[21] Today, this sort of "low-grade Gnosticism" has become "the only orthodoxy in some quarters, where 'finding out who I really am' is the ultimate imperative, and any challenge to this project is seen as the ultimate denial of one's human rights."[22]

That was a dizzying tour of the culture, a swirl of chaos like the surging waves we compared it to.

Now for the aftermath.

The Aftermath: A Christ-Haunted Age

Beyond the Numbers

"I don't believe in God, but I miss him."[23]

This is how the British writer Julian Barnes opens his 2009 memoir of mortality, *Nothing to Be Frightened Of*. It aptly captures the cultural mood. The West is not quite ready to move on from Christianity.

Let's look at the research. The majority of Americans—67 percent—still identify as Christians. And yes, the "religiously unaffiliated," sometimes called "nones"—people who "describe their religious identity as atheist, agnostic or 'nothing in particular'"—are a concerning 25 percent of the population, up from 9 percent in 2011.[24] But can a country with 67 percent of the population describing itself as Christian be called post-Christian?

A closer look at the numbers reveals a more complicated situation. For one thing, that 67 percent of Christians is down 15 percentage points from Barna's 2011 data. Church attendance is also a strong indicator of the presence and influence of Christianity in a culture—and it's slipping. In the span of a decade, those who say they attend a church service weekly dropped from 45 percent in 2010 to 29 percent in 2020 (it was just as low in 2019), as the following chart indicates. Even for less-frequent attenders, commitment waned. Those who attend church at least once or twice a month dropped from 54 percent in 2009 to 45 percent in 2019.[25]

WEEKLY CHURCH ATTENDANCE: 1993–2020

● All U.S. adults

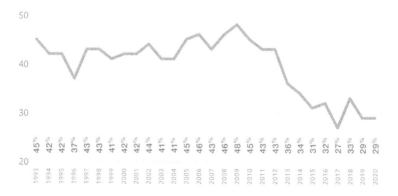

n=103,603 U.S adults, 1993–2020.

Attitudes toward pastors are, naturally, greatly tied to both church attendance and whether a person identifies as a Christian. In the new Barna study we conducted for this book, 57 percent of the general population said they at least somewhat consider a pastor to be a trustworthy source of wisdom. Those numbers rise for Christians and churchgoers. Seventy-two percent of self-identified Christians see pastors as a trustworthy source of wisdom.[26] But if you're not a churchgoer, that percentage drops to 40 percent. And if you're not a Christian, it's an abysmal 22 percent.[27] Conversely, non-Christians have the strongest reaction against pastors, with 29 percent saying a pastor is "definitely not" a trustworthy source of wisdom. That may be unsurprising in our present culture, but it is still telling and discouraging.

What about the rise of religious "nones"? Should we be concerned? Surely. Yet there are some who suggest we ought not be alarmed. Ed Stetzer wrote in 2015 that the rise is due to a move from "nominals" to "nones." "For those who have only ever considered themselves 'Christian' because they've been to church before, or because they aren't Muslim or Hindu, it is starting to make more sense to check 'none' on religious identification surveys."[28] It might make sense, but we don't want to find refuge in false comfort. I don't think we can ignore the significance of this rising segment of the population.

Then there are the changing cultural tides that come with each generation. Barna reports that older Americans (Elders, sometimes called the Silent Generation, and Baby Boomers) and Millennials differ in their levels of religious affiliation and attendance. Three-quarters of both the Elders (those born between 1928 and 1945) and Boomers describe themselves as Christians. In stark contrast, only three out of five Millennials (59 percent) and Gen Z (the youngest generation, 58 percent) identify as Christians.[29]

Gallup writer Frank Newport says these are not shifts so much as well-established generational trends. He writes:

> Generational changes in religiosity . . . happen consistently to every generation as they age and are not specific to a particular time

period or cohort. Religiosity plummets after age 18, coincident with young people leaving home and heading out into the real world of work or college. Then, religiosity begins to rise again as young people go through their 30s, coincident with marriage, children and more stable involvement in specific communities. Religiosity generally continues to rise with age, albeit with some points at which it is fairly flat, and reaches its peak in Americans' late 70s and 80s.[30]

But I'm not sure he's right. David Kinnaman and the team at Barna have been tracking faith practices of young adults for decades. Barna data on weekly church attendance by generation shows that whatever rise in religiosity there might be later in life, the relative peak seems a bit lower than it once was. Elders through Millennials have lower weekly church attendance rates than in years past.

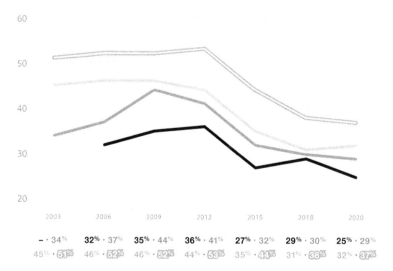

WEEKLY CHURCH ATTENDANCE BY GENERATION: 2003–2020

● Millennials*   ● Gen X   ● Boomers   ○ Elders

	2003	2006	2009	2012	2015	2018	2020
	– · 34%	32% · 37%	35% · 44%	36% · 41%	27% · 32%	29% · 30%	25% · 29%
	45% · 51%	46% · 52%	46% · 52%	44% · 53%	35% · 44%	31% · 38%	32% · 37%

n=96,171 U.S. adults, 2000–2020.
*Due to low sample size, the 2003 attendance rate for Millennials is not included in this chart.

In 2011, Barna published their discovery that "59% of young adults with a Christian background had dropped out of church at some point during their 20s—many just for a time, but some for good."[31] In 2019, Kinnaman's book, *Faith for Exiles*, coauthored with Mark Matlock, revealed that the percentage of dropouts rose to 64 percent.[32]

INCREASE IN CHURCH DROPOUTS

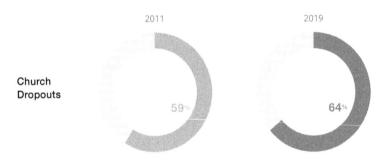

n=1,816 U.S. adults 18–29 current / former Christians, January 2011; n=1,514 U.S. adults 18–29 current / former Christians, February 16–28, 2018.

Barna's research also led them to outline four distinct categories for eighteen- to twenty-nine-year-olds who grew up Christian:

- *Prodigals* (22 percent): "ex-Christians" who "do not identify themselves as Christian despite having attended a Protestant or Catholic church as a child or teen, or having considered themselves to be Christian at some time."
- *Nomads* (30 percent): "lapsed Christians" who "identify themselves as Christian but have not attended church during the past month. The vast majority of nomads haven't been involved with a faith community for six months or more."
- *Habitual churchgoers* (38 percent): those who "describe themselves as Christian and have attended church at least

once in the past month, yet do not have foundational core beliefs or behaviors associated with being an intentional, engaged disciple."

- *Resilient disciples* (10 percent): "Christians who (1) attend church at least monthly and engage with their church more than just attending worship services; (2) trust firmly in the authority of the Bible; (3) are committed to Jesus personally and affirm he was crucified and raised from the dead to conquer sin and death; and (4) express desire to transform the broader society as an outcome of their faith."[33]

Kinnaman's analysis tells us we should not be too quick to say that the "kids are all right" (the resilient minority aside). Things are shifting, and we've got to pay attention even if we can't forecast the future.

Cross-Pressured

The complexity of this picture—a majority of Americans self-identifying as Christians, even as the percentage drops; church attendance declining; those with no religious affiliation rising; resilient disciples persisting—is part of what Taylor means by a cross-pressured age "where both our agnosticism and our devotion are mutually haunted and haunting."[34] Faith is contested, but it remains in the picture. We are "pushed by the immanence of disenchantment [think: closed-roof universe] on one side, but also pushed by a sense of significance and transcendence on another side, even if it might be a lost transcendence."[35]

The mid-twentieth-century Southern writer Flannery O'Connor called the American South "Christ-haunted."[36] That is a fitting description of many cultures in the West. The specter of the crucified Savior looms over conversations from #BlackLivesMatter to #MeToo. We might not care about victims the way we do if it weren't for the triumph of one particular victim two thousand years ago. Even many of the critiques that have been leveled against Christianity itself would not have been possible if not for

Christianity and its Christ. This is the core argument secular historian Tom Holland makes in his book *Dominion*. In an essay for *The Spectator*, Holland writes:

> Christianity had revealed to the world a momentous truth: that to be a victim might be a source of strength. . . . The commanding heights of western culture may now be occupied by people who dismiss Christianity as superstition; but their instincts and assumptions remain no less Christian for that. If God is indeed dead, then his shadow, immense and dreadful, continues to flicker even as his corpse lies cold. The risen Christ cannot be eluded simply by refusing to believe in him. That the persecuted and disadvantaged have claims upon the privileged—widely taken for granted though it may be today across the West—is not remotely a self-evident truth. Condemnations of Christianity as patriarchal or repressive or hegemonic derive from a framework of values that is itself nothing if not Christian.[37]

In fact, the notion of a human right began with canon lawyers in the 1200s. The Decretum (a compilation of church canons and teaching) concluded, "A starving pauper who stole from a rich man did so, according to a growing number of legal scholars, *iure naturali*—'in accordance with natural law.'"[38] Thus, they were not guilty of a crime. They had a human "right" to the necessities of life.[39] When the friar Bartolomé de Las Casas visited the Spanish colonies in the Americas, he rebuked Christians for thinking that they had not merely a right but a duty to conquer and "prosecute" idol-worshiping peoples.[40] Though such a view sat easily with Aristotle's doctrine that "it was to the benefit of barbarians to be ruled by 'civilized and virtuous princes,'" the Christian belief that every human had been made equally by God and had been endowed with reason made the suggestion that natives were slightly higher than monkeys blasphemy by Christian standards.[41] Thus it came to be that Las Casas coined the phrase "*Derechos humanos*"—human rights.

The great experiment of the post-Christian but Christ-haunted world is whether the fruit of justice and peace will remain when the tree of society has been severed from the roots of Christianity. Can you enjoy the fruit of Christianity—arguably, the gifts of Christendom—without the root of Christian faith and practice? To live in a Christ-haunted world is to live where (most of) the fruit of the Spirit are prized as virtues but the testimony of the Spirit that Christ is Lord is scorned.

Making Sense and Making Our Way Forward

What have we observed so far? There has been a shifting of cultural tectonic plates as many contexts have become more and more post-Christian. The clearest way to explain that in terms of the earthquake-like shift is to say that we are post-Christendom, that era when Christianity and country, the kingdom of God and a sociopolitical kingdom, were symbiotically connected. This shift—though not necessarily the total rupture of the relationship—has caused a surge in the cultural oceanic waters. These waves look like the rise of new kinds of pluralism, paganism, and individualism.

The aftermath is a mess. There are casualties—think of the programs churches would run that no longer exist, the TV shows in which Christianity was assumed as the backdrop for the family conflict, the changing laws about marriage, and more. And there is confusion. Christian impulses and values are being used to condemn Christian doctrines, practices, and institutions. The West is trying to sever the tree from its root while still demanding its fruit.

What is a pastor to do in such an age? The challenges discussed in this book are not all new. In fact, I have chosen to frame them in terms that are evergreen. We will *always* have to wrestle with our vocation, our spirituality, our relationships, and our credibility; and we will *always* have to discern how to lead our churches in worship, formation, unity, and mission. These things will always be with us. And yet, the situation is different, not perhaps unique or unprecedented—that greatly overused word of 2020. "Each day," Jesus said, "has enough trouble of its own" (Matt. 6:34). So each age has its own challenges.

My goal is to pair situational analysis with theological reflection. I'm trying to find the connective tissue between ancient wisdom—from the Scriptures and from church history—and the present challenges. But really, I'm hoping all this will provoke you to do your own situational analysis and theological reflection. Statistics alone don't tell a story. Robust empirical research requires some form of ethnography—an insider's look at how people describe things in their own words. As a pastor, you are doing this every day with your congregation. You're listening to people talk about their health challenges, political opinions, and busy schedules, and you're trying to hear the music underneath it all. Where are their fears and anxieties? What are they really hoping for or longing to find? This book is a chance for you to pay that same kind of attention to your own life and ministry. What weighs most on you? What decisions keep you up at night? What aspirations get you up early in the morning? You know the cause of the dread in your soul and the reason for the spring in your step. Think through these as you read the chapters ahead.

If you're not a pastor or don't consider yourself a church leader, think of reading this book as a kind of trust-building exercise. We're pulling the curtain back and showing you how we wrestle with some of the biggest challenges we're facing. Perhaps you'll be heartened by the honesty and the humility. Maybe by seeing the desire to be faithful shepherds in the midst of these challenges, you will find yourself willing to trust again, to put your hand back to the plow again, or at the very least, to pray more fervently for those who serve and lead the church.

It's time now to explore the challenges of pastoral ministry in a rapidly changing world.

Reflections from Dr. Russell Moore, director of the Public Theology Project at *Christianity Today*

"Why go to Sunday school, though surlily, and not believe a bit of what was taught?" asked novelist John Updike in a poem written about a month before his death.[42] The childhood on which Updike reflected was a typical one for a child of twentieth-century America. Even without belief, the mainstream American child knew the stories of, as Updike put it, the "desert shepherds in their scratchy robes."

As this chapter explains, that reality is no more—having been replaced by a pluralistic, privatized, and often disenchanted culture. In this current reality, a reference like "an eye for an eye" or "turn the other cheek" might sound as familiar as a proverb of uncertain origin, but the expectation is that the stories are not even known, much less believed. Some Christians don't take these shifts seriously enough—and think the answer is just more of the same of what worked in the 1950s, only with more enthusiasm and funding. But many other Christians take these changes too seriously—responding to a post-Christian culture with an adrenal fear expressing itself in cautious retreat or in theatrical anger.

The first-century world was quite different from our own—it was a cacophony of gods and ambitions and impulses. The gospel did not need the warm cultural incubator. Indeed, as scholars such as Larry Hurtado have shown, the "strangeness" of the Christian message—in contrast to the imperial cult or the household gods or the sexual chaos—was key to its advance. Something that could not be assumed to be a civil religion or an ancestor cult was distinctive enough that, while many walked away, many paid attention—and found, by God's grace, a light shining in the darkness.

And, as Glenn Packiam argues, when the Christian message is articulated with the clarity that comes with jettisoning the assumption that our hearers know already of what we speak and embody, the gospel addresses longings—for forgiveness, for reconciliation, for peace, for home, for life—that cannot be suppressed by a buffered self. Updike wrote of his childhood churchgoing without belief but moved quickly to write what perhaps makes the most sense to one near death:

> The tongue reposes in papyrus pleas,
> saying, *Surely*—magnificent, that "surely"—
> goodness and mercy shall follow me all
> *the days of my life*, my life, forever.[43]

A post-Christendom culture might not recognize those words as the Twenty-Third Psalm, but that doesn't mean they don't know what it is to be scared and lost and guilty and broken. And it doesn't mean there's not a Shepherd who knows how to find them in the darkest woods and who knows the way to goodness and mercy. Surely.

PART 1

Four Challenges
for Pastors

vocation

What are we called to do?

The crisis that led to the crystallization of my calling as a pastor came as I turned thirty. I knew things were beginning to shift in my life. It was time to step away from leading worship and to step toward the calling to preach, teach, and lead. I had been called a pastor as a worship leader, and I had led groups and discipled people for years in that role. I had been a pastor for eight years. But a change was coming. I knew it.

In early 2009, I was given—thanks to Pastor Brady's conviction about rest and sustainable pace—my first sabbatical. It was six weeks, but that was no small thing considering we had never been allowed to miss two Sundays in a row under the previous senior pastor. Holly and I have always tried to be intentional about our reading, but what we chose to read during sabbatical might have been the most purposeful and providential book choice yet. We read Eugene Peterson's *Under the Unpredictable Plant*. If you know the book, you know it is, as the subtitle suggests, an "exploration in vocational holiness." What we could not have known is that this book would shape our vision of the pastoral vocation in profound ways.

Peterson opens the book with a story about a crisis of vocation and faith that occurred when he was thirty. "In my thirtieth year and four years into my ordination, an abyss opened up before me, a gaping crevasse it was. . . . Who I was as a Christian was now confirmed and extended in what I would do as a pastor. . . . Then this chasm opened up, this split between personal faith and pastoral vocation."[1] I was hooked from the first page.

Using the story of Jonah as his text for this meditation on vocation, Peterson spoke with searing insight about the challenges before us. "Why do pastors have such a difficult time being pastors? Because we are awash in idolatry. Where two or three are gathered together and the name of God comes up, a committee is formed for making an idol. We want gods that are not gods so we can 'be as gods.'"[2] I began thinking about our years serving at a large church. How easily growth had become an idol! How quickly we spoke of influence and impact as if these were inherently holy things. How prone my heart was to pursue significance with an ungodly ambition.

Peterson goes on: "The idolatry to which pastors are conspicuously liable is not personal but vocational, the idolatry of a religious career that we can take charge of and manage."[3] The antidote is vocational holiness. As Peterson sees it, many pastors take personal holiness seriously but surrender their vocation to "[take] shape under the pressure of the marketplace, not the truth of theology or the wisdom of spirituality."[4] His goal in the book was to define what it means to be a pastor and then to "develop a spirituality adequate to the work."[5]

I resonated with the hollowness Peterson was describing. I knew what it felt like to be fueled by the adrenaline rush of doing "big things" for God. Now I could see that while that was fun in my twenties, it would not be enough to carry me for decades to come. My desire for or obsession with big gatherings and influential work was what Peterson would, in a later chapter, call "ecclesiastical pornography" designed to "excite a lust for domination, for gratification, for uninvolved and impersonal spirituality."[6] I needed more than a different way of seeing. I needed a different way of being, an entirely different spirituality.

> The so-called spirituality that was handed to me by those who put me to the task of pastoral work was not adequate. I do not find the emaciated, exhausted spirituality of institutional careerism adequate. I do not find the veneered, cosmetic spirituality of personal charisma adequate. I require something *biblically* spiritual—rooted and cultivated in creation and covenant, leisurely in Christ, soaked in the Spirit.[7]

Peterson's book took us by force. We returned from sabbatical *called*. Called to be *this* kind of pastor. Called to do the work in ways that were personal and local. I followed up that book with another Peterson had written, *Working the Angles*, in the same series. Once again, from the opening lines Peterson makes it clear that the situation is urgent. "American pastors are abandoning their posts, left and right, at an alarming rate. They are not leaving their churches and getting other jobs. Congregations still pay their salaries. Their names remain on the church stationery and they continue to appear in pulpits on Sundays. But they are abandoning their posts, their *calling*. They have gone whoring after other gods."[8]

The gods we have left to chase are the gods of customers and consumers. "The pastors of America have metamorphosed into a company of shopkeepers, and the shops they keep are churches. They are preoccupied with shopkeeper's concerns—how to keep the customers happy, how to lure customers away from competitors down the street, how to package the goods so that the customers will lay out more money."[9] This was stiff medicine. I would alternate between conviction and anger. He was right, but I wanted to blame someone else. I wanted to externalize my guilt by taking aim at someone else, some other church that was more consumeristic than we were, some other pastor who was more of a salesman or huckster than I was. But the weight of truth would not let me wiggle out from under it. *Was I a pastor?* I wondered.

Doing What We Don't Want to Do

Ministry life is full of administrative tasks: planning services, replying to emails, scheduling meetings, and more. And leading a team of staff or volunteers often feels more managerial than entrepreneurial. Few of us relish following up on tasks, giving and receiving feedback, or evaluating an employee pay scale. There are so many days when my colleagues and I remark to one another, "How do we ever explain to someone what it is we do?" In a single day, I can go from answering a theological question from a congregant in an email . . . to making difficult decisions with the senior leadership team . . . to lunch with a congregant grieving the deteriorating health of their spouse . . . to a slew of logistical decisions that need to be made or emails that need to be answered about various ministries and events . . . to a coaching session with key leaders . . . to attending to team dynamics and health with staff and/or volunteers . . . and cap it off with coffee with a congregant

HOW PASTORS FEEL ABOUT THEIR TIME USE

% of pastors who say "yes"

● All Pastors ● 50+ Years Old ○ Under 50 Years Old

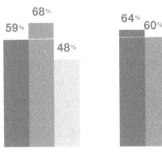

68% 59% 48%

Are you satisfied with how you spend your time during the week?

64% 60% 68%

Does your day-to-day look different than what you expected when you entered the ministry?

24% 29% 18%

Does your congregation have an accurate idea of how you spend your time during the week?

n=408 U.S. Protestant pastors, September 16–October 8, 2020.

who just needs someone to be a witness to their life with Christ. Oh, and on some days, I get to read a bit and work on a sermon.

As the world keeps moving, needs, expectations, and conceptions of a pastor change. Our 2020 study found that pastors spend about 15 hours a week in sermon prep, 7 hours a week meeting with congregants, about 6.5 hours in email or correspondence, 4 hours a week meeting with staff, another 6.5 hours a week leading services or events, and about 5 hours a week in some sort of personal development. Most of these pastors—about 59 percent—are satisfied with that distribution of time. Yet only one in four are convinced their congregation has an accurate picture of how they spend their time. People usually get the preaching bit. And they expect the counseling and guidance stuff. But they rarely comprehend the more elusive team coaching and development pieces. As my friend Pete Greig, a pastor in England and leader of a global prayer movement, remarked in a nonscientific guesstimate, "85% of my time as a pastor is spent behind the scenes building teams. Not preaching, counselling or even praying. Just quietly choreographing the space between friends, encouraging, shaping and preempting problems. This is probably not as it should be. It should probably be more."[10]

Time management aside, we also discovered that roughly two-thirds of pastors are very satisfied with their vocation as a pastor. Though interestingly, it seems satisfaction is correlated to age and experience. The older the pastor is, the more likely they are to rank their satisfaction level more highly.

When Barna pressed a little deeper, they found that the sense of satisfaction is also related to the kinds of things the job entails. In an earlier study titled *The State of Pastors*, Barna asked pastors to think about the tasks and demands that make up their weekly work and then choose a job function that best fits the description. They found that pastors who function in a responsive or reactive way tend to be less satisfied in ministry.[11]

Eighty-one percent of pastors who said they were less satisfied with their experience of being a pastor said their job felt more like a "manager" than an "entrepreneur."[12] What they mean is they enjoy the energy of inspiring vision and charting a course far more than running events and programs. In biblical terms, they'd rather be Joshua than Jethro. Eighty-nine percent of pastors who were very satisfied with their experience described their role as fitting a "leader" as opposed to an "administrator."[13]

What about the care of souls? Pastors who described a sense of fulfillment or satisfaction in ministry experience their role much more as a "doctor" than a "referee" (81 percent to 19 percent). And those who are less satisfied in their ministry describe their work as being more like a "counselor" than a "coach."[14] It sounds as though many pastors are energized by diagnosing the problem but are drained by having to be the cure.

It may be tempting to be critical of this discrepancy, to say that pastors want the easier work of pointing out problems— sins or addictions or signs of unhealth—but are unwilling or too impatient to walk with people into health. But consider the way many pastors are trained. Although 72 percent of pastors rate their ministry training as "excellent or good," only about half went to seminary, and even then, only 8 percent say that seminary prepared them very well for effective church leadership.[15] In fact, the top three things pastors wished their education—in seminary or elsewhere—had better prepared them for are "counseling burdens or solving people's problems" (29 percent), "administrative burdens" (29 percent), and "handling conflict" (27 percent).[16] In our 2020 study, the percentage of pastors who wished they had been trained in "handling conflict" and "training people" rose to about four in ten (40 percent and 41 percent, respectively), while "balancing ministry and administration" and "navigating church politics" took second place at 38 percent and 36 percent, respectively.

If you feel like an administrator or a counselor, you're less likely to be satisfied with your experience as a pastor, probably because you weren't trained for that. The role—as it has morphed into being—may be misaligned for your passion, but it's certainly ill-fitting to your preparation. Many of us don't enjoy it. We are weary from it. And it makes us want to quit.

But we don't. At least not yet. Because there *are* parts of our vocation that we love. The vast majority of pastors—roughly 97 percent—say that what they spend the most amount of time and energy on fits their sense of calling and gifting either "very well" (55 percent) or "well" (42 percent).[17] Better yet, the match between role and gift increases with age. So if you're a young pastor, hang in there. You'll learn more about yourself, and by God's grace, your church will help you step into roles that align with your gifts and passions. When the role is not a good fit, unsurprisingly, the burnout risk is high.[18]

What is it that pastors think they do well? What has their training prepared them for? Here are the top three areas in which pastors think they are "excellent": "preaching and teaching" (57 percent), "knowledge of Scripture" (48 percent), and "practical or applied theology" (42 percent).[19] When it comes to knowing the Bible and theology and sharing that knowledge, pastors shine. And why wouldn't we? It's what our training and education prepared us for. And, arguably, it's what drew us to pastoral ministry in the first place.

When I asked the pastors in my focus groups what they felt most and least prepared for, most of them responded in ways that confirmed the statistics. They were ready to preach and teach, but there were numerous organizational elements they were not prepared for. Sally, an assistant pastor in Kentucky, said she had not expected how much of her role would essentially be "event planning . . . administrating and planning events that are important to the life of the church. . . . Should I be setting up the catering or praying?" she joked. Dan, a senior pastor in the Dallas area, said the administrative and business side of things had been a burden particularly when he had worked as the sole pastor in a different region of the country and had to deal with a church building that had burned down.

Felicity shared the challenges of pastoring in rural Kentucky: "I have felt least prepared for helping my aging congregations navigate a changing culture where the church is no longer the center of the community."

Phil, a pastor in Canada, chose something a little different. "How to deal with critics," he said wistfully, "the people who put down your preaching." Two female senior pastors in my focus groups also described the hurdles their gender created for people who had different ideas of gender roles in the church. Alice, a pastor in the North East of England, said she had to learn to be herself: "God used me most when I was myself. I had to stop being apologetic about the gifts I had, even though I didn't fit the mold."

The vocational crisis facing pastors seems to be a *crisis of alignment*: our calling matches our passion and preparation but not the job itself or the expectations of the congregation. In a twist of Paul's words in Romans 7, we find ourselves doing the things we do not want to do and not doing the things we want to do. With our tongue placed firmly in our cheek, we might ask, "Who shall save us from the body of Christ?"

A Pilgrimage to Kalispell

Eugene Peterson compared the pastor's job to a triangle. The obvious and most visible elements of a triangle are the three lines or sides. These, Peterson said, correspond to the three most visible parts of a pastor's job: preaching, teaching, and administration. Based on Barna's research in *The State of Pastors*, it seems safe to say that pastors feel the best about two sides of Peterson's ministry triangle—preaching and teaching—and are troubled by how large the administrative side is. Yet the lines are not what make a triangle a triangle. A set of three lines could be arranged in any way. It is the *angles* that give a triangle its shape. The "angles" that give pastoral ministry its shape are prayer, study, and spiritual direction. As I was reading Peterson's words for the first time, I didn't know if any other pastor felt as I did. All I knew is that I was bent in the wrong shape.

Reading Peterson was messing with me. It made me want to walk away from all of it—my friendships, the congregants I knew and loved, and the city I lived in. In late 2009, Daniel Grothe, my friend and a colleague at New Life, wrote to Eugene Peterson about a visit and received a positive reply.[20] Encouraged by Grothe's bold-ness and Peterson's graciousness, I decided to write a letter of my own, but my letter contained a note of confusion. I told him that his books had left me wondering if I could be *that* kind of pastor in *this* kind of church. And I asked if he would be willing to talk more. Perhaps I could visit. I had heard that he and Jan did that sort of thing. He wrote back, gracious and generous, and said yes.

In the summer of 2010, I made the trek to Kalispell, Montana, with another friend and colleague, Aaron Stern. We spent three days and two nights in the Peterson home. Three meals a day to-gether. Long talks in the day and into the night. Laughter. Long silences. Space to journal and pray. Kayaking. Jumping in the frigid Flathead Lake with The Pastor himself. And finally, prayer together before we left. These are the fragments of a holy time, moments too monumental to be documented in a banal recounting of events. I will never forget those three days.

We went there with questions: What is a pastor, *really*? Can we truly live out the pastoral vocation in our current context—a megachurch? Were we really pastors? Eugene and Jan helped us with each one.

In answer to the first question, they helped us recognize a pastor as one who pays attention to God at work in the particular people and the particular place that God has called them to. Pastoral work is local and personal. And slow.

As for the second question, Eugene reminded us that there is no perfect context in which to be a pastor. The denomination he had served in was not a full representation of his own convic-tions and values. It had its own messes and missteps. For much of his own ministry, Eugene felt like a misfit, unsure of where he belonged, neither Presbyterian like his church nor Pentecostal like his mother. There were many times he tried to leave the church he was pastoring, drawn by thoughts of bigger cities or more stimulating contexts. And yet, he found a way to live, to stay, and to work with vocational holiness.

The beauty and mystery of how God speaks to people in encoun-ters with sages and saints is that two people can spend time with the same individual and walk away with clarity that runs in two different directions. That's what happened with Aaron and me. Could we live out the pastoral vocation in the context we were in? For Aaron, the trip was the catalyst for his realization that God was calling him and his wife, Jossie, to plant a church in Fort Collins, Colorado. For me, it was confirmation that I needed to stay at New Life. I was leading a Sunday evening service at the time, and Pastor Brady had given me the trust and authority to shepherd those people well. Aaron had a similar setup with the college and twentysomethings ministry, but he felt it was time to lead something new.

The final question was the most crucial: *Were we really pastors?* Or had our context malformed us? Had the past events at our church stained us? Had we drunk too deeply of the elixir of growth and significance, impact and influence, to be sober-minded about the unglamorous life of pastoral work? Throughout the course of our three-day visit, we had begun to sense that God had indeed called us to this kind of life and this kind of work. But the confirmation came from dear Jan in our final moments in their home. After we finished praying over each other, she looked up, misty-eyed, and said, "You could be *my* pastors." That was all we needed.

Cuthbert's Call

One night, a young boy in Scotland was out in the hills tending to sheep. A bright light began moving across the expansive northern sky, and the boy knew he was seeing a vision of a soul being carried to heaven. The next morning, he learned that Aidan, the Irish monk summoned from Iona by King Oswald in AD 635 and who had become the bishop of the small tidal island of Lindisfarne off the northeast coast of England, had died the night before. Young Cuthbert knew that the sign in the heavens was God calling him to join a monastery, to take up the mantle of service.

The process took some time. Cuthbert first served as a soldier for a few years and then entered the monastery at Melrose where he lived.[21] After some time, Cuthbert was chosen to be the master at a new monastery in Ripon. When disputes arose about Celtic versus Roman rituals, Cuthbert decided to return to Melrose in 661 and eventually became the leader of that monastery when his mentor died in 664.

But he was not there long. That same year, 664, the Synod of Whitby settled disputes about rituals and determined that the Roman rite would be used in churches and monasteries in Britain. Cuthbert, who had been trained in Celtic rites but who had acquiesced to Roman ones, was the perfect man to lead change at the priory of Lindisfarne. And so it was that Cuthbert, years after seeing the soul of Aidan being carried into heaven and hearing God call him into the priesthood, would come to Lindisfarne where he would become "Lindisfarne's greatest monk-bishop, and the most important saint in northern England in the Middle Ages."[22]

His work was not spectacular. In fact, strife from the cultural change he had led at the monastery, moving them from Celtic rites to Roman rites, left him bitter and tired. He decided to retire as a hermit to even more remote islands. But in 685, the king insisted on making Cuthbert a bishop, thrusting him "back into the world of kings and nobles."[23] It only made his reputation grow. By the time he died two years later, he was renown as a pastor, prophet, and miracle worker.

Yet even death would not end his mission. Eleven years after his passing, some monks with a curious nature opened his coffin. As the legend goes, they discovered that his body had not decayed but was "incorrupt," which they took to be a sign of his purity and power, worthy of being a saint.[24] The tomb was then excavated and set on the ground as a shrine. Reports of miraculous healings around the shrine spread, and pilgrimages to Lindisfarne grew. It became *the* holy site in Northumbria. Lindisfarne itself came to be called Holy Island.

The monastery grew as a result, attracting gifts of land and treasure from kings and nobles. In the early eighth century, the monks began creating what would come to be called the Lindisfarne Gospels, an ornate, artfully decorated, hand-copied version of the Gospels. Praised as "the most spectacular manuscript to survive from Anglo-Saxon England," the Lindisfarne Gospels were made as a tribute to God and to St. Cuthbert.[25]

Today Lindisfarne is called the cradle of English Christianity.[26] Cuthbert's most famous protégé, Bede—the Venerable Bede—is the most important historian of early medieval Christianity in Britain. Both are memorialized in Durham Cathedral.

All this was in my mind as I stood staring at the ruins at Lindisfarne on a trip with my family for my graduation from Durham in the summer of 2018. Having made over a dozen trips to Durham over the previous five years for my doctoral studies, I knew the stories of both Cuthbert and Bede and had stood at the shrines inside Durham Cathedral. I had heard of Lindisfarne; I had even seen the Lindisfarne Gospels on display at Durham. But now to stand here, with my shoes on the dirt of Holy Island, feeling my memento of Cuthbert's cross against my chest, the weight of the legend and legacy were pressed home in my soul. I stared at the reddish stones of the external walls, with arches and openings that offer a glimpse into what was once the most significant monastery in all of England, and prayed my thanksgiving to God for that young boy who saw a vision and heard a call.

THE MAJORITY OF PASTORS RECALL BEING CALLED
Can you recall a definitive moment in your life when you were "called" into the ministry?

● Yes ◉ No

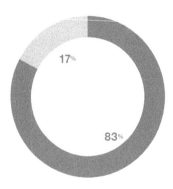

17%

83%

n=408 U.S. Protestant pastors, September 16–October 8, 2020.

Coming Back to Our First Love (John 20)

About half of America's pastors (53 percent) received their call to ministry between the ages of fourteen and twenty-one—the same age as St. Cuthbert[27] and perhaps with the same innocence and naivete. I wonder, if Cuthbert had known how much of his vocation would be about diplomacy with nobles and change management with monks, would he still have said yes? I mean, here was a guy who was more monk than entrepreneur, a man who would rather have been a hermit than a public figure. And yet he kept getting thrust into leadership, summoned from one monastery to another, and called out of solitude by a king. Even the callings that have holy and noble beginnings require some measure of persuasion from the outside in order to persevere.

In 2016, Barna found that about 97 percent of pastors said they remain confident in their calling even decades later, with about 66 percent saying that they are even "more confident" of their calling now than they were when they first heard the Lord.[28] But there is a nuance here. The less satisfied that pastors are with their vocation or church, the less confident they are in their calling.[29] Additionally, during the COVID-19 pandemic when our vocation arguably became heavier and more complicated, we saw a dip in confidence; in 2020, only 35 percent of pastors said they were more confident in their calling than when they first entered ministry. Furthermore, in 2020, only 47 percent of leaders expressed they are "very satisfied" with their ministry at their current church, down from 53 percent in 2016.[30] In a January 2021 poll, Barna learned that nearly 3 in 10 Protestant pastors in the U.S. say they've seriously considered quitting in the past year.[31] The voice of the serpent of old creeps in to ask, "*Did God really say . . . ?*" When the job seems nothing like the call we said yes to, we question why we're doing this at all. When the flood of opposition and antagonism rises over our heads, we find ourselves wanting to abandon the ship.

Your calling into pastoral ministry may not have been inscribed in the heavens as Cuthbert's was, but even he tried to quit. It's understandable if you've tried too. Your work may at times skew out of shape, looking more like the desecration of the pastoral vocation that Peterson decries than the vocational holiness he prescribes. Throughout the course of the journey we will take together in this book—indeed, in the next few chapters—we will find ways of cooperating with the Holy Spirit as he works on our interior life, shaping the angles of our work.

But things are reshaped in a fire. At times, the fire will look like crisis and challenge. These lesser flames are meant to ignite the only burning that truly matters: the fire of love for Jesus. We will spend an entire chapter on the interior devotional life of a pastor. We will look at practices and habits that lead us again and again to Jesus. For now, I want to merely set the stage by taking you back to the most unlikely pastor: Peter.

In an instance of divinely revealed clarity, Peter recognized that Jesus was the Messiah. Jesus followed this by publicly establishing Peter's call as a foundational leader of the church. But then Peter had a moment that many of us have experienced: the upending of his world, the unexpected, shocking collapse of everything he held dear. It wasn't just that the Messiah had been crucified; it was Peter's participation in his suffering. *He had denied knowing Jesus in the hour of his greatest need.* So Peter gave up on leading the charge for a new kingdom community. He went back to fishing. Even after the resurrection, Peter did not know what he was really called to do.

There, on the shores of the Sea of Galilee, the risen Jesus came to Peter, replaying a scene all too similar to the circumstances around Peter's first call. Jesus then asked Peter three times: "Do you love me?" We notice the number of times Jesus asked Peter this question, and we rightly compare it to the number of times Peter denied Jesus. Yes, this is a kind of reversal of his denial. And we reflect on the different Greek words for love that John records Jesus using.

But we often miss the most important word in the question: *me.*

You see, Jesus didn't ask Peter, "Do you love the *church*?"

"Do you love the *ministry*?"

"Do you love my *teaching*?"

Or even, "Do you love the *sheep*?"

He simply asked, "Do you love *me*?"

Peter's first call had been about a purpose: "Follow me and I will make you fishers of men." But the love of a calling is not enough to keep us from falling. It wasn't enough for Peter. The love of the mission or the ministry can't sustain us on those dark days and terrible nights. The job, as understood by the various and vacillating expectations of people, is undoable. We will all at some point want to walk away and go back to something simpler, something easier, something less complicated, less draining and costly.

Unless we return to the shore with Jesus. There, by the sea that we have fled to, comes the rescue of love. Only the love of Jesus can keep us from falling or from calling it quits. *Pastor*, Jesus asks, *do you love* me?

Our first love is our first call. It is not to a purpose, but to a Person—to Christ Jesus himself.

Pastors' Vocational Confidence

Most pastors feel satisfied and secure in their calling, though questions still creep in. Time tends to curb vocational insecurities, as older pastors report higher satisfaction and fewer doubts in their role when compared to younger pastors. Interestingly, in the height of the COVID-19 response in 2020, confidence in pastoral calling actually stabilized for more than half of pastors, perhaps an indication of how crisis brought clarity to their purpose. Still, their confidence in themselves does not exclude them from challenges with other people. Four in ten pastors say they wish they had been better prepared for delegation and conflict.

OVERALL, HOW SATISFIED ARE YOU WITH YOUR VOCATION AS A PASTOR?

● Very satisfied   ● Somewhat satisfied   ◉ Not too satisfied   Not at all satisfied

2015
72%   25%   2%

2020
67%   29%   4%

20+ years in ministry
74%   24%   2%

Under 20 years in ministry
60%   34%   6%

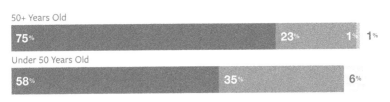

50+ Years Old
75%   23%   1%   1%

Under 50 Years Old
58%   35%   6%

n=900 U.S. senior pastors, April–December 2015.
n=408 U.S. Protestant pastors, September 16–October 8, 2020.

COMPARED TO WHEN YOU FIRST ENTERED PASTORAL MINISTRY, WOULD YOU SAY YOU FEEL . . . ?

● Just as confident about your calling   ● Less confident about your calling
More confident about your calling

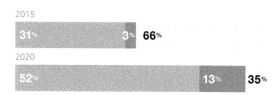

2015
31%   3%   **66%**

2020
52%   13%   **35%**

n=408 U.S. Protestant pastors, September 16–October 8, 2020.

HAVE YOU EVER DOUBTED YOUR DECISION TO BE IN THE MINISTRY VOCATIONALLY?

● Yes   ● No

All Pastors
51%   49%

50+ Years Old
40%   60%

Under 50 Years Old
63%   37%

WHAT AREAS OF MINISTRY DO YOU WISH YOU HAD BEEN BETTER PREPARED FOR?
Top Five Items

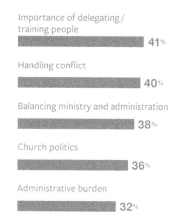

Importance of delegating / training people
41%

Handling conflict
40%

Balancing ministry and administration
38%

Church politics
36%

Administrative burden
32%

n=408 U.S. Protestant pastors, September 16–October 8, 2020.

Reflections from Ken Shigematsu, pastor, author, and speaker

When I first came to Tenth Church in Vancouver, BC, in the summer of 1996, the challenge of pastoring a historic church whose attendance had dwindled from over one thousand to one hundred and something intimidated me. Tenth had cycled through twenty pastors in twenty years. On one of my first days on the job, the church secretary walked into my office and announced, "If the ship sinks now, everyone will blame you because you were the last captain at the helm."

A couple of weeks later, my mentor Leighton Ford and I were sitting in my car outside the church. I had a desperate need for encouragement but felt too ashamed to ask. Instead, I asked for some counsel. He paused and said, "Remember that God is an artist. He will not lead you to copy anyone else. Seek God for his unique vision for this place."

I set aside my own goals and began seeking the Lord in prayer. I invited others to do the same. One day, I sensed the Holy Spirit saying, "If you will bless those who cannot repay you, I will bless you." Not long afterward, a homeless man died outside our church building on a cold winter's night. It was tragic. But we began a meal and shelter ministry for the homeless, and the Holy Spirit began drawing people of all walks of life to Christ.

Our vocation doesn't come from imitating some other "successful" pastor or ministry or even following our "bliss," it comes by seeking God for a unique vision.

spirituality

How do we renew our relationship with God?

My earliest introduction to prayer was hearing my parents praying in the Spirit every Saturday morning while a Hosanna! Music tape played in the background. I learned to intercede, to pray in a prayer language, to read the Bible and pray from it, and most of all to pray with a rhythm of regularity.

During my teen years, I often had a "quiet time" with God that lasted an hour or two. We had returned from our three years in America right before I began high school, and the only viable educational option for me was a quasi-homeschool in which workbooks and tutors helped me complete the American curriculum set by the Christian school I had attended when we lived in Oregon. I had flexibility in my schedule. I would often begin by sitting at the piano, singing my heart out to God. Then I would read a chapter or more from the Bible, working my way through the entire thing—though the Old Testament was my favorite. I'd journal reflections and ways that God was speaking to me from his Word.

By the time I left Malaysia to return to America for college, I had cultivated a habit of time with God. That would be tested in the busyness of my freshman year. I was trying to reintegrate into a country and culture that I did not grow up in but had lived in as a child. I had ambitiously taken on a full-credit load, and I was working on campus to earn some spending money. But not having a car or a TV—or a computer or Wi-Fi, for that matter—helped. On most Friday nights, when students were going out or watching movies, I made my way to the piano practice rooms in the music building. Down the dark hallway, I found the room at the end and left the lights off. I went in and worshiped my way through loneliness, insecurity, breakups, and more. My prayer life in those years may have been more intermittent than in my teens, but it was also more intense.

When I began working at a church at twenty-two, I thought my dream had come true. Hired on in the worship ministry department, I assumed personal worship time would basically be part of my job description. Though we certainly had flexibility to take a bit of time for morning devotions and prayer, what I had not accounted for is how difficult it can be to worship on a stage multiple times a week. To put your personal devotion on display in order to evoke a similar devotion in others can strain the quality of intimacy. Like a marriage on a reality TV show, the lines between authenticity and performance blur. As a worship leader, you *want* to experience God's presence in a meaningful way, but you know you also have to *display* the earnestness of that desire. It's not acting, but it can feel like it.

Sociologist Arlie Hochschild studied flight attendants to examine the toll it takes to display the expected emotion as part of your job. She identifies "feeling rules" that are at play in various social contexts, from weddings to funerals to family reunions. The expectation to conform to those unspoken rules results in "surface acting"—where we display the right emotion—or "deep acting"—where we feel the right emotion.

> Surface acting involves disguising what we feel, and pretending to feel what we do not. In surface acting, we may deceive others, but we do not deceive ourselves. Deep acting, on the other hand,

requires deceiving ourselves. In deep acting, a person changes herself by "taking over the levers of feeling production." In short, surface acting changes the display; deep acting changes the emotion.[1]

It would be a decade and a half before I encountered her work and found words for what I was wrestling with.

When the scandal occurred six years into my time on staff, the spotlight of the Holy Spirit turned onto my own soul. I was dying on the inside. I was going through the motions, riding a wave of adrenaline. I had confused influence with impact, significance with faithfulness, and the American dream with the blessing of God. One of the books I picked up in that season of profound disorientation and disappointment was Henri Nouwen's *In the Name of Jesus*. A dear friend, Jason Jackson, had given it to me a few years prior, but I had quit reading after the first few pages. It seemed worlds away from my ministry context and utterly irrelevant. That, of course, was the point, for the cure can be nothing like the disease. When I picked it up again this time, I couldn't put it down. Nouwen writes:

> I came face to face with the simple question, "Did becoming older bring me closer to Jesus?" After twenty-five years of priesthood, I found myself praying poorly, living somewhat isolated from other people, and very much preoccupied with burning issues. Everyone was saying that I was doing really well, but something inside was telling me that my success was putting my own soul in danger. I began to ask myself whether my lack of contemplative prayer, my loneliness, and my constantly changing involvement in what seemed most urgent were signs that the Spirit was gradually being suppressed. . . . I woke up one day with the realization that I was living in a very dark place and that the term "burnout" was a convenient psychological translation for a spiritual death.[2]

One line in particular jumped off the page: *"burnout" was a convenient psychological translation for a spiritual death*. That hit me hard. I became aware of the thirst in my soul, the parched condition of my own heart. I needed to renew my relationship with God.

The Slow Slide to Spiritual Death

Too many of us are on our way to spiritual death. We are in desperate need of spiritual renewal. The question is, *How?* If we're honest, there are many days as a pastor when being a monk in a monastery doesn't sound too bad! If only we could escape the onslaught of emails, the complaints of congregants, the pressure to preach an Instagram-clip-worthy sermon. But alas, our wistful glances out the study window are interrupted by the dinging of our phones.

When Barna researchers asked pastors to name two or three spiritual disciplines or practices that are most significant for their own spiritual development, 81 percent said prayer.[3] This was followed by Bible reading, a close second at 71 percent.[4] Our new study found that 88 percent of pastors pray daily, 55 percent of pastors read their Bible daily (other than preparing for sermons), with another 31 percent reading their Bible at least weekly.

But how easy is it to keep making time to pray or read the Bible? Well, that may depend on your age. If you're a pastor who is younger than fifty, you're more likely to find it difficult. Sixty

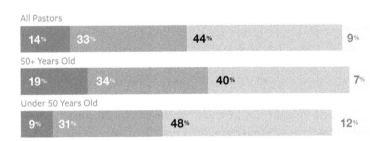

PASTORS' SPIRITUAL INVESTMENT IN THEMSELVES
How simple or difficult is it for you to find time in your ministry schedule to invest in your own spiritual development?

● Very simple ● Somewhat simple ◉ Somewhat difficult Very difficult

All Pastors

| 14% | 33% | 44% | 9% |

50+ Years Old

| 19% | 34% | 40% | 7% |

Under 50 Years Old

| 9% | 31% | 48% | 12% |

n=408 U.S. Protestant pastors, September 16–October 8, 2020.

percent of these pastors found it "somewhat difficult" or "very difficult" to invest the time in spiritual development. That's higher than the average, where 53 percent expressed difficulty, and much higher than older pastors, where only 47 percent found it difficult to prioritize time for spiritual development.

What is it that seasoned pastors know that others don't? Maybe they understand that we can't last in ministry without cultivating a deep inner life with God. I can't prove that the statistics have a causal relationship, of course. I don't know whether these pastors who have been going for more than thirty years are doing so because they've found it simple to practice spiritual disciplines. It may be the other way around: the longer we're in ministry the easier it is to say no to other things so that we can say yes to our own life with God. Either way, there's wisdom here for us. We cannot be people who simply work *for* God; we have to be those who know what it means to be *with* God. Jesus called his disciples "so that they might be with him"—that came first—and then so that "he might send them out to preach and have authority to cast out demons" (Mark 3:14–15 ESV).

Earlier, we explored what it means to return to our first call, the call to a person and not simply a purpose. We may understand that in theory. In practice, however, it's easy to miss the ways we are being driven by the cause and not by Christ himself. It's tempting as pastors to think that we're *always* with God, and because we're doing God's work, then *surely* we are in God's presence. So we keep going, we keep working, we keep answering phone calls and replying to text messages and emails and DMs on social media. We're communing with God on the go, we say.

But there are warning signs that all is not well. Pete Scazzero, founding pastor of New Life Fellowship in Queens and author of the Emotionally Healthy Discipleship materials, opens his book *Emotionally Healthy Spirituality* by listing "the top ten symptoms of emotionally *unhealthy* spirituality":

1. Using God to run from God
2. Ignoring anger, sadness, and fear

3. Dying to the wrong things [that is, denying yourself the joy of God's good gifts in your life]
4. Denying the impact of the past on the present
5. Dividing life into "secular" and "sacred" compartments
6. Doing *for* God instead of being *with* God
7. Spiritualizing away conflict
8. Covering over brokenness, weakness, and failure
9. Living without limits
10. Judging other people's spiritual journey[5]

Read through the list again *slowly*. Can you relate? When I first came across it, number 3 stopped me in my tracks: *dying to the wrong things*. I had thought I was being committed, sacrificial. But what if I was really running on fumes, operating on an unhealthy premise that because heaven and hell are on the line, I need to work like there's no tomorrow?

Which is why number 9 got me too: *living without limits*.

Ruth Haley Barton, a seasoned retreat leader and spiritual director for pastors and leaders, dives deeper into the pattern of living without limits in her book *Strengthening the Soul of Your Leadership*. She discusses several indicators that we might be living *beyond* our limits:

- irritability or hypersensitivity (think about your responses on Facebook or to Monday morning emails!)
- restlessness
- compulsive overworking
- emotional numbness
- escapist behaviors (these may range from bingeing on Netflix to mindlessly scrolling social media)
- disconnection from our identity and calling (referring to the loss of meaning, the frequency of "going through the motions")

- inability to attend to human need (such as exercise and sleep)
- hoarding energy (the tendency to feel overly protective of our energy, as though any request or invitation were a threat to our well-being)
- slippage in our spiritual practices[6]

Are you squirming yet? We don't want to admit it, do we? Our rebuttal is at the ready: we *can't* just stop. *Who will care for these people? Who will preach the sermon? Who will inspire the volunteers? Who will lead the staff? How can we possibly pray in the middle of all this?* But we must stop in order to interrupt the slow slide toward spiritual death.

Digging New Wells

In early 2007, I found myself parched. I read the Bible more diligently, devoured books that took me deeper into the text, and joined our church in prayer meetings and worship services. It was all good. But I needed something more.

It was about that time that my wife and I began to engage in some spiritual practices that were well known in other church traditions but foreign to us. Praying the Psalms was one. Our new study found that about 25 percent of pastors pray the Psalms at least weekly. As for the younger me, I loved the Psalms; I had mined them for song ideas. But praying them—just saying the words *as* my prayer each morning—that was new. It felt a bit strange, a little cold. Yet as I kept going, something began to unlock in me. Then we stumbled upon the *Book of Common Prayer*, the legacy of English reformer Thomas Cranmer. Those special "Collects"— prayers meant to be prayed collectively in Sunday worship—moved me. That was, of course, Cranmer's goal. Years went by, and we stayed on our quest, never abandoning the practices we loved— praying in the Spirit, worship songs, Bible reading—but adding to the repertoire: Sabbath, Rule of Life, and the prayer of *Examen*.

These were rich practices that opened up our hearts in new ways to the life of God.

New Testament scholar Gordon Fee wrote that the experiential dimension of the Holy Spirit is dynamic and renewable.[7] It makes sense if you remember that the Holy Spirit is the Third *Person* of the Trinity. All relationships with persons are dynamic and renewable. That's why there's a difference between the friend you've known for twenty years and the friend you knew twenty years ago and just bumped into on the subway. Every Christian—not just every pastor—needs ways of renewing our relationship with the Holy Spirit. The Holy Spirit is how we *know* God. The Spirit reveals Christ to us, guides us into all truth, convicts us of sin, reminds us of the teaching of Christ, empowers us to do the mission of God, and so much more. The New Testament church would not have known a Christianity without the Spirit. Though trinitarian theology developed in a full-fledged way later, already in Paul's letters we see the church grappling with the Spirit as the way the Father and the Son become present to us.

But here's what happens to us in ministry. We get tired of the services we're leading. Barna's *State of Pastors* report found that "a pastor experiencing worship at their church as personally meaningful tends to correlate with a lower risk of burnout, relationship trouble and declining spiritual well-being."[8] The research could not determine a causal relationship. That is, we don't know whether being at a higher risk of burnout leads to less frequently finding worship meaningful or whether finding worship meaningful less frequently leads to a higher risk of burnout. Nevertheless, "the correlation is undeniable."[9]

Maybe you have found yourself cold and unmoved in the very services you are leading. That could be from the toll that "deep acting" or "surface acting" has taken on you as you conform to the "feeling rules" that you yourself have set or that others have set. Or maybe it's from the weariness that comes from living without limits. I've been there. Worse yet are the times when we finally do get alone with God and *feel nothing*. Now, I'm not suggesting that we *have* to feel something. The stories of saints—Mother Teresa most famously—who continue to serve God without the warmth of his presence rightly offer us a corrective and an inspiration. But not every calloused heart is going through the dark night of the soul. Sometimes we just need to drink from a different well than the one from which we're serving others.

That's why the contemplative practices of the *Examen* and prayers from the *Book of Common Prayer* were life-giving to me. They were so different from my ministry context. There was nothing for me to "make happen" or lead. It didn't require speaking into a microphone or speaking at all.

But if those are the practices you're familiar with, perhaps you should consider a different path. One of the assignments I gave in a doctor of ministry class I taught at Denver Seminary was to have the students choose two spiritual practices that were newer or less familiar to them, practice them daily for two weeks, and then journal about it. When we met for the one-week intensive, students—all of them pastors or lay leaders at local churches—took turns sharing their experiences. One pastor assumed that modern worship music was all shallow pop and was pleasantly surprised. He said he would continue to play it during his morning routine of preparing breakfast for the family. Another worship leader said she had never actually prayed the prayer of *Examen*, though she had heard of it. It would now be part of her repertoire of practices. It can be hard to drink from the same well that you're drawing water from for others.

One more thing. You know when the best time is to dig a well? Before you need the water. Too many of us wait until the well we've been drinking from has run dry or ceases to satisfy. We walk away thirsty and sad, wondering if water is the problem. But water is not the problem. And frankly, most of the time, neither is the well. That's why there's no need to poison the well that isn't quenching us anymore. We don't have to criticize modern worship or the liturgy. It is still offering water to others. We simply need to find another way into the great underground water source. The river of life comes from the same Lord and the same Spirit. We may just need another way of drawing from it. We need more wells if we're going to last in the wilderness that ministry sometimes is. Eugene Peterson referred to a stretch of difficult years as a pastor as "the badlands." We will go through the badlands. There will be desert seasons. There will be a time when the wells you knew seem to be dry. It will happen. *Dig another well before you need the water.*

Getting Alone with God

The particular practices that Ruth Haley Barton recommends for pastors and leaders are the twin disciplines of solitude and silence. They are how we keep centered on God amid the onslaught of demands. I was a little surprised to learn from our study that 52 percent of pastors practice solitude or alone time at least weekly. I hadn't guessed the number would be that high in our busy and distracted age. Several pastors in my focus groups mentioned regular personal retreats and days away. Brittany, in Illinois, said that once a quarter she goes away for a couple of days. Alice, in England, takes a weeklong retreat once a year with a group of women she had trained for ministry over a decade ago. They also meet for a day every quarter. "This has been essential for me," she says. Gary, in Belfast, uses a biblical number; every forty days he detaches from everything and goes up a mountain or on a long walk. He finds somewhere private and dedicates that day to spending time with God. Barton finds this practice to be essential for leaders. She writes:

> The only way to begin facing these challenges is to keep seeking tenaciously after God through spiritual disciplines that keep us grounded in the presence of God at the center of our being. Solitude and silence in particular enable us to experience a place of authenticity within and to invite God to meet us there. In solitude we are rescued from relentless human striving to solve the challenges of ministry through intellectual achievements and hard work, so that we can experience the life of the Spirit guiding toward that true way that lies between one polarity and another. In silence we give up control and allow God to be God in our life rather than being a thought in our head or an illustration in a sermon. In that place

of our seeking we listen for the still, small voice of God telling us who we really are and what is real from a spiritual point of view. Then we are not quite so enslaved by the demands and expectations of life in leadership.[10]

Jacob, the patriarch of Israel, understood this. Scripture tells us that *when Jacob was left alone*, a man wrestled with him until daybreak (Gen. 32:24). It must have been hard for Jacob to actually get alone. He was traveling with two wives, multiple servants, eleven sons, and livestock so plentiful that his appeasement gift to his brother was "two hundred female goats and twenty male goats, two hundred ewes and twenty rams, thirty female camels with their young, forty cows and ten bulls, and twenty female donkeys and ten male donkeys" (vv. 14–15). I mean, I've got one wife and four kids, and it's pretty tough to find the space for solitude!

Jacob sent them across the stream and was finally alone after being on the run from his father-in-law. After being tricked into marrying a different daughter. After working out plans to get the wife he wanted and the freedom he had earned. His recent history was chaotic and messy enough. But now he was about to face his difficult past: the brother he had cheated.

It's difficult to face our failures when life is full. We won't notice our wounds or confess our sins when we're moving quickly. Maybe that's why we don't want to stop. When Jacob was left alone, a man came to him and wrestled with him until daybreak. We all remember the moment when Jacob asked the man to bless him and what the man said to him in reply, changing his name from Jacob to Israel. But what I missed in the text for so many years was that before he blessed Jacob, the man asked him what his name was. Jacob had been asked that question once before. In the cover of night when he approached his father in his tent for the patriarchal blessing, the aging and nearly blind Isaac asked Jacob, "What is your name?" "Esau," came the reply. Thus began the deception, the fleeing, the game playing and manipulating. It had been at least twenty years since he had been asked that question. Now here it was again: "What is your name?"

Who are you, *really*? This time, Jacob comes clean. He says his name. The heel grasper. But no longer. He would now be Israel, the one who has struggled with humans and with God, and the one who overcomes. The encounter altered the trajectory of his life and redeemed the failures of his past. And it happened when he was *left alone*.

If we're going to deal with our fears and failures—no, more than that: if we're going to come face-to-face with the only one who can heal us and restore us—we're going to have to make time to be alone with God. In the noisy swirl of life, we just keep moving, hoping we can push past our frailty. But pain and shame are a combustible combination, and it's only a matter of time before something explodes.

Pastors, we can't wait for the breakdown, for the caving in of our soul or the acting out in destructive behaviors. We have to name our darker selves in the presence of God in order to receive a new name. We have to find ourselves alone with God. And we don't need a monastery to do it.

A Monastery in the World

Prayer was never his strong suit. Given over to the "vanities of this world" and consumed with "a great and foolish desire to win fame," the young man had visions of becoming a great soldier and charmer of women.[11] He was conscious of fashion and of his appearance, so much so that after receiving a terrible wound on his leg during a battle, he underwent multiple surgeries to attempt to restore his leg so that it would once again dazzle in the tights so popular in his day. But medical procedures in Spain in the early 1500s were not what they are today, and Inigo was left with a limp for the rest of his life.

While recovering in the family castle in Loyola, he was given a book on the lives of the saints. The next year, he made a pilgrimage to a Benedictine abbey. He remained in the region for a year, staying in a nearby town sometimes with monks, sometimes in a hospice for paupers, and sometimes in a cave in the hills praying.[12] This was a dark time, a wrestling with God and with his own sense of doubt about the possibility of genuine transformation. But there were also mystical experiences in prayer that marked him. He took notes on it all.

Eventually his educational journey led him to Paris, where several friends bound themselves to one another in "a communal vow of poverty and chastity."[13] This was the beginning, in August of 1534, of the *Compania de Jesus*, or the Society of Jesus, known today simply as the Jesuits. Inigo himself was now going by a different name, a name he mistakenly thought was a Latin variation of his name: Ignatius.

When they sought the pope's approval for the creation of a new religious order, there were many skeptics. That's because the Jesuits wanted to be active *in* the world, not removed from it. They wanted to find God in all things, to practice contemplation in action. As prominent Jesuit author Father James Martin writes, one of their core beliefs seemed to many as nearly heretical:

> Some prominent clerics believed that members of religious orders should be cloistered behind monastery walls, like the Cistercians or Carmelites, or at least lead a life removed from the "follies of the world," like the Franciscans. That a member of a religious order would be "in the world," without gathering for prayer every few hours, was shocking. But Ignatius stood firm: his men were to be contemplatives *in action*, leading others to find God in all things.[14]

There were over one thousand Jesuits at the time of Ignatius's death, and today, there are over sixteen thousand in 112 countries.[15] The man who wanted to be a soldier and a nobleman became a servant of God and something of a social worker, starting schools and orphanages and safe houses for rescued prostitutes. But perhaps the most widespread legacy of Ignatius of Loyola was a way of prayer that helped people find God in all things. He spread a spirituality that does not seek a monastery apart from the world but sees the world as a monastery.

Union with Christ

Ignatius can help us. About ten years ago, I realized the discomfort of being the lead person in most meetings—or as Andy Stanley puts it, the most powerful person in the room. I felt the temptation of vanity and the pitfalls of ego near at hand. I decided I needed to talk with someone off the grid of our local church and its network of relationships, someone who didn't go to our church and was not employed by the church, someone who had been in ministry and was trained as a counselor or spiritual director. I found just the right person. Early in our sessions together, he told me I needed to explore more about Ignatian spirituality. The indifference toward anything but the will of God could be a pathway to freedom from the many anxieties that plague a leader.

I picked up a book by Father James Martin, a Jesuit priest in New York. It was inspiring and enlightening. But then it started to sound familiar—hearing the voice of God, a personal relationship with Jesus. *Was this guy an evangelical?* And then it occurred to me—there is one beating heart of both the contemplative and charismatic traditions, one common center to all Christian spirituality: union with Christ.

If my exploration of ancient practices was a move away from the forms of worship and prayer I knew *too* well, then pushing further along that path led me back to the start. It was a circle. Or perhaps a spiral, circling back to where I was but with new depth, insight, and appreciation. Either way, the two were not opposites. I need not pit loud prayer meetings against silence, worship music against psalm praying, Sabbath keeping against hard work. These and more are of one fabric.

In a sense, this is what Ignatius set out to demonstrate. The contemplative and the active are organically connected. You can find God in all things. The road to knowing God did not require a monastic life. It could happen in the world. Ignatius was not saying we don't need solitude and silence. Nor was he saying one should never stop to pray. Quite the opposite. The prayer of *Examen* is a daily stopping, pausing, and reflecting on God's presence with us that day and how we participated with him or failed to. The Ignatian revolution was the way he and his followers sought to live monastically *in the world.*

That means that right here, at the church in which you serve, right now, in this season of life and ministry, *you can know God.* You can draw near to him, renew your intimacy with him, and drink deeply of living water again. Ultimately, this is true not because you have mastered an array of spiritual practices or perfected the art of discipline, but because the Spirit says, "Come"; and we the bride answer, "Come." "And let the one who is thirsty come! Let the one who wishes receive life-giving water as a gift" (Rev. 22:17).

Pastors' Spiritual Practices Outside Church

Naturally, many Christian practices are part of a day's work for pastors. But how often are pastors making time for spiritual disciplines on their own and beyond ministry activities? Most pastors say the Bible is a mainstay of their routines, even outside of writing sermons. Worshiping with music and finding solitude, too, are regularly features of their lives. After these core spiritual practices, about half of pastors begin to make room for their hobbies and leisure—far more so than for focused faith activities like fasting or taking a solo Sabbath.

PERSONAL BIBLE READING
(OTHER THAN PREPARING
FOR SERMONS)

LISTENING TO OR SINGING
WORSHIP MUSIC APART
FROM CHURCH SERVICES

● Daily ● A few times a week ● Once a week ● A few times a month
Once a month ○ A few times a year ◎ Less often

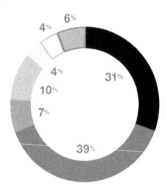

OTHER PERSONAL PRACTICES

% who do so at least weekly

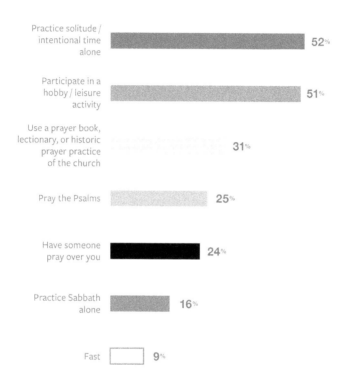

Practice solitude / intentional time alone — 52%

Participate in a hobby / leisure activity — 51%

Use a prayer book, lectionary, or historic prayer practice of the church — 31%

Pray the Psalms — 25%

Have someone pray over you — 24%

Practice Sabbath alone — 16%

Fast — 9%

n=408 U.S. Protestant pastors, September 16–October 8, 2020.

Reflections from Ruth Haley Barton, founder of the Transforming Center

"I'm tired of helping others enjoy God, I just want to enjoy God for myself!" With the utterance of these words in an uncensored conversation with a friend, I knew I was in trouble. Why? Because what I was really saying was that my leadership, which usually flows from what is going on in the depths of my soul, was *at that moment* disconnected from the reality of God in my own life. It was not the first time I had noticed such slippage, nor would it be the last, but it was certainly one of the most clearly articulated! And it points to what I believe is one of the most subtle dangers of life in pastoral ministry, and that is doing ministry disconnected from the place where God is present to us and the practices that keep us listening and responsive to what we hear there.

The soul-full leader pays attention to these inner realities and to the questions they raise, rather than ignoring them, judging themselves harshly, or continuing the charade that all is well. Spiritual leadership emerges from our willingness to stay involved with our own souls—that place where God's Spirit is at work stirring up our deepest questions and longings in order to draw us deeper into relationship and further in our own journey of transformation. Paying attention in this way is not mere narcissistic navel-gazing or morbid introspection; rather, this kind of attentiveness helps us stay on the path of becoming our true self in God—a self that is capable of a truer and ever-deepening "yes" to God's call upon our lives in the crucible of ministry. The only thing that will sustain us for the long haul, giving us the direction we need as we navigate the challenging and ever-changing landscape of leadership, is to keep returning to our own tenacious seeking after God through spiritual practices that keep us grounded in the presence of God at the center of our being.

Reflections from Marlena Graves, author and speaker

Here is the danger for shepherds: to be full of God-talk while living godless lives. To have it become all about us while we're preaching that it is not all about us. Any one of us can talk endlessly, cleverly, and expertly about God. We can pray without praying. We can be rotting inside, burnt out, and far, far away from God and our very lives. From those who love us most. What do we do? We begin by admitting the truth, confessing it to trusted others. No need for self-loathing. It's important to let our congregations know, and we must insist that they help us implement a weekly time of re-creation. Re-creating silences and solitudes that allow us just to be and that fill us with wonder—apart from our days off. It will save our lives. Our rest and contemplation will fill us with the energy to love those about us well. Fruitful contemplation is necessary for fruitful action. Maybe block off three hours once a week until lunch time to practice disciplines that revive. Being outside in nature is a good choice. Remember too that you can't do this all alone. Jesus had his inner circle of friends. Of course, it can be hard for shepherds to have friends outside of their church. So become intentional about getting to know other clergy and community members so that your life doesn't revolve around the church alone. God is your very life, not the pulpit, council room, or endless meetings.

relationships

How do we cultivate meaningful relationships?

sat there in a beautiful old auditorium in Queens, New York, with a pen in my hand but unable to think of what to write. All around me, others were busy filling in the box, listing items. My wife, seated next to me, was apparently having no trouble. But there I was, drawing a blank.

We were in the sanctuary of New Life Fellowship, where my friend Rich Villodas serves as lead pastor, attending an Emotionally Healthy Leader conference led by Pete and Geri Scazerro for pastors and church leaders. The assignment for that session was to create a "Rule of Life," the Scazerros' version of the old Benedictine practice of ordering your time with rhythms of prayer and service. The worksheet had four boxes: Prayer, Rest, Work, and Relationships. I had no trouble writing down the practices I'm engaging in to seek God, and when and how often that would occur. I didn't even struggle with detailing how we *try* to observe a Sabbath in the midst of life with four kids. Holly and I had talked about that and worked on that for a few years at that point. And, of course, as you might suspect, it was not difficult to write down rhythms of work. The only trouble was whittling down *which* work to focus on!

The box that froze my writing was the one about relationships. To be more precise, it was when I came to the part about friendships. I had written down scheduled dates with my wife and one-on-one time with the kids. *But I had no intentional designated time with friends.*

The longer I sat there, the deeper the realization sank in. *I did not think I could make time for friendships.* I mean, isn't ministry about being available to those who are in need, being ready to be there for the congregant who has gone through a divorce or lost a loved one? Shouldn't our meals be with the staff we're leading and investing in? To be sure, the lines blur in all this. Many of our friends *are* the people in our church. I don't think of them as "sheep" and me as their "shepherd." That's a little too patronizing for my taste. And our staff are dearly loved friends with whom we've been through the fire. There is quite a bit of mutuality in those relationships.

And yet. Each of those relationships is asymmetrical. There is, to put it plainly, a power differential. With our staff, as close as we might become as friends, at the end of the day, I have quite a bit of say into whether they continue in their jobs or what the compensation for their work should be. They don't have the same influence over my job. With congregants, they're hearing me open up the Word of God to them on most Sundays, but I'm not hearing teaching from them in any sort of regular way. No matter how hard we try to close the gap, the power dynamic is asymmetrical.

Furthermore, these relationships are not truly fully mutual. Would we have met if they had not been in the hospital or needed premarital counseling or prayer in a difficult season? It's hard to say. I'm sure I'm not alone in saying that there may be things I think or feel in my darkest or most fragile moments that a congregant may not be able to handle knowing about their pastor.

Perhaps I'm not being trusting enough. I think pastors have come a long way toward humility and vulnerability with their churches. The illusion of the pious perfect pastor is long gone, thanks be to God. Yet while we should strive toward authenticity in all our relationships, there is a deep level of vulnerability that can take place with only a few.

This is not unlike what we see of Jesus and his relationships in the Gospels. He walked freely among the people, touching and being personal with even those on society's margins. He welcomed children, spoke with women, hung out with tax collectors and sinners. But he was intentional with the Twelve, and vulnerable with only three—Peter, James, and John. Of course, it is hard to say *any* relationship with the incarnate Son of God is mutual or symmetrical!

As I sat there that day in Queens several years ago with my pen frozen inches above my workbook, I realized that I had not prioritized relationships of mutuality and symmetry. And I had not done so because I did not think I could. That would be indulgent or a luxury. Remember the list from Scazerro that I referenced in the previous chapter about signs of emotionally unhealthy spirituality? One of them is denying yourself good things, things that are gifts from God. I had been unconsciously denying myself the good gift of time with close friends. And the crazy thing about it is that I have the great gift of having friends I've truly known for twenty years who live in the same city as I do. *Why would I not make regular time to be with them?*

Friendship, Loneliness, and Becoming Human

Pastors are not struggling to find good friends. Or so they say.

According to Barna's 2016 research, two-thirds of pastors are "happy with their friendships," with 34 percent rating their sense of satisfaction with these friendships as "excellent" and 3 percent as "good." These results track with wider cultural trends in America, where 28 percent rate their feelings about their friendships as "excellent" and 33 percent as "good."[1] Still, that means that roughly one-third of pastors—and one-third of Americans in general—have a low sense of meaning or satisfaction with their friendships.

The Barna research team rightly asks why people who are in "such a relationally driven vocation are not better than the norm when it comes to intimacy with friends." Interesting question, isn't it? Why are the people who work with people, who are shepherd of the flock, not much better at developing close and meaningful relationships than the wider world? COVID dealt these relationships a bit of a blow. Our new study found that only 20 percent of pastors rated their satisfaction with friendships as excellent, 42 percent rated it as good, and 12 percent rated it as below average or poor.

Pastors are also more likely to feel lonely and isolated from others than the general adult population. In 2016, Barna found that while the same percentage (14 percent) of pastors as American adults report frequently feeling lonely or isolated, 38 percent of pastors report feeling that "sometimes," compared with 25 percent of all adults. In fact, a much smaller percentage of pastors than all adults say they "never" experience loneliness or isolation—16 percent of pastors as opposed to 33 percent of all adults.[2] Once again, things got a little worse in 2020. Our new study revealed that 20 percent of pastors frequently feel lonely and 25 percent frequently feel isolated—both numbers up from 14 percent just a few years prior. Nearly six out of ten pastors have experienced depression during their time in ministry. Think about that. This

**THREE IN FOUR PASTORS FEEL ISOLATED
AT LEAST SOMETIMES**
This year, how often have you felt . . .

● Frequently ● Sometimes ● Seldom   Never

Isolated from others   25%   48%   18%   9%

Lonely   20%   40%   27%   12%

n=408 U.S. Protestant pastors, September 16–October 8, 2020.

confirms what you have no doubt felt in your bones: pastoral ministry is lonely work.

The pastors in my focus group agree. "That's been hard, really hard," said Sam, a senior pastor in Pennsylvania, when asked about cultivating real friendships. Not only is it hard to find deep friendships, but the "dual roles" he often has with people in his church make it challenging. His wife has also struggled. Rick, a pastor in Alaska, said that he and his wife found online groups where they can share openly and honestly. "We're both verbal processors, so it's hard because we can't do that with anyone here in person." Sally in Kentucky has been fortunate to have "maintained old friendships from college." She says, "We have not established any new friendships that we maintain." Tim in London agrees. He and his wife have loads of great friendships outside the church, but most were built up before he became a pastor. "It's very difficult for people to not see you with that title," he admits.

We know we won't last long if we don't somehow learn to cultivate meaningful relationships. We probably know too that the research affirms our intuition. Barna found that being at low spiritual and burnout risk correlates to having an "excellent" situation with true friends.[3] In fact, if you are that satisfied with your friendships, you are more likely to also be satisfied with your "vocation" and your current church. Again, it's difficult to prove causation; we don't know which produces the other. Nevertheless, those who have true friends also love their work and their church. Friendships are not auxiliary or ancillary. They are essential.

My senior pastor, Brady Boyd, often says that when he retires, his goal is to still be a human being. He doesn't want to turn into a preaching machine or a dispenser of God-advice; he doesn't want to become a "leader" or a decision-maker or an authority figure. He doesn't want to be a persona; he wants to be a person.

It reminds me of another passage that jumped off the page at me when I was reading Nouwen's *In the Name of Jesus* after the scandal of our founding senior pastor in 2006: "Much Christian leadership is exercised by people who do not know how to develop healthy, intimate relationships and have opted for power and control instead. Many Christian empire-builders have been people unable to give and receive love."[4] Is there anything more inherently human in our creational design than to be able to give and receive love? To be truly and fully human is to love and be loved. *"The greatest thing you'll ever learn is just to love and be loved in return."*[5]

And we can learn this lesson, once again, from seasoned pastors. According to the Barna *State of Pastors* study:

> Overall, older and more seasoned ministers report higher levels of satisfaction than younger and greener pastors. Those 50 and older are more likely to rate their satisfaction with "having true friends" as excellent and less likely to rate it below average or poor. Similarly, those who have been in ministry 30 years or longer or at their current church 10 or more years characterize the state of their friendships as excellent more often than the norm.[6]

There may be several reasons for this. For one, younger pastors are often living in the busiest season of their lives—kids, church planting or transition, managing the peaks and troughs of a marriage beyond the sunny early years, learning a new city or community, and a myriad of other possible competitors for their time and attention.

And time *is* what it takes to cultivate close friendships. In two groundbreaking studies from the University of Kansas published in the *Journal of Social and Personal Relationships* in 2018, communication studies professor Jeffrey Hall found that it takes "between 40 and 60 hours to form a casual friendship, 80–100 hours to transition to being a friend and more than 200 hours together to become good friends."[7] Right away, you're probably thinking of the people you're in ministry with—worship leaders, children's ministry leaders, youth workers, and such. But here's the kicker about that study: the hours it takes to build friendships are best when they are unstructured leisure time rather than hours spent working together. According to Hall's study, the hours spent at work together don't count as much. Again, we *know* this instinctively. But we hope for shortcuts; we wish for an exception or to be the outlier. There's no getting around it, however. We need meaningful friendships if we're going to last in ministry and if we're going to stay fully human, and cultivating those friendships takes time.

A Constellation of Voices

Years ago, I read a book by Paul Stanley and Robert Clinton called *Connecting: The Mentoring Relationships You Need to Succeed in Life*. They employ a metaphor early in the book that has stuck with me over the years. When it comes to mentors, we tend to look for one "North Star," one brilliant and trustworthy voice who can guide us through the dark nights.[8] But sailors know that it takes more than one star; it takes a constellation. Yes, some stars may shine more brightly within it, but even so, it takes a constellation to guide.

The book of Proverbs tells us:

Without guidance, a people will fall, but there is victory with many counselors. (11:14)

Plans fail with no counsel, but with many counselors they succeed. (15:22)

You should make war with guidance; victory comes with many counselors. (24:6)

Many pastors know this. We understand the need to have trusted voices in our lives. In fact, Barna and I found that half of pastors receive some form of direct spiritual support at least once a month, though it's not likely a counselor or spiritual director. Nevertheless, seeking outside spiritual support is a healthy practice. Those pastors who receive regular, personal spiritual guidance are at low spiritual and burnout risk.[9]

PASTORS' SUPPORT SYSTEMS
% who do the following at least once a month

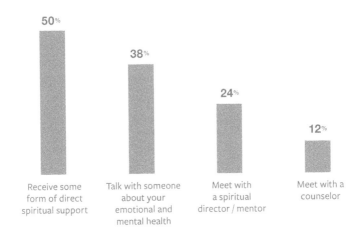

n=408 U.S. Protestant pastors, September 16–October 8, 2020.

I think the constellation image goes beyond the search for mentors. We actually need different kinds of relationships in our lives. So far, we've established that we need friends—relationships of mutuality—and we need mentors and healers—asymmetrical relationships in which someone is investing in us or caring for us. What else? Well, let's have some fun with this for a moment.

Are you a Lord of the Rings fan? Even if you've only seen the movies and never read the books, you may recall some of the characters. Frodo is the Ring-bearer, the one chosen for the dangerous mission of destroying the One Ring in the fires of Mordor. He is chosen because of his pure heart and trustworthy character. But even Frodo can't complete this mission alone. He needs a *fellowship*. As pastors, let's imagine for a moment that we are Frodo, entrusted with a power too great for a mere mortal to handle—though in our case it isn't the power to rule but the power of speaking for God to the people of God. Such sacred stewardship requires a fellowship, a constellation of relationships around us.

In my mind, this is how the Fellowship of the Ring represents the various types of relationships we need:

- *Sage*: This, of course, is Gandalf. He is the wise wizard who appears at all the right moments—at the beginning of the quest, at perilous points along the way, and when all is done. The sage represents the wisdom of those who have come before, those who see what's in us and what lies ahead and who summon us to the journey anyway. These are the mentors, the faithful women and men who have loved well and lived well and are truly and fully human. Many sages have already passed on, and we can glean from their lives through stories and writings. But others are among us, hidden in plain sight. They are, as my colleague Daniel Grothe wrote, like Simeon and Anna in the temple, faithfully serving the Lord.[10] They are not the celebrities or the superstars. They are the steady and the persistent.

- *Companions*: These are Merry and Pippin, but above all, Samwise. In fact, it's best to think of Sam and *not* the two mischievous cousins! He is the faithful, loyal friend who never leaves Frodo's side, the one whose most famous line is "I can't carry [the ring] for you, but I can carry you."[11] We all need a friend like that. Someone who doesn't try to take the weight from us, who is not looking to take our role or our job, but who will carry us as we carry it. For the pastor, these are the relationships that are mutual, that are not asymmetrical in power even if there is differentiation in gifting and function. Eighty percent of pastors said they already have someone in their lives who knows them well and who isn't part of their church or family. Usually it was a pastor in another city or a friend from the past.

- *Peers*: These would be the dwarves and maybe the elves, others who are in the war but not in the same battle. We fight on different fronts. Every so often, our paths converge, and we compare notes, sharing sorrows and multiplying joys. For the pastor, these are other pastors around the country, friends we stay in relationship with, hop on a call with, or attend conferences or roundtables with.

- *King*: In Middle Earth, this is obviously Aragorn. But who is that in the life of a pastor? Think of the people who can tell you no. Maybe that's the presbytery or the elder board. Maybe that's your senior pastor if you're an associate. The idea here is a person who is not simply an "accountability buddy," good as that may be, but rather a person who carries authority in your life—spiritual and actual. Someone who can tell you when you're wrong; someone who can tell you to turn down a speaking request or to take more time off. For me, that person is Pastor Brady Boyd. For many of my peers, it's a team of people—an outside group of overseers. If you're in an Anglican or Methodist context, it's clearly your bishop.

- *Healer*: Finally, you need someone to see when you're sick and on the verge of spiritual death. In the Lord of the Rings, this is Elrond and Arwen—the elvish healers. For the pastor, it's a therapist or a counselor or a spiritual director. The main thing here is to find someone who is *trained* for this work. A sage will share their experience and pray with you; a friend will sit with you and listen and bring you soup. But a healer will get to the root of the problem. They may prescribe medication or uncover a deep wound or trauma. Without healers in our lives, we will be tempted to spiritualize our emotions or ignore our hurts. We'll just keep moving until one day the poison that was working beneath the surface has immobilized us. Make sure there is a healer in your life. The enemy's arrows are real.

There you have it: a constellation of voices, a fellowship of the pastorate. But there's one more circle of relationships to explore.

Closer to Home

For many pastors, there is a small circle of people who love them the most and whom they love the most but who often get relegated to last place. It's their family. For pastors who are married, it's their spouse and children, if they have them. For those who are single, it may be siblings or parents. Somehow, those closest to us get the leftovers. Pastors and their spouses tend to internalize a narrative of sacrifice—*we need to do this for the sake of the church or the ministry.*

Eugene Peterson recounts a story early in his pastoral life of his five-year-old daughter coming to him after supper on a Tuesday evening, asking him to read her a book. He told her he couldn't because he had a meeting at the church. She replied by saying that it was the "thirty-eighth night in a row" that he had not been home. "I woke up," Peterson said, and soon after turned the running of the church over to his elders.[12] His wife, Jan, reflecting back on the toll pastoral ministry takes on marriages, wrote, "We've always subordinated our marriage needs for others because our marriage is so solid and good. But . . . it's a wonder more pastors . . . don't end up in the divorce courts. This is dangerous business."[13]

Dangerous, indeed. But pastors don't always feel it acutely. Barna researchers found that a whopping 96 percent of married pastors reported feeling satisfied with their marriage, with 70 percent rating their marriage as excellent.[14] Compare that to only 46 percent of U.S. adults who say their marriage is excellent.[15] Even COVID-19 didn't do much to shake this reported relational optimism among pastors (in spite of the fact that, as already mentioned, their sense of loneliness and isolation climbed during this time). In our new study, 91 percent of pastors said their relationship with their spouse was excellent or good in 2020. To top things off, pastors divorce at a lower rate. Only 10 percent of pastors have been divorced, compared to 27 percent of the U.S. population.[16]

Several pastors in my focus groups described their spouse as being a "safe place" for them during the turbulent season of the pandemic. Calvin, a pastor in Grand Haven, Michigan, said that over the years his "family relationships have actually grown stronger through the seminary and ordination process. . . . My wife has been my biggest cheerleader, and we're also totally transparent about our experiences with each other." Part of the key for them has been shielding her from the pressures and expectations of his denominational context that come with being a pastor's spouse. On the other hand, Stefan shared the challenge of having a spouse who works a demanding job as a physician. Her role takes up sixty to ninety hours a week and leaves her little time to be at church gatherings with him or even in weekly worship. Though he encourages her to trust that hers is a ministry of healing in the wider community, the separateness of their vocational lives is something to be overcome. Felicity in Kentucky serves as senior pastor in a different congregation from her husband. Their serving different rural congregations has its challenges and blessings—they can certainly relate to each other, but they feel the loneliness of not being with each other.

How about pastors' relationships with their children? About a third of the pastors Barna studied have children who are under eighteen; 60 percent say their relationship with their children is good and 36 percent say it is excellent.[17] Furthermore, even during the pandemic when our measuring sticks for success with our children had adjusted to the complications of remote life and learning, 47 percent of pastors with children who are under eighteen report that their relationship with their children is excellent. These are astounding numbers, and it's good news. Carolyn, a pastor in my focus group in New York City, shared a story about her teenage son being welcomed in by the twentysomethings in the church. They would take him out to lunch and mentor him. Alice in England had a similar story about her teenage son finding friendship with college students in the church. It was a blessing since there were few teens in their town.

But is it the whole picture? Not quite. Gary in Belfast recalls a time when they were serving in a "wee country church" and loneliness and homesickness put a strain on their marriage. Many of the pastors in my focus group described more pronounced moments of loneliness and sadness in 2020 than normal.

The truth is ministry does take a toll on families. The new study Barna and I undertook found that about one in three married pastors say they have experienced significant marital problems at some time in their ministry tenure. This is up from the roughly 25 percent who said the same a few years ago in the *State of Pastors* report.[18] Our new research also found that 39 percent of pastors with kids report having experienced major parenting difficulties, a number that is also up from the previous research (27 percent). Three years earlier, when Barna asked whether their "current church tenure has been difficult on their family," 40 percent said it's "somewhat true."[19] That data tracks with even previous studies done in the early 1990s. In short, ministry is tough on the family. Not much has changed.

Now here's the kicker: "Those who report low overall vocational satisfaction, or low satisfaction with their current church ministry, are much more likely than the norm to say that ministry has been hard on their family. Pastors high on the burnout risk metric also assess higher-than-average negative family impact."[20] It makes sense, doesn't it? If ministry has been tough on your family, it makes everything miserable. It's hard to enjoy a job that is crushing the people you love. "The leading factor that pushes pastors into the relational high-risk category is that ministry at their current church has been difficult for their family."[21] The data is clear. If ministry is good for your family, you're going to love it; if it's not, you won't.

There are several implications for all this, not least of which is for church boards or compensation committees to make sure they are taking care of their pastors and church staff. But the element that is relevant to our purpose in this chapter is to think about what you *do* have control over. You can't control who emails you or when, but you can control when you read the messages and reply. You can't control who complains about what, but you can decide how much it matters.

Early in my time of seeking spiritual direction, my director gave me a parable. He said, "Imagine a prince who lives in a castle where there is a feast available to him every day. Yet every morning when he wakes up, he takes off his royal robes, puts on some filthy rags, and heads to the marketplace to beg for bread. It's ludicrous, isn't it?" His point was that this is what we do when we look for approval outside the Father's house, where a bounty is always available. But I think we experience something similar in our closest relationships. Our families love us—not because of how well we preach or sing or lead children's ministry or recruit volunteers— but because of who we are. They can help return us to our fully human selves. We know this, but we don't always act like it. We keep leaving the castle, hoping to find bread somewhere else. But the feast is closer than we think.

The Fellowship of the Apostle

For all the sermons that have been preached on Paul's letters, I wonder how many of them are about the people he names—his friends, the ones who co-labored with him. Sosthenes was a brother and coauthor. Silas was a companion and jail mate and duet partner. Timothy was like a son and was also his most prolific collaborator. Epaphras was a fellow servant, faithful minister, and fierce prayer warrior whom Paul loved (Col. 1:7; 4:12; Philem. 1:23). He mentions Erastus and Gaius, church leaders and companions (Rom. 16:23). Lydia was a patron and friend (Acts 16:14, 40). Euodia and Syntyche were church leaders in Philippi who had been in the trenches with Paul, struggling in the ministry of the gospel (Phil. 4:1–3). Clement too (Phil. 4:3). Tychicus was a beloved brother and faithful servant who knew intimately what was going on in Paul's life and ministry (Eph. 6:21–22). Paul knew the people in Stephanas's household (1 Cor. 16:15) and cherished visits from Stephanas, Fortunatus, and Achaicus (1 Cor. 16:17). There was Titus, a true child of the faith, someone Paul could trust to carry on the work he had begun (Titus 1:4–5).

There was Priscilla and Aquila, that dynamic duo who helped teach and develop leaders. There was Philemon, a dearly loved coworker with whom Paul could speak frankly and at times sharply about his runaway slave, Onesimus. Philemon was in Paul's debt, though for what we do not know (Philem. 1:17–19). But the language of his appeal is the language of friendship. And Paul counts Onesimus as his own child, whom he loves as a father (Philem. 1:10). In that same church were Apphia, a dear sister, and Archippus, a fellow soldier (Philem. 1:2). And then, of course, there is Barnabas, that "son of encouragement" who believed in Paul early and often, standing with him in the controversy of the gospel spreading to the gentiles. Even though their friendship had a parting—ministry is tough on intimate relationships, as we've established—still their relationship shaped Paul.

We imagine Paul as a heroic individual, striking out on his own through stormy seas and desert roads, planting churches, preaching publicly, and enduring persecution. But *none* of those things happened alone. None of them. At Paul's lowest moments, God met him not only in prayer and worship—though these are surely ways that Paul found strength. God met Paul through *people* as well. In 2 Corinthians, a letter that is possibly Paul's most vulnerable, written after an experience that had left him shaken and discouraged, Paul describes how God's comfort came: "Even after we arrived in Macedonia, we couldn't rest physically. We were surrounded by problems. There was external conflict, and there were internal fears. However, God comforts people who are discouraged, and he comforted us by Titus' arrival" (2 Cor. 7:5–6). It was Titus! But not just Titus. "We weren't comforted only by his arrival but also by the comfort he had received from you" (2 Cor. 7:7). It was a chain of love, the dynamic force of fellowship. Their love for Paul and Titus came through Titus to Paul. In prison or with his pen, Paul was never alone. He lasted because of the grace of God and the people God placed around him.

Paul was surrounded by a constellation of relationships. Early on, Ananias was the *healer*, quite literally. Perhaps Barnabas was the *sage*, the one who saw the call on his life and who vouched for him to the church. His *companions* were numerous, from Silas and Silvanus to Timothy and Epaphras. His *peers* were, perhaps most notably, Peter, with whom he had sharp conflict (see Gal. 2), and from whom he received high praise (see 2 Pet. 3). The *king* would likely, early on, have been a role filled by James, the head of the Jerusalem church. When you read Acts 15, the story of the Jerusalem Council trying to sort out the gentile issue for the first time, it's slightly humorous to think that Paul—the man who would be the greatest apostle to the gentiles—is there, and yet James is the decision-maker who, after hearing from everyone, gives a letter to be sent—a letter of which Paul is merely the carrier! Surely James was the one who could have told Paul no in those early years.

Intentional Intimacy

These relationships do not flourish by accident. They require attention and intentionality. Go back with me to that day in Queens when I did not know what to write in the Scazerro "Rule of Life" relationships box. I started to imagine what could be. What if I gathered once a month with some like-hearted, sharp-minded friends to share what we were reading and writing? I immediately began a text thread. The response was instant enthusiasm. *Yes! I would make time for that!* So on the third Thursday of each month, we meet for the TAFT Society—Thursdays Are For Thinking. Though we have struggled to keep the time slot each month, it has helped the writing process of at least three books from among us. We also have occasionally done day retreats as a group of friends but with no set rhythm or expectation. I began texting them about doing our retreat days three times a year with one of them being an overnight. Again, everyone was in. A year or so later, Rich Villodas approached me about a monthly Zoom call—this was pre-pandemic and before Zoom became ubiquitous—with us and two other pastors to exchange notes. I did not realize how hungry I was for that kind of connection.

Little by little, my own constellation was being filled in. Whether or not you use a tool like the Rule of Life and write down those rhythms of connection, the point is to be intentional about it. Life is too full of the demands of ministry, the chaos of kids' activities, and the many unpredictable events for us to just hope that meaningful connection will happen.

In our home, I am greatly helped by the fact that my wife *lives* intentionally. She schedules time in our calendar for us to be together—sometimes a year in advance. Of course, even the best-laid plans of mice and men get overthrown, but that is not an excuse to give up. We set a time in our week for us to go on regular dates, even if it's a long walk around the neighborhood. (The quarantine weeks gave us a fresh appreciation for this sloweddown simple practice.) We mark a time in our calendar for us to take one of the kids out on a date. And we schedule a getaway for a couple of nights—usually in town—for time to rest, pray, and play together. Those retreats are when we revisit our own version of the Rule of Life, which we have simply called "rhythms of intentionality."[22] These practices have sustained us over the past decade and more.

Anything worth having is worth pursuing. The chase for deep friendships and intimate relationships is a lifelong quest. But it can begin today. If we really want to last in ministry, if we want to emerge from this as truly and fully human beings, then we must take seriously the human vocation of loving well. Love is purposeful and intentional. Love is sacrificial and costly. Love is faithful and persistent. No matter how good we are at preaching or leading or counseling, we are nothing without love.

The Pastor's Inner Circle

Overall, pastors report feeling supported and intimately known. The data suggest that, in the home, pastors are striving for time with their kids or spouse. Even so, serious challenges to marriage and parenting are increasingly common.

THIS YEAR, HOW OFTEN HAVE YOU FELT WELL-SUPPORTED BY THOSE CLOSE TO YOU?

● Frequently ● Sometimes ● Seldom ● Never

All Pastors

| 54% | 38% | 6% | 1% |

50+ Years Old

| 62% | 31% | 6% | 1% |

Under 50 Years Old

| 45% | 47% | 7% | 2% |

IS THERE SOMEONE IN YOUR LIFE WHO KNOWS YOU WELL WHO ISN'T IN YOUR CHURCH OR FAMILY?

● Yes ● No

20%

80%

HOW OFTEN DO YOU DO THE FOLLOWING?

% of pastors who do the following at least weekly

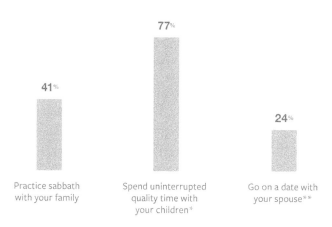

41%
Practice sabbath
with your family

77%
Spend uninterrupted
quality time with
your children*

24%
Go on a date with
your spouse**

AT ANY TIME DURING YOUR TENURE IN MINISTRY, HAVE YOU PERSONALLY STRUGGLED WITH THE FOLLOWING?

% "yes"

 2015 ● 2020

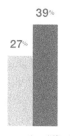

27% **39**%

Major parenting difficulties

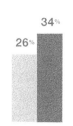

26% **34**%

Significant marital problem

*of those who have children under 18 living at home.
**of those who are married
n=408 U.S. Protestant pastors, September 16–October 8, 2020.

Reflections from Holly Packiam, pastor of parenting ministries, New Life Downtown

Cultivating deep, meaningful, and long-lasting relationships can be challenging, especially in ministry. And they're even harder to maintain. Life is full, and there is no shortage of things to be involved with or people to serve.

For years I desired to have consistent friendships, and I finally recognized that I needed to step out and invite people in rather than wait to be invited. I'm not naturally an initiator, but I took the advice of a mentor who encouraged me to intentionally invite friends to be in a small group with me. Glenn and I also began inviting friends over for dinner, even if it was once a month. I currently meet with good friends regularly over coffee for intentional conversations about what we're reading and what's going on in our hearts.

There will always be reasons not to cultivate friendships. Too many nights at the church, exhaustion from a crying baby who kept you up all night, a stacked day of meetings, and the list goes on.

And if having a full schedule isn't enough of a barrier, it's hard to lean into friendships when conflict arises. And it will. What happens when you initiate and the friendship isn't what you hoped for, or your feelings were hurt and you're not sure if you'll recover? Maybe a friend lets you down or you find that you need to take a step back from the relationship for a while. That's OK. Ask yourself if this friendship is worth fighting for. Can you accept the gift of the friendship even if it isn't everything you hoped for?

It's also helpful to prayerfully think about relationships in concentric circles. Your smallest circle might be your family and a couple of your closest friends. These are people who know everything about you and can ask you anything. Share what's making you mad, sad, glad, and anxious. The next circle might be friends you're getting to know better or ones you want to build a stronger friendship with. The outermost circle might be specific relationships you sense the Lord is calling you to pursue in this season for a particular purpose. These may be less mutual but still enriching. Or they might be pastors in other cities, people who get your life and can empathize with what you're going through.

We need different types of relationships and different rhythms and levels of investment. We can't be close to everyone, and no one friend can be everything we need. Take a small step today toward sharing your life with others in an intentional way.

credibility

How can we regain credibility and trust?

For decades, "America's Pastor" was not actually a pastor. Billy Graham earned this title during his years of faithful ministry, and after his death, virtually every news outlet used the moniker to describe him. The evangelist met with and offered counsel to every American president from Harry Truman to Barack Obama, crossing boundary lines between parties, denominations, and at times races. It did not matter that he did not lead a church or shepherd a congregation. He was a Christian who preached the gospel with boldness and clarity. That was enough to be pastor to the nation.

Today, America does not want a pastor. As I write amid the summer of a global pandemic, the voices that garner respect are those of science and commerce. We want to hear from entrepreneurs and financial advisors who can save the economy or from scientists who can tell us how this accursed virus spreads or affects us. And if we need a spirituality of sorts, it must be as personal as it is pragmatic—it has got to work *for me*.

Even among Christians, a pastor is not the primary voice of influence. One Sunday morning, a congregant came up to me and asked if I was getting ready to rob a bank or a train. I was wearing a mask as was expected of people when in close indoor spaces during the pandemic of 2020. I smiled, though he couldn't tell, and said I was trying to set a good example. He said he understood there was political pressure on leaders. If I was puzzled by what exactly he meant, his next words left no doubt. He recommended I listen to a sermon by a particular pastor in Texas who had recounted how Hitler seized control in Germany prior to World War II by manufacturing fake crises. The compliance of a docile public allowed the monster to have his way. We in America, that pastor had said, need to wake up and take a stand before that happens here. "It's scary!" the congregant said. "I'm not wearing a mask. If God wants to take me, he'll take me." Then he went on to compare his imagined courage to the three Hebrew men thrown in the fiery furnace for refusing to bow to the idol of Nebuchadnezzar. This congregant had disavowed idolatry to the State but not to his understanding of the American ideal of individual freedom.

He never asked what I thought or why I was wearing a mask. He didn't ask me to explain how the way of Christ is to protect the weak and the vulnerable. I never got to say that just as no one took Jesus's life—he laid it down—so no one makes us wear a mask; we choose to do so out of love. I had so many things to say. I had thought through it; I was prepared. He didn't seem to care. Even when people *do* want to hear from pastors, it's not necessarily *their* pastor. They'll find one who agrees with their political view or the talking points of their news outlet of choice and consign all other pastors who disagree—even their own—to the category of "coward" or "clueless."

On Twitter or Facebook, when a major social issue occurs, it's only a matter of time before someone posts what pastors *should* say about it that Sunday. And *"if your pastor doesn't speak out about . . ."*—then it's time to find a new church. The media and the mob set the criteria for what a pastor should or should not say. Either way, the pastor is no longer the locus of authority or credibility.

That same Sunday morning, on my way out the door, a volunteer introduced himself to me. He told me his son-in-law worked in our county public health department and had been in a few Zoom meetings with me. He had told his father-in-law that I was one of the few pastors he could respect and that it was changing his impression of our church. I shrugged off the compliment and praised the many pastors in the city who were in unity about decisions in how to handle the pandemic. Then I noticed that the man telling me this story had tears in his eyes. He wanted his son-in-law to come to know Jesus. And if a pastor had restored credibility to the church in some small way, then that just might be the first step.

How America Views Pastors

Restoring credibility will be an uphill climb.

According to a 2016 Barna study, 28 percent of Americans view pastors in a "somewhat" or "very" negative light.[1] Only 24 percent of Americans think of pastors in a "very positive" way. Still, just about half of Americans—48 percent—view them in a "somewhat positive" light. As the Barna study states, "Most don't actively hate pastors, not at all. They just don't especially care."[2]

When a person knows a pastor personally and thinks specifically of them, however, their opinion rises. Among practicing Christians, 87 percent view the pastor they know in a "very positive" light.[3] For Americans in general, the percentage who view pastors in a "very positive" light nearly triples—from 24 percent to 64 percent—when they move from thinking about pastors in general to the particular pastor they know personally.[4] Even for the self-described "unchurched," the percentage of positive perception rises from 9 percent to 38 percent when they think of a pastor they know.[5] (Of course, there's another implication of this: if you're unchurched and you don't know any pastors personally, you're not very likely at all to think of pastors positively.)

Generally, a pastor does not hold the place of community esteem as they once did. Today, only about one in five Americans think of a pastor as very influential in their community, and about one in four think they are not very influential or not influential at all.[6] But what kind of influence is it? Are pastors *good* for their communities? Through even that marginal influence, do pastors benefit their neighborhoods? Forty percent of Americans say yes, pastors bring a "significant benefit" to their community, while an additional 26 percent say they bring a "small benefit." Well, that's roughly two-thirds of Americans who still think pastors are a force for good locally.

Don't get too excited though. Things are changing along generational lines. Millennials are the least likely group to see pastors as bringing a benefit to the community—half as likely as the Elders.[7] And, where faith is absent, the view is bleaker. If a person has no faith, they are about twice as likely as the average American to see a pastor's presence as a "disadvantage" to the community.[8]

What about a pastor's words? Do Americans want to hear what pastors have to say? Not really. Only 21 percent of Americans consider pastors to be "very credible" on the "important issues of our day." Even among those Barna defined as evangelicals, the number only rises to slightly over half.[9] Think about it: *nearly half of American evangelicals don't see their pastors as being an authoritative voice for navigating current affairs.*

If people are going to listen to pastors, it might be about how to live according to God's will. The plurality of Americans—though still a mere 36 percent—think pastors are "very reliable" on that topic.[10] Pastors are counting on this, albeit with perhaps a bit too much confidence. Our new study found that most pastors (78 percent) believe people see their wisdom as at least "somewhat reliable" when it comes to "God's will for human beings and the world," and most also feel they are trusted to be a reliable source when it comes to "how people can live out their convictions privately and publicly" (70 percent).

What people don't want to hear from pastors, though, is "how Christianity should inform our political and justice systems." In fact, 56 percent of pastors—the largest segment on either end of the spectrum—see themselves as "not very reliable" on those is-

THE PASTOR'S MIXED RELIABILITY, ACCORDING TO PASTORS

● Very reliable ● Somewhat reliable ● Not very reliable ○ Not at all reliable

Are pastors reliable as sources of information and counsel for how people can live out their convictions privately and publicly?

Are pastors reliable as sources of information and counsel for how Christians should inform our political and justice systems?

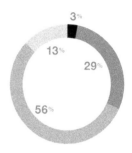

n=408 U.S. Protestant pastors, September 16–October 8, 2020.

sues. Where the general opinion about what pastors have to say is a bit of a yawn, people feel strongest about a pastor sharing his or her political theology or political opinions. And what they feel is "I don't trust you." Pastors seem to know this. In our 2020 study, we found that more than two-thirds of pastors don't think Americans view them as a reliable voice on how Christianity should inform our political or justice systems.

My focus group conversations confirmed this. Michelle has been a senior pastor in a small community in eastern Colorado for almost two decades. That longevity has given her a respect in the community and a credibility that is not easily eroded. Yet she laments the "loud voices" of social media, news outlets, and more that have made people question her when she says something that does not align with their political talking points. Similarly, Felicity, who generally enjoys the trust of the community due to the Appalachian culture that views pastors as honorable figures, felt the erosion of that trust in 2020.

Not surprisingly, those with no faith don't want to hear what a pastor has to say on much of anything. At least 94 percent of those with no faith don't think pastors are "very reliable" about knowing how relationships work, how to live out one's convictions, how to know God's will for human beings and the world, or much else.[11]

When I asked the pastors in my focus groups whether they thought their congregations viewed them as trustworthy sources of wisdom, they were unsure. It depended on the topic. Sally, in Kentucky, definitely felt like a credible voice to her church when answering their questions about family ministry, which is her area of specialty. But she was quick to add that she has felt "put in a box" because of her role and gender. And there were definitely those who were cautious about her opinions on social or political issues because she was deemed "progressive." Gary in Belfast, Ireland, said his church thinks of him as a "font of all wisdom" on anything related to Scripture. But because the culture equates age with wisdom, no one older than him (he's in his early forties) would consult him for life decisions. To them he's just "a boy."

Michael had a different experience than anyone else in my focus group. As a British-born, ethnically Chinese curate in the Church of England, he has far more respect from the community with his "dog collar" on than he ever did as a pastor in nondenominational Chinese churches where to be Chinese was less than being White. With the reservoir of institutional trust held by the Church of England, he experienced an honorable welcome into the parish from local magistrates and other county leaders. Stefan, a pastor at a multiethnic church in Toronto, Canada, described a general place of honor given to religious figures depending on the ethnic background of the community. "They respect the religious aspect of the pastor even though the credibility doesn't come for the church." He chalks this up to the "honor-shame" culture of many of those communities. "Even non-Christians respect religious figures" even if "they are skeptical of what [they] believe."

The attitude toward pastors is not overwhelmingly positive or negative; it's tepid. There is no one who is "America's Pastor" because America no longer cares if it has a pastor. If a person goes to church, they likely know a pastor and are generally interested to hear their thoughts on so-called spiritual matters. But even so, they aren't the only voice. Younger people are less likely to know a pastor from involvement in church, and those who don't have any faith at all could not care less what pastors think—about anything. It's fine if there are churches in the neighborhood. They're probably a good influence. But no one thinks of a church as the center of a community. I'm not sure if people are really seeking out a pastor as a credible voice in uncertain times. In fact, we found that only 21 percent of pastors strongly think their church's community/neighborhood considers them to be a trustworthy source of wisdom. Pastors, for the most part, are peripheral and ornamental. Quaint, but not entirely necessary. Kind, but not wholly credible.

Credibility in a Digital World

Living in a digital age has added further complications. In one sense, the internet has been a great equalizer, disrupting traditional hierarchies of power and granting anyone the access and the potential to amass a following. Economic historian Niall Ferguson notes that while networks have always existed in some form of a system, they were typically always hierarchies.[12] It's the internet that made networks possible without the grossly uneven distribution of power. Anyone can post; anyone can search; anyone can learn. The access to information—much to the chagrin of doctors who have to respond to patients' questions based on Google searches—has had a democratizing effect, so much so that authoritarian regimes around the world implement heavy-handed censorships and firewalls.

Social media platforms, however, have created another disruption. Without erasing the democratizing effect of the internet and without eliminating the possibility of digital upward mobility, social media has reshaped power in the form of followers and "likes." Now the number of followers on Instagram is enough to make a person an "influencer." A viral video can launch a career or end one. Popularity has replaced credibility.

What does this mean for church leaders, for those who carry a kind of "religious authority"? Pauline Hope Cheong, professor of Human Communication at Arizona State University, notes that "religious authority is eroded by online religious activities."[13] One reason is that "the internet allows access to information previously . . . only understood by elites who are certified and/or ordained."[14] Such access by nonprofessionals can "undermine the plausibility structure of a religious system."[15] If anyone can google their questions about the Bible and theology, why do they need to ask their pastor? Why do they need a pastor? There is a positive side here: power dynamics can be held in check. Pastors can't spit out claims without a congregant fact-checking them on their phone in the middle of a sermon. People who don't think the gifts of the Spirit are for today may watch YouTube videos of charismatic worship and question what they've been told about the Holy Spirit.

But this access to information is a double-edged sword. It does not simply tear down or destabilize existing structures of authority. It creates new ways of establishing authority and gives rise to new authority figures such as "online forum leaders and web masters."[16] Instagram influencers, right-wing bloggers, videos and memes floating around Facebook—these have been created and curated by new figures of authority. And with new "leaders" come new "tribes." This can lead to the dangerous assumption that all views are equally valid. Each person becomes their own arbiter of religious truth, each doing what is right in their own eyes or in the eyes of the podcast they listened to this morning. Jim, a pastor in one of my focus groups who serves as the senior pastor of the church he grew up in, described his struggle in rural northeastern Missouri. During COVID-19, when all church services went online-only, he reported losing people to the "hot preacher" online whom he couldn't compete with.

Authority in the digital age, however, is not simply a story of disruption. Cheong also notes a kind of "continuity and complementarity" in authority when traditional religious authority

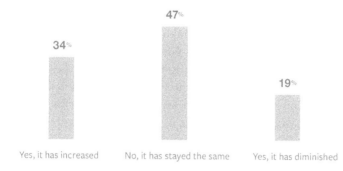

HAS YOUR INFLUENCE IN THE LIVES OF YOUR
CONGREGANTS SHIFTED DURING THE YEAR 2020?

47%

34%

19%

Yes, it has increased   No, it has stayed the same   Yes, it has diminished

n=408 U.S. Protestant pastors, September 16–October 8, 2020.

figures—from the pope on YouTube to Buddhist priest bloggers to pastors on Twitter—enter these spaces with their own content and campaigns. This sort of "strategic arbitration" reflects an adaptation to new conditions, and thus pastors seem to be "adjusting their social identity from that of commanders and sages, to guides and mediators of knowledge and encounters both online and offline."[17]

In short, online platforms have disrupted traditional forms of ecclesial authority, but many church leaders are filling the same spaces to extend or reinforce their authority. In both cases, people may gain and protect power dishonestly through crafted self-presentations. The digital age does not solve the problem of the misuse of power; it simply creates new conditions in which such abuse may occur. Thus, the pastor's loss of credibility may indeed be the fruit of a misuse of authority—whether that occurred by the vain quest for online popularity or in private but is now being exposed in the digital world. What is needed is for the historic and global witness of the church to be a mitigating influence, to hold some sense of authority. The creeds and confessions of the church can become guardrails and boundary lines in this wild frontier.

Misusing Authority

The path to regaining credibility begins with taking responsibility. We must face the reality that we have contributed to the crisis of credibility. Yes, there are cultural headwinds that have changed the social standing or cultural power of a pastor. But we have made a mess of things too. From small country churches to uber-megachurches, many pastors have been found to be bullies and hypocrites, alcohol abusers and womanizers. The crisis of credibility is a symptom. The misuse of authority is the root cause.

The Old Testament reflects on the use of power in the way it tells the story of Israel's first king. Saul's story reveals three classic ways of mishandling authority: using it for our own benefit, overstepping the bounds of our authority, and exercising it rashly.

The first misuse comes in a warning from God. When the people ask Samuel for a king, he warns them that kings *take*. They will "take your sons"; they will "take your daughters"; they will "take your best fields, vineyards, and olive groves"; they will "take your male and female servants"; they will "take one-tenth of your flocks" (1 Sam. 8:11–17). God warned Israel that rejecting Yahweh as King and seeking a human ruler—giving a human the kind of power that belongs to the Lord—comes at a cost. Kings *take*. Saul does some taking, but the Hebrew verb shows up most strikingly when David *took* the wife of Uriah, Bathsheba (2 Sam. 11:4).

How have we taken from our people? How have we taken their time, their hopes, their trust, and used it for our own ends? Maybe we have treated good-hearted people who serve our churches as though they are cogs in the machinery of our ambition. Perhaps we have dismissed our sacred congregation as dumb "sheep" who annoy us. We are all too willing to take their time but slow to give ours. For some of us, this hits close to home.

The second misuse of power is in overstepping its bounds. Saul, impatient for Samuel's arrival, decided to act like a priest and offer sacrifices. But this was not his role. Samuel did not mince words in his rebuke: "'How stupid of you to have broken the commands the Lord your God gave you!' Samuel told Saul. 'The Lord would have established your rule over Israel forever, but now your rule won't last. The LORD will search for a man following the Lord's own heart, and the LORD will commission him as leader over God's people, because you didn't keep the LORD's command'" (1 Sam. 13:13–14). Saul had been anointed king. Though it was not God's intended way of ruling his people, he made a concession, accommodating their desire. But Saul had trouble submitting. He did not want to obey. Mostly, he was afraid of what the people would think of him if he did not act. "'I saw that my troops were deserting,' Saul replied. 'You hadn't arrived by the appointed time, and the Philistines were gathering at Michmash'" (v. 11).

In the attempt to be strong leaders, we can become disobedient fools. Saul was afraid of looking weak, so he tried to do it all—even though that was *not* what God had called him to do. How many of us, in the effort to live up to people's expectations, step into roles for which we have neither the training nor the calling to perform? We tend to think of disobedience in terms of moral failures, but we are unfaithful to the call every time we act like we can fulfill someone else's vocation. I'm thinking about the temptation to pretend we are counselors, when many of us are not trained that way. When a pastor speaks dismissively of counseling or mental health, saying from the pulpit that a person who is anxious or depressed simply needs to pray more, they are eroding their own credibility by overreaching with their authority.

Others attempt to make major financial decisions that have massive implications for the business operations of the church when they really have no understanding of such matters. The temptation is to show that we can do it all, that we can be the savvy CEO, the brilliant theologian and teacher, the incisive counselor and therapist. We are the anointed one, after all. But the king was meant to work in tandem with the prophet and the priest. Saul needed Samuel. We need to trust that God is at work in the lives of others so we don't keep overstepping the bounds of our authority.

The third misuse of power comes by exercising authority rashly. In the very next chapter of 1 Samuel, Saul and his army had won a battle with the Lord's help. Instead of being attentive to their condition, weary after the fight, he doubles down on bravado. "Anyone who eats anything before evening when I have taken revenge on my enemies is doomed" (14:24). Exhausted and in need of replenishment, some soldiers came across a honeycomb on the ground. Saul's son, Jonathan, had not heard his father's hasty vow, and ate some honey. The soldiers, aghast at what had happened, told Jonathan about his father's pledge. Jonathan recognized the folly of it right away. "My father has brought trouble to the land. Look how my eyes lit up when I tasted just a bit of that honey! It would have been even better if the troops had eaten some of their enemies' plunder today when they found it! But now the Philistine defeat isn't as thorough as it might have been" (vv. 29–30). Not only was the defeat not as thorough as it might have been; the soldiers were set up to fail. After completing their conquest, they sinned against the Lord by eating the animals immediately, without draining them of their blood as was Israelite practice. Saul saddled himself with the dilemma of keeping his word or saving his son. And he made it more difficult for his troops to honor God because of the command he had given them.

There are a few ways that using authority rashly relates to us. How often do pastors speak with bravado about a politically partisan fight? How many times do we cash in the capital of a congregation's trust by calling them into a culture war? We have a tendency to announce with certainty whose "side" God is on, and in doing so we smear God's name and diminish our credibility. The text also speaks to our overly driven attempts to do God's work. Our teams may be exhausted and in need of replenishment after a long fight, but we drive them harder and push them to work longer hours—all "for the sake of the lost" or "the call." But when we act in a way that imposes our will on others, we are both hasty and foolish.

The shoe may not fit on all of us. But we can all take a hard look at ourselves and ask the Lord what measure of responsibility we must take for the loss of credibility of pastors. Have we stewarded power well?

The Source and the Shape of Authority

If the mishandling of power has led to the loss of credibility, returning to the source and shape of a pastor's authority is the way back home. I don't mean that we can find a way to return to a central place in our communities. But we can once again become trustworthy people when we rediscover the source and the shape of pastoral authority.

During the medieval centuries, the pastor—the *priest*—was anointed with special powers. They could heal the sick through prayer and anointing with oil, hear from God and interpret the Scriptures, and, of course, turn bread and wine into the body and blood of Christ. But as reformations led to rationalism, the pastor in the post-Enlightenment West found authority in his learning. As Andrew Root maps the shift in perceptions of pastors in America, he notes that "the pastor no longer had magical powers, but he could read; he was no longer a superhero but now was just a learned man."[18] Jonathan Edwards, perhaps the first of America's Pastors, devoted himself to study for thirteen hours a day! This began a long tradition of education as the basis for credibility. If a pastor went to the right seminaries and had the right degrees, if they devoted themselves to hours of study, they were to be trusted.

But Root notes a shift that began in the late twentieth century. The authority of a pastor began to come from the institutions they created. "The power of the professional office of pastor rests not in a divine order or a disciplined will (bound to education) but solely in the strength of institution. . . . Just as a CEO has the power of her office due to the societal or economic strength of the company, so too the pastor's power depends on the size and influence of the congregation."[19] With long sermons as a detriment and seminary education as a potential liability, pastors began to seek other ways of establishing their presence in a community. The answer was in building strong and influential churches. The pastor now "has to spend time and energy winning a cultural place for his congregation, not encountering (and inviting people into) divine action (he's unsure how to even do that)."[20]

But none of those things are the actual source of our authority. When God anointed David, he was a boy who knew how to seek God. That practice left him later in life. Shortly after his coronation, David hastily made plans to move the ark of the covenant without first "inquiring of the Lord," as he had done when he was a fugitive on the run from Saul. Jesus, the true Son of David, had no such lapses. He taught as "one who had authority, and not as the scribes" (Mark 1:22 ESV). Right until the end, he was stealing away to be with the Father. Hours before his arrest, he was in prayer.

The disciples took note. When Peter and John answered the high priest about the healing of the lame man at their command, the crowd was in awe. "Now when they saw the boldness of Peter and John, and perceived that they were uneducated, common men, they were astonished. And they recognized that *they had been with Jesus*" (Acts 4:13 ESV, emphasis added). Their authority had not come from their education or their institution—they were the ones being questioned by those with institutional power! Their confidence came from having been with Jesus.

The source of our authority, ultimately, comes not from our popularity or influence (though without influence, one could hardly be a leader), not from our education (though training and preparation are good things), and not from the institutions we lead (though creating institutions is part of having presence and place). The source of our authority is Jesus, and it comes from being in his presence.

But that is not all. By being with Jesus, we learn from him what power is *for*. We rethink how our authority is used. Jesus, "knowing that the Father had given all things into his hands, and that he had come from God and was going back to God" (John 13:3 ESV), got up, removed his robe, took up a towel and a basin, and began to wash the feet of his disciples. Jesus knew where he had come from and where he was going. Jesus had been with the Father and was going back to the Father. Jesus knew that the mission and the ministry were what the Father had entrusted to him. And so he took the form of a servant and washed their feet. When you know the *source* of your authority, you understand the *purpose* for it.

Pastors, if we have misused power—using it for our own gain, overstepping its bounds, or exercising it rashly—it's because we have forgotten its actual source. If our authority really did come from our education or the size of our institutions or the scope of our influence, then we could boast in it. *We did this. We earned this. We worked for this.* But if we recognize it as a gift, if we understand that the only authority we have is that which comes from the anointing of the Spirit of the Lord, then that same Spirit works to form Christ in us. The source of authority determines its shape. Our authority comes from Jesus, and it is to be used as Jesus used his power: to empty ourselves in service and self-giving love. As Paul would later write, our "strength is for service, not status" (Rom. 15:1 MSG). To recapture this perspective is to begin to return to credibility before Christ and his church. Credibility is the result of the good and right stewardship of power. When you understand the purpose of your power and the limits of your authority and act accordingly with humility, you earn trust and gain credibility.

The Pastor's Trust Factor

There is a sense that pastors can be counted on, whether one is looking for general wisdom or advice more specific to relationships or God's will. That is, if you are a Christian or a pastor yourself—non-Christians rarely regard pastors as trustworthy or reliable. Pastors may have picked up on the fact that congregational trust far exceeds the community's trust. Just one in five say their neighborhood "very much" sees them as a source of wisdom, compared to two-thirds who say their congregation sees them this way.

WOULD YOU CONSIDER A PASTOR TO BE A TRUSTWORTHY SOURCE OF WISDOM?

● Yes, definitely ● Yes, somewhat ○ Not really ● Definitely not ● Not sure

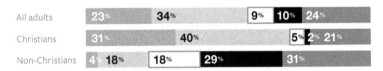

All adults	23%	34%	9%	10%	24%
Christians	31%	40%		5% 2%	21%
Non-Christians	4% 18%	18%	29%		31%

n=909 self-identified Christian U.S. adults, n=611 non-Christian U.S. adults, October 9–20, 2020.

● Yes, very much so ● Yes, somewhat ● No

Pastors: Would you say that the community / neighborhood where your church is located considers you to be a trustworthy source of wisdom?

21%	61%	17%

Pastors: Would you say your congregants consider you to be a trustworthy source of wisdom?

67%	33%

n=408 U.S. Protestant pastors, September 16–October 8, 2020.

IN YOUR HONEST OPINION, HOW RELIABLE DO YOU
THINK AMERICANS SEE PASTORS AND PRIESTS AS A
SOURCE OF INFORMATION AND COUNSEL FOR . . .

● Very reliable ● Somewhat reliable ⬚ Not very reliable ○ Not at all reliable
● Not sure

How the church can help people live according to God's will?

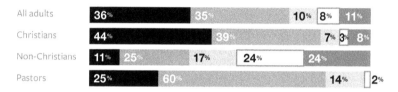

	Very reliable	Somewhat reliable	Not very reliable	Not at all reliable	Not sure
All adults	36%	35%	10%	8%	11%
Christians	44%	39%	7%	3%	8%
Non-Christians	11%	25%	17%	24%	24%
Pastors	25%	60%	14%		2%

God's will for human beings and the world?

	Very reliable	Somewhat reliable	Not very reliable	Not at all reliable	Not sure
All adults	35%	33%	10%	11%	12%
Christians	43%	38%	7%	4%	8%
Non-Christians	9%	18%	18%	32%	23%
Pastors	17%	61%	20%		3%

How relationships work and how to make them better?

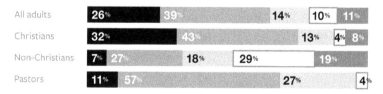

	Very reliable	Somewhat reliable	Not very reliable	Not at all reliable	Not sure
All adults	26%	39%	14%	10%	11%
Christians	32%	43%	13%	4%	8%
Non-Christians	7%	27%	18%	29%	19%
Pastors	11%	57%	27%		4%

n=1,025 U.S. adults, April 29–May 1, 2015.
n=408 U.S. Protestant pastors, September 16–October 8, 2020.

Reflections from Tara Beth Leach, pastor, author, and speaker

Pastors are losing credibility at an alarming rate, and too much is at stake not to ask the critical question, *What can we do to restore our credibility?* Credibility isn't just about our own egotistical reputation; rather, it's about our witness. As pastors, we join Christians down throughout history in bearing witness to the life-altering, world-shifting, and life-changing news. When the credibility of our witness is diminished, the world surely takes notice . . . and they already have.

Perhaps the most important starting point for pastors is to model the journey toward restoration through the important but difficult practices of humility, and prayers of *Examen*, lament, confession, and repentance. While these practices are critical to restoring our credibility, they aren't necessarily the *fun* and *glossy* ones. They require leaders to humbly face the world and admit that we don't know all that we have claimed to know (humility). They mean opening ourselves up to the Spirit who searches the crevices of our hearts and intentions and exposes them to ourselves and one another (prayer of *Examen*) and listening to understand instead of speaking to prove something must be normalized (prayer of *Examen*). They require painfully groaning our own complicity and participation in harmful systems in this world (lament). We must courageously confess before those we have hurt and not loved well (confession). Finally, we must dismantle decaying systems, deconstruct harmful theology, and turn toward the radiant Jesus who calls us to bear witness to the world's most remarkable story throughout history.

PART 2

Four Challenges for the Church

worship

Why do we gather in worship?

t might have been the most anticipated Sunday morning in recent memory. We had been on lockdown for eleven weeks. Eleven Sundays with no in-person church services. Several others had to endure much longer. Still, it felt unbearably long. Our team had rallied in a span of days to turn the sanctuary into a makeshift TV studio, adjusting lights and arranging cameras to make sure everything looked as good as it could to stream. We had always had a livestream, but now what was peripheral had become central, what was supplemental had become essential. It was working. We heard stories and saw pictures of people gathering around their TVs or computer screens to sing along and study the Bible together. Some of our church's eight congregations spread around the county used Zoom after the service time as a sort of digital lobby for people to chat and pray with one another. Like most pastors around the world, we were doing the best we could.

But we missed the smiles on people's faces, the spontaneous conversations in hallways and aisles. We missed hearing the buzz of conversation before and after service, and even during the meet-and-greet time. And we missed the sounds of voices singing, hands clapping, people shouting "Hallelujah!" and "Amen."

So on Sunday morning, May 31, 2020, I woke up with a charge of excitement. *We are gathering physically in one building as the church today!* It didn't matter that the room was set at only about 15 percent of its normal capacity, or that chairs were arranged by sets of twos, threes, fours, and sixes, or that each cluster was spaced from the others by six to ten feet, or that people were wearing masks when they entered and exited and moved around the building. As I stood in the second row, watching the countdown video that we had all grown accustomed to with our online services, the congregation began to cheer through the final twenty seconds. They were there in the room ready to worship.

Several times in the first few songs, I would just stop and look around and listen. It was the voices that got to me. Then we began singing that marvelous anthem from Andrew Peterson, "Is He Worthy?" And I lost it. I started weeping. Here we were singing about the eschatological choir that would one day gather from every tribe and tongue, from every nation and family, and we—one local church gathering in worship—were singing in anticipation of that day. It was an embodied signpost pointing forward to the completion of redemption. The goal of God's design of diversity in the beginning and God's deliverance of the cosmos from slavery to sin and death in the end is God's glory. Everything in heaven and earth will worship. Every time the church gathers in worship, we are rehearsing for that day. More than that, we are foretasting the world to come.

That Sunday, I sang and wept and sang some more; I shouted and danced and clapped. And all the saints were as one, social distancing and all.

Worship On-Demand

One Monday morning, after I had preached a sermon on worship the day before, I received an email from a friend in our church sharing his experience of being a missionary in Spain. Besides the Roman Catholic Church, the only other religious group the people in their area were familiar with were Jehovah's Witnesses. Even though his group explained that they were connected with an evangelical church in town, people did not know what to make of them. These missionaries would often gather in an apartment on the outskirts of town for a meal and for worship. My friends told me no less than ten of them had guitars and would often all bring them to these evenings. On the warm summer nights, with no air-conditioning, the windows and doors to the balcony were always open. The music would reverberate to neighboring apartments, and everyone seemed to enjoy it. Soon, the people began referring to them as *la gente que canta*, which roughly translates to "the people who sing." Eventually, this became their marker. When they were out on the streets, striking up conversations and trying to tell people about Jesus, people would ask who they were. "Are you the Jehovah's Witnesses?" "No," they would reply. "Are you the people who sing?" "YES!" they answered enthusiastically. "We are the people who sing."

The church is always singing. From the earliest moments, you find the New Testament church in prayer and worship. Luke's Gospel contains not one, not two, but four songs in the first two chapters, each of which became regular choruses for the early church. When two of the most prolific church planters and missionaries of that era found themselves in prison in Philippi, they sang. With bruises on their backs and blood on their lips, at midnight they *sang*. It's no wonder that many of Paul's letters contain eruptions into doxology, whether through a poem, a prayer, or a hymn. The book of Revelation, as already mentioned, is full of scenes of the saints singing. Not even a century after the New Testament era, when a local governor named Pliny wrote to his uncle, the Emperor Trajan, about how to handle the Christians, he spoke of how they would rise early and gather to sing hymns to Christ as if to a god. Christians *sing*.

That Sunday in late spring of 2020—Pentecost Sunday, no less—our church came together to carry on the grand and glorious tradition. We gathered to worship and to sing. And what a sound it was.

But it didn't take long for the shine to wear off. People soon complained about registering to save their seat. Others didn't like that they had to adjust to new service times and days because of limited seating and because many of our off-site congregations around the city could not yet meet in the schools that had been their place of worship. Some did not feel safe—which was perfectly understandable. We continued to make all our services available online for just that reason. But others told us quite bluntly that they had gotten used to watching online and rather enjoyed that. They could stay in their pj's, not wrangle kids, and even watch on their own schedule.

That last trend troubled me. Barna discovered a few months into the pandemic that half of "churched adults"—those who have attended a church service at least once in the past six months— had not "streamed an online service in the last month."[1] And for "practicing Christians," who typically attend a church service at least once a month, only one in three said they had "streamed an online service" in the past month.[2] When the data is broken down by generation, the picture is worst for younger Christians—the ones who presumably are more tech-savvy and digitally inclined. "When asked if they had attended church within the past four weeks, exactly half of practicing Christian Millennials (50%)" said they had not.[3]

There are pros and cons with online worship, of course. Every pastor in my focus groups admitted that it was not ideal and that it would not be central to their identity post-pandemic. Our research suggests that pastors at large carry these same opinions, as we found that only 4 percent of pastors "strongly agree" that "churches can effectively operate in an online-only format" (with another 23 percent who "somewhat agree"). But as my focus group participants shared, they all know online worship is hugely important now, and it is enabling the development of new skills that will bear fruit beyond the COVID season. Sally in Kentucky points out that it is their "most inclusive form of worship for folks with mental and physical disabilities, for folks with illness, and often for folks with kids. So I think it needs to stay and be invested in." Stefan in Toronto shares his perspective from a "post-Christian culture in Canada, particularly in Toronto": "People like the convenience of listening to services on their time and have their weekends free.

Even pre-COVID, people like to have the weekends to go to their cottage and watch the services online." Yet other pastors, such as Dan in the Dallas area, know that "digital fatigue makes it difficult for online worship to be primary." When something has to give, families give up online worship instead of "work and school."

But all this raises some fundamental questions for us as church leaders. *Why do we need to gather in worship? Can't we worship on our own? Can a worship service be "on-demand"?*

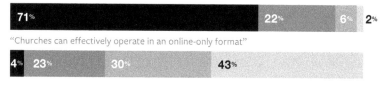

DIGITAL VS. PHYSICAL CHURCH? FOR PASTORS, NO CONTEST

● Strongly agree ● Somewhat agree ● Somewhat disagree ● Strongly disagree

"The physical gathering is essential to the church"

| 71% | 22% | 6% | 2% |

"Churches can effectively operate in an online-only format"

| 4% | 23% | 30% | 43% |

n=408 U.S. Protestant pastors, September 16–October 8, 2020.

What Are Sundays For?

What is the purpose of our gathering? What are we trying to accomplish when we come together in worship? We already have an answer to those questions. When we sit down to plan the songs in the worship set list or the sermon series or even the stage design, we make those decisions out of a framework shaped by our understanding of the purpose of congregational worship. Spoken or unspoken, conscious or unconscious, we know what Sundays—or whatever the day of our gathering—are for.

A cursory survey of the books and pamphlets and websites from scholars and pastors over the past few decades reveals three paradigms of congregational worship, three ways of thinking about the purpose for the church to gather together.

The first is *mission*. This approach has its roots in the frontier revivals in America, most notably the Second Great Awakening. "Liturgical scholar Melanie Ross writes that while Jonathan Edwards during the First Great Awakening described 'revival' as a 'marvelous work of God,' Charles Finney about a hundred years later argued that revival was the result of employing the 'appropriate means.'"[4] The goal was the conversion of souls through whatever means worked. Ross credits Finney for shifting away from the historic shape of a church service as four movements—gathering, word, table, sending—and creating instead a threefold ordo (order of service)—songs, sermon, altar call.

Without realizing it, many of us are heirs to Finney's legacy. While the move from a fourfold service shape to a threefold one may not be that significant, there is an underlying premise that we have unwittingly adopted. Finney's real legacy is the "unashamed relativization of forms," the belief that "any method can be used if it proves effective in winning someone to Christ."[5] That very legacy is what worship historian James White sees in the seeker-sensitive movement that began in the 1980s and 1990s and continues in some form today.[6]

Now, you may be thinking, "Well, what's wrong with that? Aren't we supposed to reach the lost?" Indeed, we are. And there is nothing inherently wrong with saying that part of the purpose for the church's gathering is to proclaim the good news to the world. The mission paradigm emerges from a biblical impulse found most obviously in the book of Acts, where people are being saved from the very first gathering on the day of Pentecost. The problem is not with the paradigm; it's with the emphasis we give it. But I'm getting ahead of myself.

The second paradigm for congregational worship is *formation*. The same year that Bill and Lynn Hybels and Rick Warren released their books about churches focusing their services and ministries on the seeker, Marva Dawn, a liturgical theologian, released a book called *Reaching Out Without Dumbing Down*. Whether it was meant as a direct rebuke or not, lines had been drawn. Summarizing her contribution, Alan Rathe writes, "Dawn especially stresses this deeply formative power of corporate worship. She understands that power to be, on the one hand, wholly God's. She also recognizes that the practices of the gathered community, especially in connection with worship, are powerfully formative in and of themselves."[7]

If the mission paradigm is the product of the wider evangelical movement, the formation paradigm comes to us largely through the Reformed tradition. The late theologian Robert Webber pioneered an approach he called "ancient-future worship," which he defined as "the common tradition of the church's worship in Word, Table, and song, practiced faithfully and communicated clearly in every context of the world."[8] For Webber, worship needs both remembrance and anticipation as it rehearsed the gospel. Similarly, Tim Keller sees "the built-in order of the Reformed liturgy" as "gospel re-enactment."[9]

The formation paradigm is most forcefully argued by Christian philosopher James K. A. Smith. He contends that ultimately, we are what we *love*, we may not love what we think we love, and that our loves must be shaped by the practices of Christian worship. These practices are communal—congregational—and counter-formative. What he means is that we are *already* being formed by something— the seasonal sales, the summer holidays, the drive to spend and consume, and more. Worship is where Christians get their desires recalibrated, their hearts realigned, and their loves re-aimed.

The problem with this sort of thinking is it tends to result in churches focusing on getting the song lyrics just right or incorporating a historic liturgy or adopting ancient practices. But words and prayers and practices do not automatically form us into the image of the Son. The Holy Spirit does that, and he does so in a variety of ways. As we will see below, there is a wildness to the Spirit's work that cannot be scripted.

The third paradigm is *encounter*. If the mission paradigm comes from the wider evangelical tradition, and the formation paradigm emerges from the Reformed tradition, then the encounter paradigm of congregational worship comes from the Pentecostal-charismatic streams. (I say *streams* because the five hundred million Pentecostal

Christians around the world are only one part of a neo-charismatic movement, sometimes referred to as the "Third Wave," that comprises Christians from over eighteen thousand "independent, indigenous, post-denominational" associations, networks, and groups "that cannot be classified as either pentecostal or charismatic but share a common emphasis on the Holy Spirit, spiritual gifts, pentecostal-like experiences . . . signs and wonders, and power encounters."[10])

This paradigm is evidenced less in books and more in sermons and songs. Think of all the songs that talk about meeting with God, about God being here in our midst, speaking, moving, ready to act. The musical aspect of congregational worship—in Pentecostal-charismatic tradition—"places the presence of God as the goal and the center of its practice."[11] This has led several scholars to draw comparisons between music and the Eucharist—the Lord's Table. Singing has become the new sacrament, they say. Two historians of contemporary worship, Swee-Hong Lim and Lester Ruth, make insightful comparisons between the way music and singing function in Pentecostal-charismatic streams and how the Eucharist functions in liturgical traditions.[12]

I tend to think that the encounter paradigm actually draws from something more intimate—the notion of person-to-person relationships. The Jewish philosopher Martin Buber described the sacredness of an "I-You" relationship.[13] We depersonalize the other when we treat a person as an object. When we seek to move the other but never allow them to move us, we turn our relationship into "I-It." "Praise and worship, for the pentecostal-charismatic, is an I-You encounter; the human, the collective I, meets the divine You in song and prayer."[14] But even the most sacred of interactions can become profane when they are commodified. When church is the site of a religious transaction, when a congregation becomes the consumer of an experience or the seeker of a new high, the encounter paradigm has gone awry.

By now you see that each paradigm can be defended biblically. You've probably heard many of these defenses or perhaps given one of these rationales yourself. You may not have known you held that understanding of the purpose of congregational worship, but now it's becoming clear.

So which paradigm is the *right* one?

A Generative Tension

In our new study of pastors, *encounter* (43 percent) and *formation* (41 percent) were statistically tied for the number one paradigm chosen by pastors as the primary reason for the church to gather in worship, while *mission* lagged behind at 16 percent. In our new survey of the general population, practicing Christians[15] ranked *encounter* (44 percent) and *mission* (40 percent) as a statistical tie for number one. While there is agreement between pastors and parishioners—mainly, that encounter is widely seen as very important—we are still left to wonder what the ranking *should* be.

Have you ever messed around with a photo-editing app and tried to resize a picture but ended up stretching it in strange ways? Then you discovered the little box labeled "lock aspect ratio." Aha. That's the way to change the size without messing up the proportion. I think all three of the paradigms for congregational worship are meant to exist in a kind of generative tension with each other. Not all tension between ideals is bad. Think of a guitar string. Just the right tension enables the music to happen.

All three paradigms come from the Bible. The missionary impulse of God is seen from calling Abraham to knocking down Saul on the road to Damascus. The formative intent of God is found from the Ten Commandments to the New Testament's insistence that we walk worthy of our calling (Eph. 4:1). The encounter instinct is inherent in the relational God who exists as three in one and calls humanity to enter into fellowship with him and with each other. These ways of thinking about the purpose of church cannot be dismissed as secular ideas or contemporary innovations.

But if we elevate one to the detriment of the other two, we'll have problems. The image distorts. When *mission* becomes the only paradigm, then we believe we must reach the lost at any cost and do anything short of sin to win people to Christ. Church services become the "showroom floor," staff become the performers, and congregants become the sales and marketing teams. I think about the times we've had to sell a house during our kids' younger years. Every morning, I'd wake up, head downstairs, and immediately start barking orders to quickly put away the eggs or wipe the counters. And my poor kids were simply trying to eat breakfast. But as anyone who has sold a home knows, there could be a showing any day, and any showing could be the one that results in an offer. You must be ready. That kind of living on the edge of a sale is exhausting. It is for churches too.

When *formation* becomes the only paradigm, we analyze every element to death and think that we can script spiritual formation. The services become catechism class, the staff become educators, and congregants become students who have little patience for anyone who is less serious than they are about the things of God. An occupational hazard of mine is that I'm prone to overexplain or to go on about a lesson I want my kids to learn or a point I'm trying to make. This is useful as a preacher, not so much as a father and husband. When we lead our churches this way, we can put too much weight on a single worship service, expecting our practices and prayers, our songs and sermons, to make disciples just by the people's participation in them. As we'll see in the next chapter, formation doesn't quite work that way.

When *encounter* becomes the only paradigm, we become experience junkies in search of the next high or exhausted producers who have to make each gathering epic, all the while battling the temptation to manipulate the crowd with music and lights and image and sound. The services become "experiences," the staff become event producers, and congregants become consumers or radical individualists. I was speaking at a conference once where the guest-artist worship leader opened the session by assuring us that she wanted to be the soundtrack for our personal time with God. It's a nice sentiment, but that's not what corporate worship is for. There was a reason people had come from all over the country instead of staying home and streaming her album on Spotify. But when an experience with God is all we're after, it's easy to let the subjective nature of experience devolve into a privatization of worship.

The truth is, we need all three paradigms. The question is, How do we hold them together in the right way?

The Spirit and the Church

All three paradigms come together by the Holy Spirit. The Holy Spirit is the one who empowers our mission. Jesus told the disciples to wait for the Spirit so that they would receive power to be his witnesses (Acts 1:8). The Holy Spirit is the one who forms us into the image of Christ (Gal. 5:16–23). And it's through the Holy Spirit that we encounter the presence of God when the church gathers together (1 Cor. 12 and 14). The Spirit compels us toward mission, works in us for our formation, and encounters us as the presence of God.

When I was doing my doctoral research at Durham University, I designed my method to analyze both the text and the performance of the "ritual" known as contemporary worship. My goal was to discover how Christian hope was encoded in contemporary worship songs *and* experienced in contemporary worship services. I learned that the lyrical content of many songs of hope named by worship leaders around the country are overly focused on the *present tense*, the *proximate space*, and the *personal case* (I, me, my). This falls short of a robust, historically Christian eschatology that looks "for the resurrection of the dead and the life of the world to come."[16] But when I spent time with two local churches in the fieldwork part of my research—through "participant observation" in services, interviews with pastors and worship leaders, and focus group conversations—I learned that when people came to worship, their experience of hope was *consistent* (they could count on leaving church feeling better than the way they came in), *resilient* (they could summon that hope again throughout the week via worship and prayer), and *variant* in the means by which that experience came (for some it was the music and the energy, for others it was the silence and the prayer).

How does one account for that disparity? My proposal was that we understand it when we have a robust theology of the Spirit. The Holy Spirit, after all, is God's *eschatological* presence—the Spirit is how we foretaste the future! And the Holy Spirit is also God's *powerful* and *empowering* presence. We know that God is able and that in him we have all the strength we need. Remembering and experiencing this power is another major component of the experience of hope. Finally, the Holy Spirit is God's *sacramental* presence—the Spirit works through creation to communicate God's presence to us (think of anointing oil or the waters of baptism or the bread and the wine). In short, *the Holy Spirit is the wild card in congregational worship.*[17]

But when we try to define what the Spirit's work in a group of worshipers has to look like, we get ourselves into trouble. The Presbyterian focus group said the things that brought them the most hope when they came to worship were the time of silence and the fellowship and prayer for one another. The charismatic focus group said those things were the energy of the room and the emotion of the service. Here's the point: let God show up however God shows up. There are many ways to encounter God. And there are many ways to pierce the canopy and break the immanent frame.

A few of the pastors in my recent focus groups talked about their struggle with narrow definitions of encounter in particular. Marvin in Springfield leads a church that is connected to the Pentecostal tradition. People have pushed back against some of the changes he's made—such as weekly communion—because they haven't recognized them as moments of encounter. Calvin in Grand Haven feels that the congregation's expectation of what encounter looks like is shaped by sources beyond their church or church tradition.

The Spirit is not only the X factor in our encounter with God but also the active agent in our mission and formation. Sociologists Donald Miller and Tetsunao Yamamori studied fast-growing churches in the developing world with effective social programs and community outreach initiatives. They discovered that 85 percent of the churches nominated by global church leaders as exemplars of social engagement and service were Pentecostal or charismatic. But that fact was not incidental. Miller and Yamamori are convinced that the "'single most important element that empowers Progressive Pentecostals' is 'unequivocally' the 'energizing experience of worship.' . . . 'It is where, according to Pentecostals, the Holy Spirit speaks to them about their duties as Christians.'"[18]

In worship, the Spirit is how we encounter God, are formed as disciples, and are sent into the world on mission. All three paradigms of congregational worship are fueled and sustained by the Holy Spirit.

Not only that, the Holy Spirit helps us discern which way to lean for our particular congregation in a particular season. The goal is not to give each paradigm even weight and attention.

For example, Gary in Belfast came into a church that he guessed was 98 percent about formation. When he took over as senior pastor, he felt they needed to swing the "pendulum right to the other side." He has asked his church the question, "When was the last time someone came to Jesus in a service?" Jason, an associate pastor in Tennessee, resonated with Gary's context as his church was mostly about formation. But he saw the need to help them value an encounter with God. As a former worship leader, Jason believes that encountering God is missional. Tim in London had a different perspective. As the pastor of a church plant, he has had several people come to faith through the church—people who have no framework for Christianity. So while they started with a mission paradigm, Tim sees the need to move to an emphasis on formation. Dale, a pastor in East Portland, also described a shift from an "altar call" and "sinner's prayer" each week to embracing discipleship rhythms. A few other pastors described a 50–50 split between two of the three paradigms.

Holding the paradigms in tension does not mean equal splits into thirds. Just as the Spirit is the author and animator of each, so the Spirit helps us discern the context of our church and the season in which we find ourselves.

Practices for the Presence

Paul, writing to the church in Ephesus, one of the pillar congregations of the early church, tells them how to think about their shared life together. In typical Pauline fashion, he draws three very powerful but very different images together so quickly that a middle school English teacher might chastise him for mixing his metaphors. He first describes them as citizens; then they are members of a household, a new family that is being formed in Jesus; then he switches again to say that the household is not just a family but a building: "So now you are no longer strangers and aliens. Rather, you are fellow citizens with God's people, and you belong to God's household. As God's household, you are built on the foundation of the apostles and prophets with Christ Jesus himself as the cornerstone" (Eph. 2:19–20).

Paul goes on to say that the church is not just any building but the temple itself: "The whole building is joined together in him, and it grows up into a temple that is dedicated to the Lord. Christ is building you into a place where God lives through the Spirit" (Eph. 2:21–22).

This temple imagery stretches throughout the letter. In Ephesians 3 Paul prays for the church to be able to grasp the width and length and height and depth of God's love because in knowing God's love they will be filled with God's fullness: "I ask that you'll know the love of Christ that is beyond knowledge so that you will be filled entirely with the fullness of God" (Eph. 3:19). To be filled with the fullness of God is an echo of the glory of God filling the temple at key moments in Israel's history. There are many ways to think about the glory of God. The Hebrew notion is about God's weightiness, the very substance of his being.

Paul believes that the primary manifestation of God's glory happened through Christ Jesus (see 2 Cor. 4:6; Col. 1:5). He references in the letter to the Ephesians the ascension of Christ as the precursor to him filling all things: "The one who went down is the same one who climbed up above all the heavens so that he might fill everything" (4:10). Christ came, died, was buried, and was raised up and exalted so that he would fill all things.

But the church is the place where God dwells *now* in advance of the day that he fills all things. Christ is *already* filling the church through the Holy Spirit; Christ is building us into a place that God can dwell by his Spirit (Eph. 2:22). As we experience his love—which the Spirit pours out in our hearts (Rom. 5:5)—we become filled with the fullness of God.

Now we see one final piece: the filling by the Spirit is ongoing. "Instead, be filled with the Spirit in the following ways: speak to each other with psalms, hymns, and spiritual songs; sing and make music to the Lord in your hearts; always give thanks to God the Father for everything in the name of our Lord Jesus Christ; and submit to each other out of respect for Christ" (Eph. 5:18–21).

The imperative to be filled is not a one-and-done kind of thing. It is a regular experience. But more than that, it is a *congregational* experience. I did not simply say a "communal" experience, or even a "collective" experience, though it is true that it happens with others rather than only individually. Paul is describing a specific context, a specific gathering of people: the church. This challenges our modern Western notion of God being everywhere and thus the church being any get-together of Christians. Certainly, God's presence *is* everywhere, and it is truly a spiritual discipline to learn to become aware of him. And it is definitely true that wherever two or three are gathered, we can begin to "have church" or even "be the church" in that space. And yet, the New Testament repeatedly draws on temple language (almost every time we are called the temple of the Holy Spirit, the noun is plural) to help us understand that there is a particular way God is present when the church gathers—with those we would have chosen and those we would *not* have chosen—in worship.

Not only is there a *place* and a *people* for this infilling—the gathered church—but there are *practices* that facilitate this infilling. The early Christians read the Scriptures, often expounding on them. They sang hymns—the New Testament offers us several—and prayed. They received bread and wine in remembrance of Christ, sometimes as the final course of a large feast. And they had a deep fellowship with one another, where food and possessions were shared. Preaching. Prayer and song. Eucharist. Fellowship. These are the practices of the church in worship that both result from and renew the Spirit's presence in us.

One of these practices became central for the early Christians: the Eucharist. Coming to the Lord's Table was the high point of their reenactment of the drama of the gospel, of Scripture itself. There, they remembered how the God of creation made a covenant with Israel to rescue, redeem, and renew all things. Israel's unfaithfulness could not derail God's plan and promise. This covenant came to its fulfillment in Jesus Christ, who was faithful on Israel's behalf, yet carried the suffering for their—and indeed the whole world's—unfaithfulness and sin and bore the judgment of evil in his own body on the cross. But God showed his faithfulness to Jesus by raising him from the dead. Christ will come again in glory, and the church celebrates this feast in anticipation of it. At the Lord's Table, the early Christians remembered his death, encountered his presence through the Spirit, and anticipated his coming. This is why it became Christian practice to confess the "mystery of faith" every time they participated in the Eucharist: Christ has died; Christ is risen; Christ will come again.

There is one other thing early Christians would pray when coming to the Lord's Table. It is called the *epiclesis*, the prayer inviting the Holy Spirit. *Come, Holy Spirit.* The Spirit would make the meal the occasion for God's presence. The Spirit at the Lord's Table holds together past remembrance, present encounter, and future hope.

The Lord's Table is not only the church's central practice but also its core paradigm for understanding our life in Christ and the church's presence in the world. When the bread is taken, the words describing Christ's actions at Passover are spoken. He *blessed* it, *broke* it, and *gave* it. It is at the Lord's Table that we remember we too become the body of Christ for the world. We have been *blessed*—we have been rescued and redeemed! We have been *broken*—by our frailty and failure and the fallenness of the world itself, yet we find grace and wholeness through confession. We have been *given*—our purpose and calling to bring flourishing into the world are restored and reaffirmed.[19] Indeed, every time the church gathers in worship, we rehearse our blessedness, we remember our brokenness, and we reenact our givenness.

To pull all these threads together, we might say it like this: we gather as the church to be a witness in the world of the world to come; we gather to be formed as the family of God and filled with the Spirit of God; we gather to be sent back into the world as carriers of the kingdom of God. In an age that has lost its understanding of why the church gathers, may we be those who call aloud, "Come, let us worship the Lord together!"

The Patterns in Worship Paradigms

Why might a pastor prioritize mission, formation, or encounter in a weekend service? Barna presented pastors with definitions of these mindsets and asked them to rank the three as purposes for congregational worship. Here, let's look at how influential aspects like church budget, racial makeup of a congregation, denomination, neighborhood, and education relate to a pastor's perceived intent for service.

Encounter: experiencing the presence of God
Formation: making disciples
Mission: reaching the lost

ENCOUNTER

● Ranked 1 ● Ranked 2 ● Ranked 3

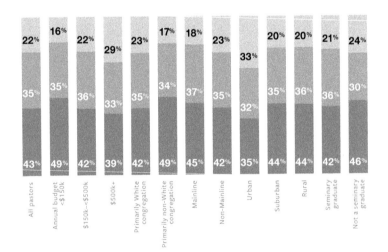

	All pastors	Annual budget <$150k	$150k–<$500k	$500k+	Primarily White congregation	Primarily non-White congregation	Mainline	Non-Mainline	Urban	Suburban	Rural	Seminary graduate	Not a seminary graduate
Ranked 3	22%	16%	22%	29%	23%	17%	18%	23%	33%	20%	20%	21%	24%
Ranked 2	35%	35%	36%	33%	35%	34%	37%	35%	32%	35%	36%	36%	30%
Ranked 1	43%	49%	42%	39%	42%	49%	45%	42%	35%	44%	44%	42%	46%

FORMATION

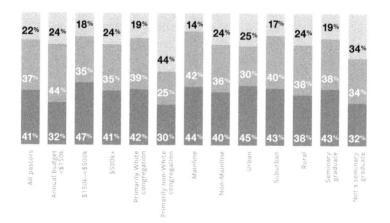

Categories (left to right): All pastors, Annual budget <$150k, $150k–<$500k, $500k+, Primarily White congregation, Primarily non-White congregation, Mainline, Non-Mainline, Urban, Suburban, Rural, Seminary graduate, Not a seminary graduate

Top segment: 22%, 24%, 18%, 24%, 19%, (44%), 14%, 24%, 25%, 17%, 24%, 19%, 34%
Middle segment: 37%, 44%, 35%, 35%, 39%, 25%, 42%, 36%, 30%, 40%, 38%, 38%, 34%
Bottom segment: 41%, 32%, 47%, 41%, 42%, 30%, 44%, 40%, 45%, 43%, 38%, 43%, 32%

MISSION

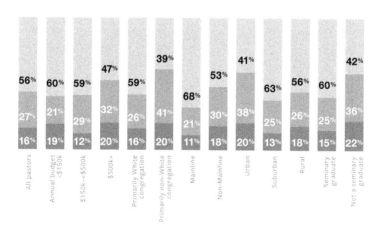

Categories (left to right): All pastors, Annual budget <$150k, $150k–<$500k, $500k+, Primarily White congregation, Primarily non-White congregation, Mainline, Non-Mainline, Urban, Suburban, Rural, Seminary graduate, Not a seminary graduate

Top segment: 56%, 60%, 59%, 47%, 59%, 39%, 68%, 53%, 41%, 63%, 56%, 60%, 42%
Middle segment: 27%, 21%, 29%, 32%, 26%, 41%, 21%, 30%, 38%, 25%, 26%, 25%, 36%
Bottom segment: 16%, 19%, 12%, 20%, 16%, 20%, 11%, 18%, 20%, 13%, 18%, 15%, 22%

n=408 U.S. Protestant pastors, September 16–October 8, 2020.

Reflections from Bishop Todd Hunter, C4SO Diocese in the ACNA

In the Jesus Movement, worship was for reaching the lost. The Vineyard's intimate songs revealed that worship was for God. In Anglican worship, I have used elements of the *Book of Common Prayer* (*BCP*) as spiritual disciplines for spiritual transformation.

God has blessed all three of these approaches.

After many years of using the *BCP*, I see in its richness a way to keep a lesser trinity consistently in view: God, me, and others.

God *is the focus of Anglican worship.* For most of the church year, our first words in worship are "Blessed be God." We confess what we believe about God; we pray to God. In Eucharist we celebrate his work in and through Jesus.

But **we** *are not left out.* We ask for our hearts to be cleansed. In confession we agree with God about the state of our sinful lives. In absolution we experience the forgiveness and freedom of God. We receive the body and blood of Jesus.

Others *are included too.* We pray for the world in all its iterations. We give money for the sake of others. Those who may feel like outsiders, but who are making their way in, are given *comfortable words* of assurance. We are blessed and sent out as agents of God's kingdom for the sake of others.

Maybe we don't have to choose a single worship style. Maybe there is a way, in any church, to keep God, personal growth, and love for others held together in worship.

144

formation

How do we make disciples?

found out on Facebook. They had commented on a post I made in a way that made me wonder if they were leaving the church. I reached out personally to ask if their comment had meant what I thought it meant. They confirmed it did. They were leaving the church. I was being farewelled. And for what? Because I had posted about how Black Americans do not want to live in fear of the police, about how as Christians our role toward government is not simply to submit but also to humbly hold policymakers and the police who enforce those policies accountable. This did not fit their perception of the world. They could not help importing extreme views held by others who had made similar remarks as mine into my carefully measured words. The mere overlap of language led to assumption about which tribe I belonged in. I had been lumped with "liberals" and dumped with deserters of the faith.

Beneath my anger was a deep sadness. These were people who had volunteered and served in our church. Our kids were in activities together. I had baptized their children. We had given them financial assistance when they were in need. Now I found out they were leaving by a cryptic comment on my Facebook post.

This story is neither unique nor rare. In the summer of 2020, I heard from several pastors about members of their church leaving.

Some told them via email or text; others arranged for a meeting to discuss things before going. For some, it was about the pandemic. The departing congregants believed COVID-19 was fake or politically fueled or media hyped, and they were disappointed that their church was not meeting in person. For others, it was about the conversations about race. They believed the media or the liberals or both were mischaracterizing events in order to sow seeds of discord and division and to stir an uprising against the police. Or they were disappointed that pastors weren't saying more, that their silence was complicity. There were those who couldn't believe their pastor was not speaking out against abortion or in favor of Trump, while others wanted their pastor to denounce Trump. From COVID to QAnon, people were firmly committed to their values and worldview. If their pastor aligned, great; if not, it was time to go. The reasons for each departure may have seemed disparate, but there was a common thread. More than a conspiracy theory or a viral video, the common denominator in the reasons for the trickle exodus was tribalism.

What is revealed by this tribalism is *a failure of discipleship*. It is a failure evident not in their disagreement but in the inability to think theologically about social issues and current events. We have predetermined our views by our "in group" and squeeze everything through the prism of our politics. There isn't a single issue that is not politicized. And because politics is war, a point cannot be conceded or ground will be lost. This may be the end of civil discourse, but more alarming is the crisis of formation that it reveals.

The problem with discipleship in America is not that we lack the resources to reflect biblically or theologically on relevant issues. Those are plentiful. The problem is that we refuse to listen to anything—even "biblical teaching"—that contradicts or challenges our tribal identity. The Bible no longer has the power to shake us, to wake us up, to open up our eyes and ears.

When people are being discipled by their favorite podcaster or blogger or Instagram influencer or by a news network or their social media feed at rates that blow time in church out of the water, how can a pastor compete? When these various influences fertilize their opinions and demands, the fruit they bear is division and dissension in the church or departure from the church. Our congregants' lack of commitment and their low level of spiritual maturity are among the most draining things pastors deal with.[1] For pastors who are already at risk of burnout and spiritual or relational deterioration—and about one-third of pastors are[2]—the pain of church politics is particularly acute.[3] Half of pastors at risk of burnout feel underprepared for handling conflict.[4]

While the toll all this takes on pastors is heavy, the burden of non-discipleship is heavier. We cannot rely on attendance or involvement in programs to gauge our efforts. But that's what many pastors continue to do. In our new study, we found that the most common way churches measure the effectiveness of their discipleship efforts is through overall attendance at church programs and events (54 percent) and by the proportion of those involved in "discipleship pathways" (51 percent). Older pastors are more likely to point to the number of new salvations (35 percent vs. 24 percent of younger pastors) and engagement through serving (50 percent vs. 38 percent). But attendance, engagement, and even conversion are not the same thing as formation and discipleship.

How do we participate in the work of spiritual formation in the age of identity politics and tribal loyalties? We must start by rethinking our goal.

What Is the Goal?

The vast majority of church leaders say that the goal of discipleship is "being transformed to become more like Jesus."[5] When we discussed the goal of discipleship in my focus groups with pastors in North America and in the U.K., the responses centered on Jesus—and not just because that seems like the right Sunday school answer. "Becoming more like Jesus," "to do for others what Jesus has done for us," "a way of life," "companionship on the journey with Jesus," "being conformed to the image of Christ," "to walk with God in our everyday lives"—these were some of the responses they shared. It makes sense, then, that the preferred language to refer to the process of spiritual formation or discipleship is "becoming more Christ-like."[6] Barna found that practicing Christians agree with this terminology but differed on the goal itself. The top stated goal of discipleship for practicing Christians is "learning to live a more consistent Christian life."[7]

This is a matter of semantics, right? What's the difference between wanting to become more like Jesus and wanting to live a more consistent Christian life? Well, ideally, there is no difference. But what happens along the way is the "Christian life" becomes an abstraction, a collection of virtues or a set of ideals that we aspire to. Jesus, however, is a historical being, the incarnate Son of God who was born, crucified, and raised on the third day.

Chasing conformity to the "Christian life" makes us vulnerable to whatever iteration of that ideal is presented to us. The American vision of the Christian life may include living a cozy life in the suburbs and voting to preserve that life at all costs. Ideals are easily co-opted by partisan politics. *Faith, Freedom, Family. God and Country.* Examples abound.

But Jesus is less easily hijacked. If we are in doubt about a particular version of who Jesus is, we return repeatedly to the four evangelists. In the pages of the Gospels, we are met again and again by the Christ of their proclamation who does not fit neatly in our camps. The brilliant and provocative theologian and ethicist Stanley Hauerwas writes:

> To be a disciple of Jesus, it is not enough to know the basic "facts" of his life. It is not enough to know his story. Rather, to be a disciple of Jesus means that our lives must literally be taken up into the drama of God's redemption of this creation. That is the work of the Spirit as we are made part of God's new time through the life and work of this man, Jesus of Nazareth.[8]

Studying the Bible is not an end in itself. Confessing one of the creeds or memorizing the catechism is not the point. Becoming like Jesus is the goal.

Jim McClendon told a story about two brothers, Clarence and Robert Jordan. Clarence, a pacifist and an integrationist, was the founder of Koinonia Farm, an interracial community near Americus, Georgia, that operated long before the civil rights movement. When he needed some help fighting discrimination from the local gas company that had refused service, Clarence enlisted the help of his brother Robert who was a lawyer. Robert, however, was unwilling. He had political aspirations and could not jeopardize losing his job or his house. His brother pleaded that they too might lose everything. Robert replied, "It's different for you."

> "Why is it different? I remember, it seems to me, that you and I joined the church on the same Sunday, as boys. I expect when we came forward the preacher asked me about the same question he did you. He asked me, 'Do you accept Jesus as your Lord and Savior.' And I said, 'Yes.' What did you say?"
> "I follow Jesus, Clarence, up to a point."
> "Could that point by any chance be—the cross?"
> "That's right. I follow him to the cross, but not *on* the cross. I'm not getting myself crucified."
> "Then I don't believe you're a disciple. You're an admirer of Jesus, but not a disciple of his."[9]

A disciple is one who actually gets on the cross. Not one who simply believes in the cross or is grateful for Jesus's cross. A disciple is one who follows Jesus so closely that they take up their cross. Their life has taken on the same shape as Jesus. To be a disciple is to be cruciform.

The cross is the difference between keeping a vague notion of the Christian life and actually becoming like Jesus. The central act of Christ is the bearing of the cross. He is known in heaven as the Lamb who was slain. The imitation of Christ is nothing if it is not the tracing of our lives around the contours of sacrificial, self-giving love. Hauerwas puts it this way: "Discipleship is quite simply extended training in being dispossessed. To become followers of Jesus means that we must, like him, be dispossessed of all that we think gives us power over our own lives and the lives of others. Unless we learn to relinquish our presumption that we can ensure the significance of our lives, we are not capable of the peace of God's Kingdom."[10]

It is common to say that people want the kingdom—the righteousness, peace, joy, and more that come with God's reign—without wanting the King. That may be true of those outside the church. They seek justice without judgment, freedom without surrender, or love without forgiveness. They want the fruit of the kingdom without the rule of the King. That is true enough. But for those inside the church, we want the King and his kingdom without a cross. We'll take a Savior who gets us to heaven, a Lord of the afterlife. And we like all the blessings of forgiveness and peace that come with his rule. But we have not reflected deeply enough about the *nature* of his rule. Jesus is the King who conquered by dying, who won by losing, who rescued by giving. All this is made manifest in the cross. If the world wants the kingdom without the King, the church wants the King without a cross.

The cruciform life is what becoming like Jesus looks like.

How Movements Are Sustained

How do we learn to take up our cross? How do we become formed in the way of sacrificial love and forgiveness?

In the early 1960s, when the civil rights movement was finding its stride, child psychologist and educator Kenneth B. Clark sat down to conduct an interview with the Reverend Dr. Martin Luther King Jr. It had been a few years since Rosa Parks stayed in her seat, since the Montgomery bus boycott, and since voting rights were granted to African Americans. But the work was far from over. Prejudice found more vicious ways of baring its teeth, and violence had spilled into the streets. White people found ways of keeping Black people out of their neighborhoods through redlining and out of the voting booth through literacy tests. Peaceful protests were met with mass arrests and beatings. Yet Dr. King was leading a movement with a commitment to nonviolence at its core. They would be a "creative minority" just as the early Christians had been, subverting the power of an unjust empire, provoking it to repentance.[11]

In the interview, Clark asked about how the movement had largely retained its commitment to nonviolence. He pressed Dr.

King about the relationship between "direct-action nonviolence" as a technique and the love of one's enemy as an ethic. Dr. King was clear about the link. One was "a method of acting to rectify a social situation that is unjust"; the other accepts nonviolence as "a way of life."[12] Clark pressed King about how one could actually love the perpetrators of violence and oppression. Reaching for the language of the New Testament, Dr. King responded that love is not "an affectionate response" but rather the *agape*, a kind of "understanding, creative redemptive good will for all [people]."

What baffled Clark the most was how this movement with no police force and no uniforms could "maintain this type of discipline, control and dignity" among "people who are voluntarily associated," despite voices like Malcom X and James Baldwin that contradicted or questioned Dr. King's nonviolent approach.[13] This was not an "authoritarian organization." Clark wanted to know: "How do you account for this . . . beautiful dignity and discipline?"[14]

King responded, "Well, we do a great deal in terms of teaching both the theoretical aspects of nonviolence as well as the practical application. We even have courses where we go through the experience of being roughed up and this kind of sociodrama has proved very helpful in preparing those who are engaged in demonstrations." King continued, "I think there is a contagious quality in a movement like this when everybody talks about nonviolence and being faithful to it and being dignified in your resistance. It tends to get over to the larger group because this becomes a part of the vocabulary of the movement."[15]

In essence, when asked how the movement he was leading was so effectively formed in their "way" and discipled in their values, even at great cost to themselves, Dr. King pointed to *teaching*, *practices*, and *community apprenticeship*. More on all three in a moment.

It Takes a Church

A few years ago, when Barna asked pastors what they thought were the essential elements of discipleship, they listed time with

God (93 percent), prayer and meditation (93 percent), a personal commitment to grow in Christlikeness (92 percent), attending a local church (89 percent), and a deep love for God (88 percent) as the top five.[16] Notice that three have to do with *action*—time with God, prayer and meditation, and attending a local church—and two have to do with *attitude*—commitment to grow and a deep love for God. Furthermore, only one requires others—attending a local church. When asked directly about a method that would have a "significant impact on developing disciples," pastors said that personal Bible study, small-group Bible study, and one-on-one mentoring relationships were the top three methods for developing disciples.[17]

Barna's data on what practicing Christians find helpful for their spiritual growth parallels what pastors said. Regular prayer (59 percent), attending church worship services (55 percent), having a quiet time (40 percent), studying the Bible on their own (38 percent), and studying the Bible with a group (31 percent) round off the top five practices.[18] In this list, two are *communal*—attending church worship services and studying the Bible with a group—while the other three are *individual*. And yet, of the 90 percent of Christians surveyed who said that spiritual growth is important in some way, only 25 percent prefer a small group, while 16 percent prefer a one-on-one approach. Thirty-seven percent actually prefer to pursue spiritual growth on their own.[19] The solo climb ideal of spiritual growth runs deep in the American Christian imagination.

A list of potential obstacles to spiritual growth was presented to practicing Christians. They were asked to mark which ones were major and which ones were minor. The number one major obstacle to spiritual growth is the "general busyness of life."[20] Next is the hard work that they knew spiritual growth would require. But then comes a bevy of factors, all nearly equal in response, from their friends not being interested in spiritual things to not wanting to think about mistakes made in the past, from bad experiences with groups to not wanting to get too personal with others, from not being able to find a good church to having other priorities at the moment.[21] They know spiritual growth is important, but so are lots of other things.

In Barna's 2020 study of the general population, we learned that Christians think the most essential practices for discipleship are a "deep love for God" and "prayer and meditation," followed closely by "time with God."

THE ESSENTIALS OF DISCIPLESHIP: FIRST COMES LOVE

Which spiritual disciplines do you believe are essential to discipleship (i.e., becoming more like Jesus)?

% among Christians

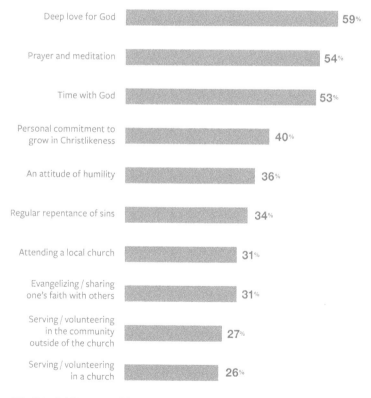

Deep love for God	59%
Prayer and meditation	54%
Time with God	53%
Personal commitment to grow in Christlikeness	40%
An attitude of humility	36%
Regular repentance of sins	34%
Attending a local church	31%
Evangelizing / sharing one's faith with others	31%
Serving / volunteering in the community outside of the church	27%
Serving / volunteering in a church	26%

n=892 self-identified Christian U.S. adults, October 9–20, 2020.

I'm going to make a radical observation: we have shaped our vision of discipleship in a way that is *individual* and *internal*. Church leaders repeatedly point to motivation and desire. *If only they had a deep love for God and a stronger commitment to spiritual growth.* Pastors keep insisting that with the right vision casting from the senior leader and the right structure, they can motivate people to embrace discipleship and growth. But that's not quite right. Then you have the leading voices on discipleship repeatedly beating the drum of one-on-one relationships. The key is mentoring, they say. That is closer to the mark. But not enough people find the right spiritual father or mother, and few are even willing to try.

As long as we focus on the *individual* and the *internal*, the obstacles will repeatedly be *circumstantial* and *seasonal*: *We're too busy. We don't have the right people around us. It just isn't a priority right now.*

What Dr. King knew is that discipleship is not simply about the custom-made plans or well-structured programs. It takes a movement—a movement rooted in a particular ethic, a way of seeing the world. Dr. King's followers were a group of people who worshiped together, prayed together, marched together, and even got arrested together. He had patterned his movement after the early Christians. Formation in the early church was not focused on the individual or the internal but rather the *communal* and the *habitual*. Evangelicals are fond of saying that going to church doesn't make you a Christian. True enough. But perhaps in emphasizing personal faith we've forgotten what the first centuries of Christians knew: *it takes a church to make a Christian.*

The Patience of the Early Church

"We do not preach great things; we live them."[22] This was a common saying among North African Christians in the early 200s. Christianity was spreading by the appeal of its community to the world around them. Long before it became socially acceptable, pagans—at great cost to themselves and despite great disincentives to do so—were becoming Christians. Even more remarkably, they were becoming Christians without ever attending a church service. Christian worship in those days took place behind locked doors. Outsiders could not be trusted to protect the identity of the Christian community.

How did the church grow?

Tertullian, a pastor in the early years of the third century in the North African city of Carthage, remarked that non-Christians would look at Christians and say, "Look . . . how they love one another . . . and how they are ready to die for each other."[23] Something about the way they cared for the poor, conducted their business, and restrained their appetites and sexuality appealed to the pagans. These people were different. As Alan Kreider, a professor of church history and mission, puts it, "It was not Christian worship that attracted outsiders; it was Christians who attracted them."[24]

To the Romans, Christianity did not seem like a religion—a prescribed set of rituals that had to do with relating to a god in order to obtain blessings. Roman religions had little to do with what we might call ethics.[25] Christianity seemed much more like a philosophy, a way of living. Christianity was concerned with one's behavior in the marketplace and in the household. In a Christian letter from the 200s, the writer notes that Christians are not all that different from everyone else in "local customs" of "dress and food," yet they "demonstrate the remarkable and admittedly unusual character of their own citizenship" in the kingdom of God.[26] The writer cites specific examples of this by stating how Christians don't abandon their babies on the streets as was common in the Roman Empire for unwanted offspring. Moreover, since at least the time of Paul's letters to the Corinthians, it was Christian practice that husbands and wives have sex only with their spouse, unlike the Greek and Roman double standard of demanding a faithful wife but allowing men to have courtesans and concubines for pleasure and slaves for their "daily needs."

Kreider, drawing on the work of French sociologist and philosopher Pierre Bordieu, boils down the difference between Christians and pagans to their *habitus*—the set of "predispositions and practices."[27] If the main way that people became Christians was through the witness of their unique way of living, then the reflexive responses of Christians had to be intentionally shaped. The church knew they could not have people who claimed to be Christians who did not live like Christians—let alone like Christ himself. A Christlike *habitus* had to be formed.

This conviction led to the creation of preparatory processes for conversion. In the third century, a document emerged from Christian communities in North Africa, Rome, and possibly even Egypt, called *The Apostolic Tradition*. It would have a wide reach, appearing in several languages from Latin to Syriac to Arabic. The text reveals a model for becoming a Christian that could be mapped in four stages: *welcome, instruction, preparation*, and *initiation*. Kreider, using different terms for these stages, describes each one in detail. During the first stage, a nonbeliever who knows a Christian from their work or neighborhood becomes curious about this group known as the Way. The Christian functions like a kind of sponsor, explaining things to them and introducing them to Christian teachers. After a period of months or sometimes years, the teacher would grill the sponsor about their non-Christian friend to see if they were teachable and willing to change their behavior. In fact, some change needed to already be evident. Then they would be admitted into the second stage where they would receive instruction or *catechesis*. The focus here is less on doctrine and more on becoming like Christ. They would learn about Christ and about the practices of the church in worship and in the world. They would then face a "Second Scrutiny," addressed once again to the sponsoring Christian. Kreider is emphatic about the content of this examination, perhaps to show how this method differs from our contemporary versions of discipleship: "The leaders did not ask about the candidate's orthodoxy, about their mastery of doctrine, about their memorization of biblical passages, about their piety or prayer life. . . . They did not ask about the candidate's opinions and attitudes. . . . They did, however, want to know how the candidate treated poor people. Actions said it all."[28]

To be clear, sound doctrine and memorization of Scripture were indeed part of the instruction stage, but parroting the right words in an oral exam was not the goal. A changed life was.

After passing this second assessment, the candidates proceeded into a preparation phase in which they would "hear the gospel." This phrase may have meant a special immersion in the teaching of Jesus or the candidate's inclusion in worship services or a deeper round of doctrinal instruction. Whatever it was, the imitation of Christ was now coming into sharper focus. The "Third Scrutiny" was now between the bishop and the candidate. Here the candidate renounced sin and evil and turned toward Christ in fullness. The bishop would drive out demons and affirm the right living of the candidate. They would then proceed to the fourth and final stage: initiation into the community through the waters of baptism.

If we set aside the rigidity of the stages in the Apostolic Tradition and don't fret about when baptism occurs—at the beginning for many of us rather than at the end—we see the larger patterns that may be helpful to us today. The goal and indeed the premise of the Apostolic Tradition, as Kreider sees it, is that people don't think their way into a new way of living; they "live their way into a new kind of thinking."[29] Cyprian, the bishop of Carthage after the time of Tertullian, saw the goal of catechism as the formation of habits. Kreider paraphrases Cyprian's words to a Christian teacher in charge of creating a curriculum for those who wanted to become Christians:

> Habitually, Christians will share economically and care for the poor and the sick, widows and orphans; habitually, they will engage in business with truthfulness, without usury, and without pursuing profit to the extent of going before pagan judges; habitually, they will be a community of contentment and sexual restraint; habitually, they will behave with the multifaceted nonviolence of patience.[30]

Practicing a Long Obedience Together

Since Dr. King was inspired by how the early church grew under the boot of the Roman Empire, it's no surprise that the insights we noted from his civil rights movement correspond to what we might say about the church in the 200s in Carthage in particular. We might distill and synthesize the wisdom of both for the church today by saying that formation in a Christlike way also involves *teaching*, *practices*, and *community apprenticeship*.

Entire books could be written about each, but a few remarks are necessary in the short space we have left. The teaching of the church in the third century focused on the narrative of Scripture— the big story arc of God's redemptive work in the world—and the teachings of Jesus. Large chunks of Scripture were memorized. But again, the goal of every teaching was to reveal Jesus and to produce a life that imitated Christ's. To do that, the teaching had to tell the story, employing a Christocentric hermeneutic and applying a cruciform ethic of love.

There are long lists of embodied, communal, and habitual practices that were part of the catechetical process. Generally, the practices could be grouped into three categories: *practices of worship*, *practices of prayer*, and *practices of service*. Chief among the practices of worship that were formative for new believers in the early church were baptism and the Eucharist. The weekly celebration of the Eucharist served not just to remember and encounter Christ's sacrificial love but also as a way of reinforcing their imitation of that love. After serving small portions of bread and wine to everyone who was present, the deacons would take it to members who were absent. "The meal spreads outward, forming the character of the worshipers and playing an essential part in the life of their community, which is committed to care for orphans, widows, prisoners, and sojourners."[31] In a similar way, when the believers would pray together, they prayed vigorously and collectively for all Christians everywhere.[32]

Both of the first two practices took place behind closed church doors, and were therefore invisible to non-Christians. But they produced practices that were visible to the world. The practices of service were exemplified in the way Christians fed the poor and cared for widows. "Some congregations . . . had replenishable stocks of food and clothing for their members."[33] Christians—even Cyprian himself—simplified their own lifestyles in order to make their generosity possible. Their service extended to everyone. In one remarkable story of Christian women bringing food and drink to captured peasants who had been forcibly conscripted into military service, one of the prisoners reported that their help had come from Christians who "were merciful to everyone, including strangers."[34]

Finally, an apprenticing community was a key path to formation. From a sponsor for curious seekers to teachers to the diverse community of the church itself, disciples were made not in isolation or even in one-on-one mentoring but through the church. An apprenticing community may take the shape of a small group, a very intentional kind. The kind of community that makes disciples is focused not only on thinking the right things but also on doing the right things. Such a community is not afraid to ask probing questions about one's line of work. Converts to the early church who had been idol makers or gladiators were told to "cease or be cast out." Businesspeople were urged not to charge interest and to pay their workers in a timely fashion. When Cyprian was baptized, he spoke of his sponsor as the "parent of his new life." Paul's wish that the Corinthians would have not just a myriad of teachers but fathers and mothers in the faith had come true for the church in Carthage.

I want to pause here to stress that even as we explore creative ways of engaging in "digital discipleship," there is no true substitute for embodied community. Apprenticeship happens through bodily copresence. This is what the oft-used church phrase "life on life" is meant to indicate. Though technology can help us approximate this sort of apprenticing community, it can never rise to the level of holistic formation that happens through an embodied community.

I sat down one Monday morning to meet with a congregant going through a hardship. We talked about the struggles his wife was experiencing and how the family was doing in the midst of the turmoil. From time to time, the conversation would drift to his hobbies or what the kids were into. I found myself wondering, *What does he need from me? Why did he want to meet? He already has a counselor.* But then it hit me. He wants to feel normal, even if for a few minutes. I took the detours with him.

But there was something more. He needed me to be a witness to his life. As I asked him questions about what a day was like, what a week was like, what the "work" of healing would mean for her and for him, he offered up glimpses into his world. After an hour or so of listening and chasing conversational rabbit trails, I looked him in the eyes and said, "You are living the cruciform life."

Instantly tears welled up in his eyes. "Not very well." He sighed.

"It doesn't matter," I insisted. "You are. The cross is on your back." Then, from some Spirit-inspired place, I said, "Even Jesus stumbled as he carried the cross. But the main thing is, you're carrying it." His tears were streaming now.

This was why I was meeting with him. To help him feel some semblance of normalcy. And above all to be a witness to his life. To show him what he could not see himself: Christ was being formed in him.

There is no formula for formation. Making us like Jesus is the work of the Spirit. But it is not a solo effort. It will not be the result of focusing on the individual and the internal. Becoming like Jesus requires teaching that is Christocentric and cruciform; becoming like Jesus is embodied in reflexive responses to practices that are communal and habitual; and becoming like Jesus is forged in the fire of a community that will not shy away from speaking the truth in love about our behavior. These three things are interconnected and interrelated. They do not occur sequentially but rather simultaneously and symbiotically. The community is formed by the story and sustained by its habits. Yet there is no way to receive this story or practice its habits without a community. These three elements are ways of cooperating with the Spirit's work that have served the church well in days that were darker than ours. As we have reflected on the teaching, practices, and community that made not just converts but disciples against all odds, we have something to assess our own efforts against. May God give us the grace and the courage to call people to follow Jesus, cross and all.

Making (and Measuring) Disciples

Discipleship success, pastors say, is largely determined by the numbers of church engagement (attendees, volunteers, and so on). The larger the church, the more exploration of possible metrics of discipleship, especially through group pathways like small groups and classes. More than one-quarter of small churches (under 100 people) don't measure discipleship efforts at all.

HOW DOES YOUR CHURCH MEASURE THE EFFECTIVENESS OF DISCIPLESHIP EFFORTS?

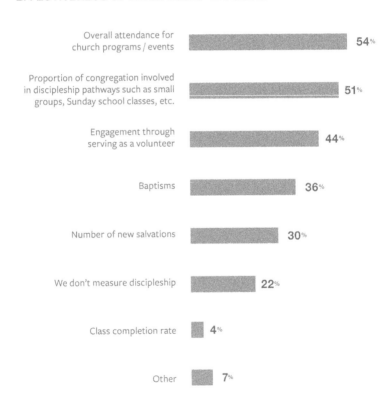

Overall attendance for church programs / events — **54**%

Proportion of congregation involved in discipleship pathways such as small groups, Sunday school classes, etc. — **51**%

Engagement through serving as a volunteer — **44**%

Baptisms — **36**%

Number of new salvations — **30**%

We don't measure discipleship — **22**%

Class completion rate — **4**%

Other — **7**%

BY CHURCH SIZE

● <100 Attendees ● 100–249 Attendees ● 250+ Attendees

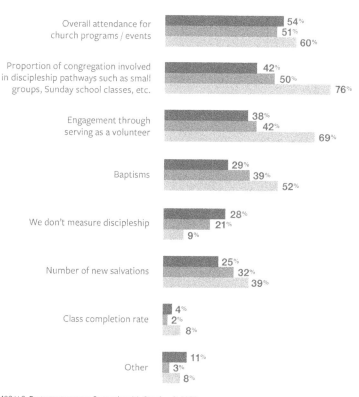

Overall attendance for church programs / events
- 54%
- 51%
- 60%

Proportion of congregation involved in discipleship pathways such as small groups, Sunday school classes, etc.
- 42%
- 50%
- 76%

Engagement through serving as a volunteer
- 38%
- 42%
- 69%

Baptisms
- 29%
- 39%
- 52%

We don't measure discipleship
- 28%
- 21%
- 9%

Number of new salvations
- 25%
- 32%
- 39%

Class completion rate
- 4%
- 2%
- 8%

Other
- 11%
- 3%
- 8%

n=408 U.S. Protestant pastors, September 16–October 8, 2020.

Reflections from Rich Villodas, pastor, author, and speaker

The cultural challenges before leaders of the church are minimally twofold: reactivity and restlessness. By *reactivity*, I'm referring to the anxious, automatic ways we engage those we lead in our community and the larger world around us. By *restlessness*, I'm identifying the perpetual sense of "not enoughness" every pastor will encounter at some point. In the face of these two ubiquitous realities, the cultivation of *presence* is desperately needed.

Formation is not simply about thinking the right things, having the right experiences, or engaging in the right practices of mission. All these things are critically important but must ultimately flow from a life of *presence*—presence with God, ourselves, and with the people we lead.

A life marked by *presence* is one shaped by the steady, ongoing work of prayerful reflection and communion with God. Why do we often have a hard time navigating the terrain of racial injustice, political hostility, and the everyday tensions we encounter within our communities? I think it has much to do with our lack of prayerful self-examination and abiding with Jesus.

Pastoral ministry is often fraught with massive conflicts and microcriticisms. This is why apart from this commitment to *presence*, we will be swallowed up whole. This work is strengthened through the habits of silence and interior examination, leading to the often-challenging task of nondefensively holding space with others. The important and comforting truth to remember, however, is that this is not something we achieve; it's something God works in us. Amen.

unity

How do we preserve unity in the church?

When Paul began planting churches in the first century, he was sowing the seeds of revolution. No, he was not inciting violence or plotting an insurrection. But he was challenging the very order of society.

The church was radical for several reasons. The first was the way it approached what we call "religion." The late Christian historian Larry Hurtado wrote that religion in the Roman world "was virtually everywhere, a regular part of the fabric of life," and "from the lowest to the highest spheres of society, all aspects of life were presumed to have connections with divinities of various kinds."[1] Hurtado drives his point home: "There was really nothing like the modern notion of a separate, 'secular' space of life free from deities and relevant ritual."[2] Cultic practices and rituals were for personal piety and blessings. But that display of piety was an essential part of a collective Roman identity. In fact, one of the ways Rome united various ethnicities was through assimilating the many gods of each region and people. Hurtado writes:

> Indeed, for people in the Roman era generally, "piety" meant a readiness to show appropriate reverence for the gods, any and all the gods. That meant, as the occasion called for it, reverencing any of those recognized as gods by any of the peoples that made up the

empire. So, for example, on a visit to some other city or land, you might be invited to take part in rites associated with the deities of that place, and you would typically accept the invitation without hesitation. Outright refusal to worship deities was deemed bizarre, even antisocial, and, worse still, impious and irreligious.[3]

The gods represented diversity, symbolized piety, and effected a kind of unity.

Jews were already living against this grain with their belief in only one God, and one who could not be represented with an image or an idol. Strange as this was to Roman sensibilities, Rome granted Jews an exception on account of the ancient nature of their beliefs. They were a well-established people with a long history of monotheism. Christians, however, were viewed with suspicion. Who were these people who refused to worship the gods? Why did they follow a crucified *Messiah* who they claimed was now alive and reigning as *Savior* and *Lord*—terms used in imperial propaganda for Caesar? Why did their worship center on "eating his flesh" and "drinking his blood"? But above all, it was the exclusive worship of Jesus that set them apart from "most other religious groups."[4]

Beyond their strange worship practices, the church was markedly different in the way they lived. As a result, many early Roman writers thought of Christianity not simply as a religion—which in the ancient world was more about rituals than about ethics—but as a philosophy. It was a teaching about a way of life. And the Christians' way of life was different from the Roman one. Christians did not discard babies. Christians only had sex with their spouses—not with prostitutes, courtesans, and slaves as was Roman practice. All these choices and more puzzled Roman observers.

These teachings about idolatry and ethics were found in the letters Paul wrote to the churches and in other New Testament documents. But there is one more reason that the churches Paul founded were so revolutionary. It was the nature of the churches themselves. To use the terms we've used in previous chapters, the church was not just radical in its *worship* and in its *formation*; it was also groundbreaking in its *unity*.

The Greco-Roman world was well stratified by class and by gender. The churches Paul planted shattered those divisions. Commenting on Paul's missionary preaching and writing to the church in Galatia, the secular historian Tom Holland remarks, "The fabric of things was rent, a new order of time had come into existence, and all that previously had served to separate people was now, as a consequence, dissolved."[5] He goes on to quote Galatians 3:28, "There is no longer Jew or Greek, there is no longer slave or free, there is no longer male and female; for all of you are one in Christ Jesus" (NRSV).

To the Corinthians, Paul embodied Christ's radical flattening of the stratified world by his identification as one who is weak and foolish. Holland again observes the remarkably countercultural nature of Paul's preaching:

> In a city famed for its wealth, Paul proclaimed that it was the "low and despised in the world, mere nothings," who ranked first. Among a people who had always celebrated the *agon*, the contest to be the best, he announced that God had chosen the foolish to shame the wise, and the weak to shame the strong. In a world that took for granted the hierarchy of human chattels and their owners, he insisted that the distinctions between slave and free, now that Christ himself had suffered the death of a slave, were of no more account than those between Greek and Jesus.[6]

The early church was a revolutionary community in part because of their remarkable unity. They held together Jew and gentile, male and female, and slave and free as equals, as one new family in Christ. Ethnicity, gender, and class could not segregate the early church. Diversity and difference remained, but the division was torn asunder.

But a casual observer of Christianity in America might not find the same phenomenon. Today, the church is divided by racism, political tribalism, differing convictions about gender roles in the church, and more. Compounding that, in the new frontier of the digital age, social media algorithms reinforce our echo chambers, escalate our tensions, and elevate our anxieties.

Even in our cities, churches feel divided along these fault lines. Nearly half of pastors tell Barna the leaders in their city are "not really" connected and unified. Ironically and tragically, this is a response that garners much agreement across different segments of pastors. What we have in common is our experience of division.

DO YOU THINK THE CHURCH LEADERS IN YOUR
CITY ARE CONNECTED AND UNIFIED?

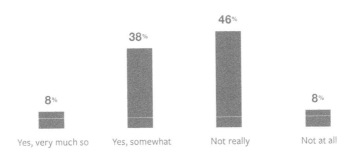

n=415 Protestant pastors, January 22–27, 2021.

There is no way to adequately grapple with every threat to the unity of the church in a single book, let alone one chapter. When I tweeted a simple poll in January of 2021, asking my followers what the biggest threat to unity in the church was—racial tensions, political tribalism, gender roles, or economic disparity—634 people responded. Seventy-nine percent chose political tribalism, 10 percent chose racial tensions, 8 percent chose economic disparity, and 3 percent chose gender roles. This, of course, is a completely unscientific poll, and I had no basis for selecting the options I did. Many took the trouble to comment things like "all of the above" or to reference the intersectional nature of many of the options.

But my conversations with pastors in my three focus groups confirmed the poll and added more details to the picture. Most of them said "politics," "worldview," "current events," "the politicization of benign things." Included in the references to politics and current events were the cultural conversations about racial justice that boiled over in 2020. A few also mentioned sexuality and same-sex marriage.

Between my Twitter poll, my focus groups, and my own experience as a pastor, I've chosen to zoom in on two threats to the unity of the church that rise with particular urgency today: racism and nationalism. But instead of discussing racism in general, I will focus on the tensions that come from different perceptions of the problem and thus different notions of a solution. Similarly, rather than talking about political tribalism in general, I am going to focus on one specific kind of toxic element that is not to be reconciled but removed. Brace yourself: there is bad news ahead. What follows contains important situational analysis aided by good sociology, but it won't be easy to read.

Divided by (Structural) Racism

The summer of 2020 saw city streets across America filled with marches and protests. Most were peaceful; some were destructive. #BlackLivesMatter became a rallying cry in basketball arenas and social media, TV commercials and street art. The demonstrations were provoked by the video footage of a Minneapolis police officer holding his knee on the neck of an African American named George Floyd. This came mere months after the release of a video of two White men in a truck who chased down an African American jogger named Ahmaud Arbery in the country roads of Georgia and shot him in broad daylight. Enough was enough. The video evidence made it plain for the world to see that Black people were still suffering as victims of prejudice and violence. The motto seemed simple enough: Black lives matter. Yet the organization by the same name has questionable aims, to say the least. In what should have been the easiest occasion for White Christians and Black Christians to come together in solidarity, the summer of 2020 instead drew the dividing lines more deeply. Many White Christians rationalized the instances of police brutality as owing to other factors than race and blamed Black people for stoking the fires of division by speaking out. Black Christians, tired of explaining their perspective and their position, began exiting White spaces and exhorting others to do the same, giving up on the fight for a multiethnic church. Many stayed the course, trying to build bridges and facilitate listening, lamenting, and learning.

But the crux of the issue both for those who walked away and for those who decided to stay is about the nature of racism. Is racism structural and systemic or *only* personal and relational?

The truth is this question has persisted and plagued the church for decades, if not much longer. In the late 1990s, sociologists Michael Emerson and Christian Smith conducted surveys on the phone with over twenty-five hundred Americans and then traveled around the country to conduct extensive face-to-face interviews with nearly two hundred evangelicals in twenty-three states. After analyzing the data on the spreadsheets from their surveys and framing it through the words and stories of the individuals they had met and spoken with, they published their findings in 2000 in a groundbreaking book called *Divided by Faith*. They arrived at three clear conclusions about what the majority of White evangelicals think about racial tensions in America. First, they think of racism as "the result of sinful individuals who harbor personal prejudice."[7] Second, they think racial tensions are caused by the tendency of certain racial groups—such as African Americans—to take isolated incidents of prejudice and project them onto a wider scale so that the conflict is between groups and not individuals. Third, they think racial tensions are exaggerated at best or fabricated at worst by "minority groups, liberals, the media, or the government."[8] Sounds as if Emerson and Smith could have been conducting their research in the summer of 2020.

To make matters worse, evangelicalism's emphasis on personal sin, personal repentance, and personal faith inadvertently backfires when they are used as a way of denying the social dimensions of sin. The Scriptures are under no such illusion. The Old Testament is full of instructions, corrections, and provisions for the social and structural nature of sin and its effects—from Cain and Abel to Israel and Edom. And the New Testament speaks of salvation that comes to rescue and reorder households. Yes, sin, repentance, and faith are deeply personal, but they are not private or individual. We are not atomistic creatures. Our sin—and God's salvation—creates a ripple effect.

Then there's the compounding factor of social distance. No, not the six-feet-apart kind experienced during the COVID-19 pandemic. The distance that occurs because of old racist rules, like the Jim Crow laws, and racialized economic policies, like redlining and more, have made it unlikely for many White Americans to know what the Black experience of America is like. This distance is fatal to empathy.

Emerson and Smith conclude:

> We stand at a divide. White evangelicals' cultural tools and racial isolation direct them to see the world individualistically and as a series of discrete incidents. . . . Ironically, evangelicalism's cultural tools lead people in different social and geographical realities to assess the race problem in divergent and non-reconciliatory ways. This large gulf in understanding is perhaps part of the race problem's core, and most certainly contributes to the entrenchment of the racialized society.[9]

In another study that mapped attitudes over thirty-three years, from 1977 to 2010, Emerson and Smith's thesis was confirmed. More than that, it was shown to persist even a decade after their work.

> Despite a great intellectual awareness about racial problems that began to grow in the evangelical community after the publication of *Divided by Faith* and more strident activity to eliminate prejudice, . . . white racial attitudes have remained largely the same: an individual's perceived lack of prejudice or an individual's attention to issues of personal race relations *always* trumps the structural. Hearts often matter more than bodies and certainly more than systemic problems.[10]

This is evidenced in the way evangelicals are least likely to think that "racial economic gaps" are due to "discrimination" and gaps in "education" and most likely to blame "motivation" and "ability."[11]

CURRENT PERCEPTIONS OF RACE RELATIONS IN AMERICA, BY ETHNICITY

Do you think our country has a race problem?

% who say "definitely"

● All U.S. adults ● Self-identified Christians

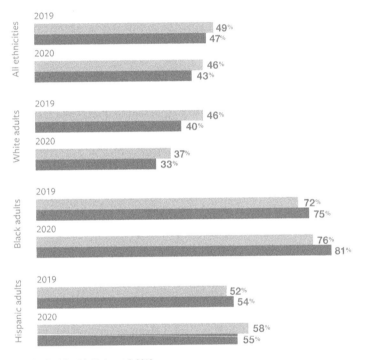

All ethnicities

2019
49%
47%

2020
46%
43%

White adults

2019
46%
40%

2020
37%
33%

Black adults

2019
72%
75%

2020
76%
81%

Hispanic adults

2019
52%
54%

2020
58%
55%

n=2,289 U.S. adults, July 19–August 5, 2019.
n=1,525 U.S. adults, June 18–July 17, 2020.

Barna repeated a study of attitudes toward racism—past and present—in 2019 and 2020 to see if the events of 2020 would impact perceptions. What they found was a mixed bag.

First the bad news: Christians aren't any more likely to think racial injustice is an issue than non-Christians; in fact, the number of Christians who think race is not a problem rose.

As of the July 2020 survey, practicing Christians—self-identified Christians who say their faith is very important in their lives and have attended a worship service within the past month—are no more likely to acknowledge racial injustice (43% "definitely") than they were the previous summer. There is actually a significant increase in the percentage of practicing Christians who say race is "not at all" a problem in the U.S. (19%, up from 11% in 2019). Among self-identified Christians alone, a similar significant increase occurs (10% in 2019, 16% in 2020).[12]

And then there's the issue of motivation "to address racial injustice in our society." That too is moving in the wrong direction. "In 2019, one in five U.S. adults was 'unmotivated' (11%) or 'not at all motivated' (9%); just a year later, in the summer of 2020, that percentage has increased to 28 percent (12% 'unmotivated,' 16% 'not at all motivated')."[13]

Still, there is some movement in the right direction. Barna found "a boost in Christians' willingness to strongly agree that, historically, the U.S. has oppressed minorities—from 19 percent in the 2019 survey to 26 percent in the summer of 2020 (for both self-identified and practicing Christians, respectively)."[14]

And churches are getting more diverse. The National Congregations Study reports that "the number of multiracial congregations is on the rise."[15] And megachurches are becoming more multiracial, which according to one new study is defined as "having 20% or more minority presence in their congregation."[16] In 2020, 58 percent of megachurches report being multiracial, up from 21 percent two decades prior.[17] For fifty years, pastors from Howard Thurman to Henry Buchanan and Bob Brown have sought to cultivate multiracial worship as the key to "affecting change on the racialized and racist social landscape."[18] Evangelicals are getting better at the solutions they believe in: changing hearts through conversion and breaking down individual prejudice by building personal relationships within a Christian community. Yet Korie Edwards, a sociologist at Ohio State, has strong words about the failure of multiracial churches to do anything about racialized

SELF-IDENTIFIED CHRISTIANS' CURRENT MOTIVATION TO ADDRESS RACIAL INJUSTICE, BY ETHNICITY

How motivated are you to address racial injustice in our society?

● Very motivated   ○ Motivated   ● Somewhat motivated
● Unmotivated   ● Not at all motivated   Not sure

White self-identified Christians

2019: 14% | 18% | 35% | 12% | 11% | 12%
2020: 10% | 15% | 29% | 14% | 22% | 9%

Black self-identified Christians

2019: 33% | 30% | 29% | 4% | 1% | 4%
2020: 46% | 24% | 19% | 2% | 3% | 6%

Hispanic self-identified Christians

2019: 24% | 27% | 27% | 8% | 8% | 6%
2020: 23% | 18% | 28% | 12% | 12% | 7%

n=2,889 U.S. adults, July 19–August 5, 2019.
n=1,525 U.S. adults, June 18–July 17, 2020.

social structures and White norms and privilege: "Symbolism, evangelism, and interracial relationships are not what changed our country. None of the major changes to the racialized social structure resulted from multiracial worship."[19]

The church may be less divided by racism today, but it is just as divided—if not more so—on what kind of racism remains and how to address it.

Political Tribalism and "Christian" Nationalism

The hostility between the political left and right has caused a chasm in the church. One pastor bragged on Twitter after the 2020 presidential election that his senior pastor had refused to serve communion to anyone who had voted Democrat. Because political alliances seem to fall along denominational lines, with "progressive" Christians voting Democrat and evangelicals voting Republican, the assumption is that anyone who voted Democrat must also be theologically liberal. It's an old assumption that continues to find new life. As one of the pastors in my focus groups shared, "We're now keenly aware that cable news has more influence to disciple our church family than the church does, and these channels are creating a politicized tribalism. This comes with all its trappings: idolize the tribe's celebrities, fight on the cultural battleground against other tribes, and more."

But the threat to the unity of the church is not simply political partisanship. There is something more sinister at work.

On January 6, 2021, a mob of Americans stormed the Capitol building in Washington, DC, to interrupt the certification of the electoral college votes on the next U.S. president by Congress. Fueled by claims of a fraudulent election, people who were convinced they had been the victims of a great injustice allowed their resentment to boil over into an attempted revolution. What grieved me most was the sight of banners that said "Jesus Saves" hanging on the Capitol and signs that read "Jesus is my Savior, Trump is my president" as people stormed the steps. A cross was erected outside, along with gallows and a noose ostensibly for Vice President Mike Pence. Inside, QAnon leader Jake Angeli led a prayer in the Senate's chamber, thanking God for allowing them to come in and to bring about the rebirth of a nation. Jesus's name was invoked multiple times. The men in front may have looked like rebels, but they sounded like dazed and confused youth group kids. Nevertheless, the mob they led played the part of Visigoths and vandals, trampling, assaulting, and killing.

Though some saw this moment as the inevitable end toward which the political tribalism in America had been careening, many Christian pastors and writers paid attention to something more sinister. The profane convergence of Christian symbols and language, conspiracy theories, and a radical right-wing agenda had coalesced in an attempt to subvert the political system that day. As people tried to make sense of what they had seen, the term *Christian nationalism* appeared over and over in articles and blogs and opinion pieces in major news outlets and mainstay Christian media such as *Christianity Today* and The Gospel Coalition. But the definitions and implications were unclear.

Enter sociologists Andrew Whitehead and Samuel Perry. In their 2020 book from Oxford University Press, they offer the conversation more specificity and clarity, moving the discourse beyond the vague but indicting the label "White evangelicalism." As with any diagnosis, the better we understand the problem, the closer we are to developing a cure. The first of their three core arguments and insights is that understanding Christian nationalism matters if we are to understand the polarization in America.[20] The second argument is that Christian nationalism is distinct and must be understood in its own terms. Christian nationalism is not the same as being White or being a White evangelical, though "roughly half

HOW CONCERNED ARE YOU ABOUT "CHRISTIAN NATIONALISM" IN OUR NATION RIGHT NOW?

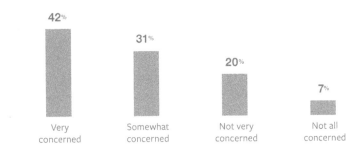

Very concerned	Somewhat concerned	Not very concerned	Not all concerned
42%	31%	20%	7%

n=415 Protestant pastors, January 22–27, 2021.

of evangelicals (by some definitions) embrace Christian national-ism to some degree."[21]

Here is where the metaphor of a diagnosis is particularly help-ful. Nobody likes being labeled. No human should be reduced to a category. Address people by their names, not the labels we assign them. But it's also important to recognize that just because someone is unfamiliar with the terminology doesn't mean they aren't ascribing to the ideas. A person may have never heard of the diagnosis and still be suffering from the sickness. There is no formal creed for Christian nationalism, but there are symptoms.

Whitehead and Perry use the term *Christian nationalism* to refer to a "fusion of American civic life with a particular type of Christian identity and culture."[22] This fusion insists "that the Christian God formed, favors, and sustains the United States over and above the other nations of the world. They proclaim the United States plays a central role in God's plan for the world."[23] In short, Christian nationalism believes that the Christian God is responsible for America's *history*, is central to America's *identity*, and is invested in America's *destiny*.

Christian nationalism is also about cultural power. Beyond simply wanting moral influence or drawing from the Christian moral vision to shape the definition of human flourishing, Chris-tian nationalism is about "seeking to retain or gain power in the public sphere."[24]

But Christian nationalism is better understood on a spectrum. Whitehead and Perry map Americans onto a Christian nationalism scale comprising four categories. Each is described with a quote from people they interviewed.

Ambassadors: "I believe [the U.S. was] founded on Christian prin-ciples, so, yes, I believe that, in essence, how we were created was the principle of Christianity. It's Christian beliefs. That's where we come from."—Trina

Accommodators: "I would agree that [the U.S.] was founded on Christian values, and maybe it was founded as a Christian nation.

But today, presently, I don't know. . . . That's a harder question to answer, right?"—Luke

Resisters: "I don't feel comfortable identifying the United States as a Christian nation even though I know that Christianity has been a major part of the history of this nation."—Deb

Rejectors: "No, I don't think the United States is a Christian nation. We are founded on a godless and secular Constitution."—Donald[25]

The third and most crucial argument in the book is that "Christian nationalism is not 'Christianity' or even 'religion' properly speaking. . . . In fact, . . . Christian nationalism often influences Americans' opinions and behaviors in the *exact opposite direction* than traditional religious commitment does."[26] Thus they insist that to "condemn Christian nationalism" as they define it "is not to condemn Christianity or religion per se."[27]

Here I must add a few words of critique for Whitehead and Perry. First, they apply their findings exclusively to the political right while ignoring the ways these assumptions are also at work in the political left. The fusion of Christian language and ideals with political agendas is not as partisan as they make it seem. Second, in trying to critique those who overplay the influence of Christianity in America's founding, they fail to give enough attention to the actual influence of Christianity on the way we think about a society. Our "Western ideals" of justice and liberty, for example, come from Christianity—from the expectation of equality among ethnicities and genders to the notion of human rights. Several historians have demonstrated this.

Third, there are other reasons for wanting to preserve a society shaped by a Judeo-Christian moral vision that don't qualify as "Christian nationalism" that Whitehead and Perry leave unexplored or unacknowledged. One such rationale is what the late former Chief Rabbi of the British Commonwealth, Jonathan Sacks, argued for in his book, *Morality*. When a society loses a shared moral framework and is left with the market and the state—arenas of competition not cooperation—the collapse of society is not far behind.

> No society has ever survived like this for very long, not even the greatest: not ancient Greece, not the Rome of antiquity, not Renaissance Italy. In each of these three cases, the release from the traditional moral restraints for a while unleashed a burst of energy and creativity, but was too quickly followed by decline and fall. A society of individualists is unsustainable. We are built for cooperation, not just competition. In the end, with the market and the state but no substantive society to link us to our fellow citizens in the bonds of collective responsibility, trust and truth erode, economics becomes inequitable, and politics becomes unbearable.[28]

Then there is the missiological twist on the rationale that argues a strong America is good for global Christian mission. From Constantine to Clovis to Charlemagne, Christian mission has been helped by a strong man who, at the very least, made conditions favorable for the church. These rulers did not wage "holy wars" or coerce conversions, but evangelistic embassies were able to follow military conquests and preach the good news. To be fair, they also built early forms of what we would call hospitals and schools, cared for the poor, and more. But the argument holds: Christians were able to do good because they had sway over the machinery and muscle of the state.

Today, there are evangelicals who make a similar argument about America. A strong America with a robust economy and policies that are favorable to Christians, churches, and religious organizations makes global missions work not only possible but exponentially more effective. According to this view, the government need not be "Christian" in order to be a propellant for Christian mission. I reject this utilitarian view. But still, this is not Christian nationalism; it's a misguided understanding of global evangelism married to a faulty theological functionalism.

These critiques notwithstanding, Whitehead and Perry's work has at least two implications for pastors. First, we must make a strong statement: Christian nationalism is not one "tribe" within a political tribalistic cultural moment. It is a movement that Christians must unequivocally denounce. It is one thing to disagree about a path to the common good or even to have differing if also overlapping visions of what the common good is. Such must always be the case in a liberal democracy. But to summon Jesus as the justification for one's political ideals is to make the Lord of the world a mascot for our party. This is anathema.

Second, there is good news. The more closely a person follows Jesus, in devotion and discipleship, the less likely they are to adhere to Christian nationalism as Whitehead and Perry define it. That means we have work to do. But as one of the pastors in my focus groups said, "Disentangling people's lives from Christian nationalism" is a work he feels "least prepared for." Lord, help us.

The Church as a Kingdom Community

What are we to do about the threats to unity in the church today? How can we bridge the gaps in both the diagnosis and the prescription for racial tensions? How can the cancer of Christian nationalism be cut from the body of Christ, and how can Christians on the political left and the political right be held together? Can the church become again a radical community in the world? These are massive questions for which there are no simple answers. But we may find clues by turning again to the early church.

The reason the early Christians were able to forge such a radical unity in such a stratified and segmented world was because they believed Jesus was the world's true Lord. He was the true King who ushered in a new kingdom, of which the church was a visible expression. The language they used for Jesus no doubt drew from the treasury of Hebrew titles and terms, from *Messiah* to *Son of God*. Yet many of these terms also had a particular resonance—especially when expressed in Greek—in the Greco-Roman world. Caesar Augustus, for instance, was called the son of God. His reign was said to have subdued all kings and ushered in a great peace—thus he was celebrated as the king of kings and lord of lords and the prince of peace.

Take, as another example of imperial language being applied to Jesus, the Christ hymn in Colossians 1:15–20. Numerous phrases can be cross-referenced to documents that apply them to Caesar: "He is the image of the invisible God" (cf. Plutarch, *Themistocles*; Ecphantes, *On Kingship*); he is "the firstborn over all creation" (cf. Letter of the Proconsul of Asia in Praise of Caesar); "in him all things hold together" (cf. Aristides, *Orations*; Seneca, *On Clemency*); "he is the head of the body, the church" (cf. Lucian, *Apology*; Seneca, *On Clemency*); "he is the beginning" (cf. Letter of the Proconsul of Asia); "in all things he might have the supremacy" (cf. Lucian, *Apology*); "for God was pleased to have all his fullness dwell in him, and through him to reconcile all things to himself making peace" (cf. Ecphantes, *On Kingship*; Calpurnius Siculus, *Eclogues*; Pliny, *Panegyricus*, *Res Gestae*; Cassius Dio).[29]

Furthermore, key terms, such as *ecclesia* (church, assembly), *eikon* (image), and *eirene* (peace), which show up not only in the Colossian Christ hymn but throughout Paul's letters, all had particular use in Roman propaganda. The use of them in the Colossian Christ hymn could hardly be accidental or incidental. Was it a way of "trolling" Rome? Walsh and Keesmat put it more formally: "In the space of a short, well-crafted, three stanza poem, Paul subverts every major claim of the empire, turning them on their heads, and proclaims Christ to be the Creator, Redeemer, and Lord of all creation, including the empire."[30]

Here's the point: if there is a new King, then there is a new kingdom. And the church is to be a "small working model" of the kingdom.[31] The church is not a gathering of individuals who have been saved from this life, passing the time with singing and good works. The church is a radical, countercultural community.

That's why the Colossian Christ hymn places the church in between the stanza about Christ as the sovereign over creation and the stanza about Christ as the sovereign over the new creation. Christ is the sovereign over a new assembly—a new body politic. "He is the head of the body, the church" (Col. 1:18 NRSV). The church exists in the space between creation and new creation. The church belongs to the created order, yet it bears witness to the new creation that has already begun. The link between *worship*, *formation*, and *unity* is this very kingdom *identity*. The church's worship should reinforce this identity, the church's ethics should embody this identity, and the church's unity should make this identity visible to the world.

The visible unity of the church that cuts across the barriers of ethnicity, class, and gender witnesses to the world that a new King and new kingdom have come. The church's radical unity is not only the outworking of the implications of Jesus's kingship, it is also an essential part of the church's mission. This is why Paul makes the reality of their unity as plain as possible to the Galatians: "You are all God's children through faith in Christ Jesus. All of you who were baptized into Christ have clothed yourselves with Christ. There is neither Jew nor Greek; there is neither slave nor free; nor is there male and female, for you are all one in Christ Jesus" (Gal. 3:26–28).

But this kind of unity must be cultivated. To live out the reality of our unity in Christ, we must embrace three postures. We find these in Sandra Van Opstal's book on the kind of worship that must shape the church in the next era. The first is *hospitality*, which says, "We welcome you." The next is *solidarity*, which declares, "We stand with you." And then comes *mutuality*, which confesses, "We need you."[32]

Multiracial churches and churches that resist becoming politically partisan are already practicing *hospitality*. "You are welcome here" no matter who you voted for and how your ideals of achieving the common good differ from mine. "You are welcome here" because ethnic diversity is part of the design of creation and the glory of redemption.

But as the research referenced above suggests, simply fostering relationships among ethnicities in church is not enough. Those relationships must allow people to take the next step toward *solidarity*. Solidarity means being willing to stand where someone else is. Hospitality allows the person with power to remain as the host, but solidarity requires giving up our power and privilege and place and entering someone else's pain. As my friend Rich Villodas, who pastors in Queens, New York, where seventy-five languages are spoken and people from 120 countries live, puts it, the "habit of incarnational listening requires something of a crucifixion." We "must undergo a painful process of leaving what is familiar territory (my perspective on the matter) and make space in my heart for a different narrative."[33] To listen to someone else's experience of America, to consider the painful reality of structural or systemic racism even when it does not affect you or even seem like a reality to you is a Christlike act of self-emptying love. The same can be said about a bridge across political lines. Curiosity about different policy paths to care for the poor or provide health care for the marginalized can go a long way. But it will require dropping our labels for one another. The church today desperately needs to "let this same mind" be in us that was in Christ.

Finally, unity is found through genuine *mutuality*. This is seen in the "one another" texts in the New Testament. The two words in English are one Greek word, and they pepper the instructions to the New Testament church. Here's a sampling:

Be of the same mind with one another. (Rom. 12:16; 15:5)

Don't boastfully challenge or envy one another. (Gal. 5:26)

Gently, patiently tolerate one another. (Eph. 4:2)

Bear with and forgive one another. (Col. 3:13)

Seek good for one another, and don't repay evil for evil. (1 Thess. 5:15)

Don't complain against one another. (James 4:11; 5:9)

Confess sins to one another. (James 5:16)

Love one another. (Rom. 13:8; 1 Thess. 3:12; 4:9; 1 Pet. 1:22; 1 John 3:11; 4:7, 11; 2 John 5)

Through love, serve one another. (Gal. 5:13)

Regard one another as more important than yourselves. (Phil. 2:3)[34]

Genuine fellowship—the sharing of life in Christ—is mutual. I need you, and you need me. I give to you and receive from you. Power dynamics are meant to be neutralized by the Spirit.

In All Honesty

Sometimes honesty has to come first. It takes an honesty about the threats to unity, and it takes an honesty about our own participation in the problems.

Steve is a pastor of a revitalized church in Alabama. We became friends a few years ago and talk regularly via Zoom. A pastor of a White-majority church, Steve is taking some brave steps to help lead his church in honest learning and lament. He wrote to me recently, describing the process that led to his action.

> I am an ordinary pastor who loves his church, loves his community, and loves this country. When I slow down to consider the deaths of George Floyd and Ahmaud Arbery and others, I am broken. When I consider the peaceful protest by men and women who long for change, when I talk to my brothers and sisters in the African American community who feel deeply hurt, I am saddened. When I consider the unacceptable acts of people who were not a part of any protest but just want to cause great division, destroy property, and drive a deeper wedge of racial division, I am angered. When I consider the police officers, the vast majority who are standing in the gap to make a difference, some of them even losing their lives, I am moved.
>
> In the face of a broken world, with broken values, and broken systems, and broken people, how does God want an ordinary pastor in a majority-White church and White community to respond?

The question has nagged at him for the past two years. He knows the Scriptures and has a clear understanding of justice. But it was more recently that he began to get a clearer picture of his own life.

"I grew up playing basketball. At many points in my life, I was the only White guy on the team, and I didn't think twice about what the others may or may not be experiencing." He had never stopped to consider how different his experiences were from his Black friends. "I have to be honest, it wasn't until my midtwenties that I started to understand how unaware I was of the experience of many of my Black brothers and sisters who were and still are deep friends of mine. . . . I have never once been called derogatory names because of the color of my skin."

This honesty, which is a precursor to hospitality and solidarity, is an honesty not only about personal experiences but also about history. "We have to be honest that we have a history," he told me. "And it is not ancient history." He was beginning to see his own place in this history. "I come to this moment in our history as a White man who grew up along the coast of Florida and Alabama. Just a few years before I was born, a Black man or a Black woman could not drink from the same water fountain I could as a White man. I am someone who has had a completely different American experience than my Black brothers and sisters."

The common rebuttal is that life is hard for everyone. "I would agree," he said. "Life is hard for everyone. Although I can share some of my own challenges in life, life has never been hard for me because of the color of my skin."

The big step Steve is leading his church to take is an act of embodied, communal solidarity. "When you hear the cries of the broken, . . . our tendency is to offer our opinions, offer our solutions, over offering our ears and our hearts to people. But the best thing we can do is to love well by cultivating a posture of listening, learning, and lamenting."

All this led him to pioneer an annual mission trip focused on prayer and processing in Montgomery, Alabama, in connection with the Equal Justice Initiative led by Brian Stevenson. Steve described it this way: "The trip serves more as a pilgrimage anchored in prayer, learning, and listening. It is deeply connected to our mission of leading people toward their next step with Jesus. My hope is the experience will foster humility, shape deeper spiritual formation, and cultivate a life of grieving well as we stand in solidarity with the broken and overlooked." Beautiful.

Humble honesty that is willing to listen, learn, and lament. Radical hospitality toward those who are not like us. Genuine solidarity with those whose pain is not our own. Humble mutuality where love and sacrifice flow both ways. This is the kind of community that witnesses to the world of a true and better kingdom. *This* is the unity that glorifies God.

Reflections from Dr. Derwin Gray, pastor, author, and speaker

I was asked by a Gen Z, "Pastor, does Jesus care about racism?" I asked her, "Why do you ask?" She said, "I just don't get my family. They say they love Jesus, but they seem not to care about the things that hurt Black people. When I hear them talk, they sound more like the nighttime cable news guy they listen to, instead of Jesus."

Young people want to know, Does Jesus care about racism? Jesus does care about the sin of racism because it is dividing and destroying our culture and his church. First, we have the honor of leading God's people to understand that Jesus not only died for our sins but also placed us in a family with different-colored skins. We are the multicolored family God promised Abraham (Gal. 3:8).

Second, we have the privilege of equipping God's people to understand that the cross of Jesus creates a humanity called the church (Eph. 2:14–16). In the first-century culture of the Second Temple era, Jewish people saw only two groups of people: Jews and gentiles. After Jesus's life, death, and resurrection, he formed a new people group composed of both Jews and gentiles and called the church.

Third, we have the honor of equipping God's people to "walk worthy of the calling you have received, with all humility and gentleness, with patience, bearing with one another in love, making every effort to keep the unity of the Spirit through the bond of peace" (Eph. 4:1–3 CSB).

Jesus cares about racism, and so should we.

mission

What is our mission in the world?

What is the mission of the church? What are the missional implications of the gospel? In the North American context and in many European contexts as well, there has been a split lasting well over a century over these questions. In the early 1900s, pastors and theologians such as Walter Rauschenbusch advocated a view of sin that was social and material and thus a vision of salvation that was as well. But because of the tendency of such voices to also reject pillars of creedal orthodoxy, their reading of the gospel of the kingdom came to be viewed as liberal. Such critiques were not without merit.

But the reaction created an opposite error. Theological conservatives came to focus on atonement, honing in on personal sin and God's forgiveness. For all the good things that came from the emphasis on personal faith and repentance, the unintended consequence was how that emphasis was framed as being *over and against* any social or material dimension of the gospel. Thus, to confess Jesus as the only way to the Father or to stress the need for repentance or to believe in the atoning death of Christ on the cross was to place one as a theological conservative over and against a theological liberal. The mission of a conservative church, then, became preaching to make converts while ignoring the pain of the community in which it existed—unless there were certain "good works" that could earn goodwill from the community. But even so, feeding the hungry or seeking to change inequitable structures was optional and ancillary; it was not endemic to the gospel itself.

The split, however, was mainly in the White Protestant church. In African American churches, there was no way of ignoring the social plight of their parishioners and of their community. The gospel was always meant to be good news for the poor. Today, social concerns shape evangelical engagement but with different actions and goals than mainline Protestants. For many White evangelicals, preserving their definition of *family values* is what drives social action. In an interview with PBS's *Frontline* a few years ago, Christian historian Mark Noll explained what *family values* refers to: "Most white evangelicals, North and South, would probably see family values as related to influence in the local schools, as preference given to traditional families, one man, one wife married. Traditional values would include protection for children. Traditional values would include protection for life."

Noll elaborated on the disparity between the priorities for social engagement between White Christians and Black Christians in America:

> Black churchgoers and white churchgoers who would share a common set of evangelical beliefs almost predictably are going to come down on different sides of the modern political debate.
>
> African-American churches, and especially urban churches in the main cities of the United States, are concerned about issues bearing in on those communities. Those issues have to do with support for public education. They have to do with the provision of welfare for stressed families. They have to do with the provision of work and government policies that support the ability to make a living.
>
> White evangelicals are—not exclusively—but they are comfortable in the suburbs, and in the small towns and rural areas of the United States. Those two environments historically and contem-

poraneously have posed different ranges of social issues, and have put different social issues in the forefront of church concern, as well.

So we have in the United States now a situation where religion is the second-strongest indicator of public partisan behavior. But race remains the number one indicator.[1]

Conservative or liberal, Black or White, we cannot seem to decide what the mission of the church is. When we asked pastors to rank a list of missional priorities into a top five, our new study showed that 72 percent of pastors rank "sharing the gospel with non-Christians locally" while 58 percent rank "local poverty" and 53 percent rank "caring for elderly and widows" in their top five. But a closer analysis reveals a deeper divide. Eighty-six percent of mainline churches rank "local poverty" most highly as their missional priority compared to 48 percent of non-mainline churches. Meanwhile, "sharing the gospel with non-Christians locally" was the top priority for 83 percent of non-mainline pastors compared to 37 percent of mainline pastors.

TOP FIVE MISSIONAL PRIORITIES AS A CHURCH
All Pastors

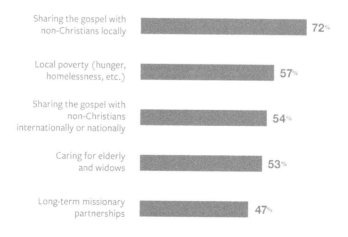

Sharing the gospel with non-Christians locally	72%
Local poverty (hunger, homelessness, etc.)	57%
Sharing the gospel with non-Christians internationally or nationally	54%
Caring for elderly and widows	53%
Long-term missionary partnerships	47%

Protestant Mainline Pastors

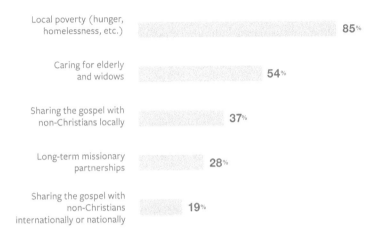

Local poverty (hunger, homelessness, etc.) — 85%

Caring for elderly and widows — 54%

Sharing the gospel with non-Christians locally — 37%

Long-term missionary partnerships — 28%

Sharing the gospel with non-Christians internationally or nationally — 19%

Protestant Non-Mainline Pastors

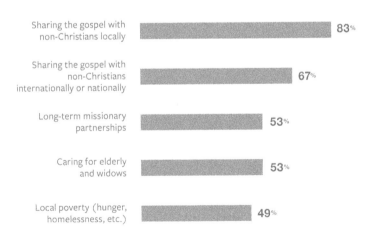

Sharing the gospel with non-Christians locally — 83%

Sharing the gospel with non-Christians internationally or nationally — 67%

Long-term missionary partnerships — 53%

Caring for elderly and widows — 53%

Local poverty (hunger, homelessness, etc.) — 49%

n=408 U.S. Protestant pastors, September 16–October 8, 2020.

The split between sharing the gospel and caring for the community continues to persist. How do we reconcile the divide and discover a vision of mission that encompasses both? For the love of God and the good of the world, we need to recover the way the New Testament church worked out its mission through the lens of the kingdom of God. A rich theology of the kingdom holds together evangelism and justice, proclamation and demonstration, and healing and hospitality.

When the Call Became a Person

I want us to take a long biblical tour of the mission of God through a kingdom lens. If the last chapter was thick on situational analysis, this one will be long on scriptural recovery. We're going to do some constructive work to reshape our vision of the mission of the church. Stay with me.

The Bible introduces us to a God on mission. From the moment of Adam and Eve's sin, God began seeking the lost. He called out to them, asking questions that were less of an interrogation and more of an intervention. To Adam, "Where are you?" "Who told you that you were naked?" (Gen. 3:9, 11). To Eve, "What have you done?" (Gen. 3:13). To Cain, "Where is your brother Abel?" (Gen. 4:9).

These questions were meant to help them recognize where they were and what they had done. But at their core, these were questions meant to remind human beings of their own vocation as image bearers who would fill the earth and reflect God's wise and loving order in the world. The mission of humans was to reflect and extend the rule of God in such a way that the earth would be fruitful and flourishing. But they chose to live apart from God. Like a mirror moving away from the light, all they could reflect was darkness. Their sin was a failure of mission, a missing of the mark of their calling to both worship and work.

Then the God who called light out of darkness and order out of chaos, called Abraham out of his father's house: "All the families of the earth will be blessed because of you" (Gen. 12:3). The mission of God to make for himself a people from all the peoples of the earth, a family from all the families in the world, begins to take shape with the call of Abraham.

We find out quickly, however, that Abraham himself is in need of saving. Not long after hearing his call, we witness his fall—his lie about his wife. The great father of faith wavers in fear. And his descendants are not much better. Isaac repeated the sin of his father by lying about his own wife, Rebekah. Jacob lies to swindle his brother out of a blessing. And Jacob's sons sell off their little brother, Joseph, and lie about it to their father. Joseph deceives his brothers in order to test them when they come to Egypt for aid during a time of famine. But somehow God works amid it all to preserve his chosen people.

Their privileged status in Egypt dies with Joseph, and Abraham's descendants now become slaves to harsh taskmasters. But God, mindful of his mission, hears the cries of his people. Why act for these Hebrew slaves when oppression was aplenty in the ancient world? Because they were *his*. So God called Moses the fugitive after he had murdered an Egyptian. Moses had anger at injustice, but his actions were not God's. Now they would be. God sent him with signs and warnings, and judgment fell on the Egyptians and on Pharaoh's house. After all, they could not *serve* God while *enslaved* to Egypt (the Hebrew word is the same). Their freedom from slavery was a freedom for worshipful service to God. The people of God were freed to worship their covenant God. Here we see another layer of the mission of God: God forms for himself a people, calling them and delivering them so that they might worship him. The Hebrew word for *worship* is the same word for *service* or *work*. Just as the call in Genesis 1 was for human beings, made in God's image, to worship and to work—to be, as N. T. Wright is fond of saying, angled mirrors who reflect God's wise and loving order into the world and creation's praise upward to God—so now the call is applied to one specific family. Where humanity had failed, Israel would be called to be faithful.

Nothing would deter God from getting the story back on track. Not the sin in Eden, not the failures of Abraham, Isaac, and Jacob, and not the captivity in Egypt. God would deal with evil, carry the weight of sin, and rescue his people. The mission of God goes on.

Once in the land, the people wanted one leader, a king who would fight for them and rule over them. This was tantamount to a rejection of God (cf. 1 Sam. 8). But if an entire nation could not faithfully worship God and carry out his work, then perhaps one representative king could. The circles keep getting smaller. From the human race to one nation to one representative. The language in the Old Testament about their king was originally meant for all humanity. Instead of humans being crowned with glory (Ps. 8), it is now one man. Furthermore, the language about Israel now gets applied to the king. Israel was God's "firstborn"; in the Psalms, the king is the son of God.

Yet even Israel's kings could not rise to the call. Saul, tall as he was, falls woefully short. David, heroic though his exploits, uses his power to take what his cravings desire. Solomon, wise though he was, was foolish enough to have hundreds of wives and concubines with their idols in tow. It gets worse from there. The failure of the kingdom is exposed by the prophets, but even the prophets are not able to call Israel back.

Yet the calling God, when his words go unheeded, does not go away. The Word became flesh and "moved into the neighborhood" (John 1:14 MSG). The call comes in a person. Jesus, the human one—"Son of Man"—sums up the human story in himself. And Jesus, the seed of Abraham and the Son of David, gathers the story of Israel together in himself, as the true King, the Son of God. The story that kept shrinking from one humanity to one nation to one king now explodes outward as it becomes embodied in Jesus.

Jesus is the mission of God in human flesh. In him, salvation reaches its climax.

The Mission of Jesus

What did the mission of Jesus look like? Jesus came announcing the kingdom of God. "And he went throughout all Galilee, teaching in their synagogues and proclaiming the gospel of the kingdom and healing every disease and every affliction among the people" (Matt. 4:23 ESV). What is the "gospel" or good news of the "kingdom"? It is the joyful announcement of God's arrival, drawing on Isaiah's vision of the messenger of good news:

> Go on up to a high mountain,
>   O Zion, herald of good news;
> lift up your voice with strength,
>   O Jerusalem, herald of good news;
>   lift it up, fear not;
> say to the cities of Judah,
>   "Behold your God!"
> Behold, the LORD GOD comes with might,
>   and his arm rules for him;
> behold, his reward is with him,
>   and his recompense before him.
> He will tend his flock like a shepherd;
>   he will gather the lambs in his arms;
> he will carry them in his bosom,
>   and gently lead those that are with young.
>   (Isa. 40:9–11 ESV)

God is coming to his people as the King! The imagery of the tender shepherd is how the Old Testament speaks about a ruler who uses their power rightly: to protect, defend, nurture, and provide for those entrusted to their care. Ezekiel uses shepherd language to talk about the wicked and self-serving kings of Israel and Judah, concluding with a promise from God that he would come and be king himself (Ezek. 34).

For Jesus, preaching the gospel of the kingdom meant saying that God had come to rule and to reign—it was the good news they had been waiting for. But Jesus does more than announce the kingdom; he *brings* the kingdom, for he is, in fact, the King. Matthew tells us that Jesus healed those who were sick. Healing in the Gospels is not a party trick or a little sideshow to draw a crowd for the "message of salvation" that Jesus wanted to preach.

Healing was a specific sign of the arriving rule of God. When John the Baptist sent word asking if Jesus was the Messiah or if he should look for another, Jesus replied, "Go and tell John what you hear and see: the blind receive their sight and the lame walk, lepers are cleansed and the deaf hear, and the dead are raised up, and the poor have good news preached to them" (Matt. 11:4–5 ESV).

When Jesus emerged from the temptation in the wilderness, which in itself was a replaying and redeeming of Israel's story because of his resistance to the enemy, he went to the synagogue and found the Isaiah scroll and read from it:

> "The Spirit of the Lord is upon me, because he has anointed me to proclaim good news to the poor. He has sent me to proclaim liberty to the captives and recovering of sight to the blind, to set at liberty those who are oppressed, to proclaim the year of the Lord's favor." And he rolled up the scroll and gave it back to the attendant and sat down. And the eyes of all in the synagogue were fixed on him. And he began to say to them, "Today this Scripture has been fulfilled in your hearing." (Luke 4:18–21 ESV)

Here is a key insight for us to recover: the results of the reign of God are not merely individual and internal. God's inbreaking rule is not simply for our forgiveness of sins. Israel's deliverance from slavery to Egypt is a paradigm of how God's redemptive mission works. Because the Exodus dealt with political, social, and economic dimensions of life in order to form a people who would worship and serve God—the so-called spiritual dimension—we must see God's redemption as a "totality of concern for human need."[2] Christopher Wright makes the case that while some have argued that the New Testament draws on Exodus imagery to allude to a spiritual deliverance and the Old Testament emphasizes a material deliverance, the whole counsel of Scripture must be held together to reveal God's redemptive mission. To "change people's social or economic status without leading them to saving faith and obedience to God in Christ leads no further than the wilderness or the exile, both places of death," but to preach the forgiveness of sins without addressing the moral implications for justice and righteousness socially, economically, and politically, is to produce a kind of "private pietism."[3] Wright points out that this too was one of Israel's sins, as the prophets showed:

> The prophets saw a people whose appetite for worship was insatiable but whose daily lives were a denial of all the moral standards of the God they claimed to worship. There was plenty of charismatic fervor (Amos 5:21–24), plenty of atonement theology in the blood of multiple sacrifices (Isa. 1:10–12), plenty of assurance of salvation in the recitation of sound-bite claims for the temple (Jer. 7:4–11), plenty of religious observance at great festivals and conventions (Isa. 1:13–15). But beneath their noses and under their feet, the poor were uncared for at best and trampled on at worst. Spiritual religion flourished amidst social rottenness.[4]

Beyond the exodus event, Israel's experience of exile also linked the spiritual need for forgiveness with the material need for deliverance. When Israel hoped for the forgiveness of sins, they were thinking of their national sins that had resulted in exile—not only the literal exile in Babylon but also the ongoing experience of exile under Roman domination even as they lived in their land. Forgiveness was not abstract. They were suffering under the weight of their sin in a tangible way. They needed God to forgive them *and* free them.

When Jesus came, he did not spiritualize these hopes, pointing them to a vision of liberated souls in the afterlife. That would have been a hope that was foreign to the Old Testament. Jesus said that his arrival would mean the beginning of a reversal, the very thing his mother had sung about when she carried the Son of God in her blessed womb.

The gospel of the kingdom—the good news of God's arriving and inbreaking rule on earth as it is in heaven—does not split what modern evangelicals call "evangelism" and "justice." These are of the same fabric. Sins are forgiven, the hungry are fed, the poor are welcomed in, the captives are freed, and a new community is born. When the Lord reigns, the earth rejoices.

The good news of the gospel is not simply spiritual and eternal; it has bearing on the physical and material. Paul, summoning more language from Isaiah and the prophets, said that God in Christ had begun putting the world back together in such a strong way that when the work culminates at Christ's return, it will constitute a new creation. The old creation will be brought through death into new life.

The mission of God is for his rule to arrive in fullness for the good of the world. Jesus announced and inaugurated that rule, the kingdom of God, as its anointed King.

Announcing the Kingdom

What does all this mean for the mission of the church? "As the Father has sent me," Jesus said to his disciples, "even so I am sending you" (John 20:21 ESV). Jesus himself embodied the mission of God in the world from the beginning. The mission of the church is the mission of Jesus continued by the power of the Spirit but with one twist: since we ourselves are not the kingdom bringers, our mission is to *announce* Jesus as King and to *anticipate* the fullness of the kingdom by living under his reign now.

The announcement of the kingdom of God is at the heart of what the gospel is. Over the past decade or so, there have been a plethora of books and think pieces quibbling over what the "gospel" really is. Some say it's "justification by faith," the good news about how we are saved by faith, not by works. Others say it's the salvation message, a call to repentance and faith. And when our congregants say, "Pastor, please just preach the gospel," they usually mean, "Please don't make me rethink my social or political opinions."

Matthew Bates, following the trail set by Scot McKnight and N. T. Wright along with many others, returns us to the Bible's use of the word *gospel*, paying particular attention to Paul's use. Bates summarizes things this way: "The gospel is the true story of how

Jesus the Son was sent by *God the Father* to become the saving king who now rules forever at his right hand through the sending of *the Holy Spirit*, fulfilling God's promises in Scripture."[5] The gospel is good news, not good advice or a transaction. Bates distinguishes between the gospel as an "announcement"—the way the word *euangelion* was used in the Roman world—and the "saving benefits" that follow from it—the forgiveness of sins, adoption, justification, and more.[6]

In the Roman world of the New Testament, the word *gospel* was used as a slogan of sorts. Five years after Augustus's death, the Galatian Commonwealth met to honor the memory of Caesar as savior and lord for the peace and order he had brought to their region and to the empire.[7] A new road south of Galatia was named after Augustus—the Via Sebastos (Greek for Augustus)—and the three newly united Galatian tribes had a "new marker of identity"—the *Sebastenos*, the ones favored by Augustus, a title given by the Caesar.[8] In gratitude for this gift, the Galatians decided five years after his death to honor him by inscribing Augustus's own account of his career on various monuments throughout their region. The word? *Euangelion*—good news, the word we translate as "gospel."[9]

To preach the gospel is to announce the good news that Jesus is the saving King.

Many Christians are losing their verve when it comes to making this proclamation. In a recent study titled "Spiritual Conversations in the Digital Age," Barna found that "one-third of all U.S. adults say they have made a 'big change' in their life because of a conversation about faith (35%)."[10] And Christians know the impact spiritual conversations can have: "One in 3 Christians says someone has come to believe in Jesus after they shared about their faith in him."[11] Yet only 64 percent of Christians agree that it is every Christian's responsibility to share their faith, down from 89 percent who agreed in 1993.[12] Nearly half of Millennial practicing Christians "strongly agree" that "it is wrong to share one's personal beliefs with someone of a different faith in hopes that they will one day share the same faith."[13] This is despite the fact that

68 percent of them "strongly agree" that "the best thing that could ever happen to someone is for them to come to know Jesus."[14]

Could this change in attitudes about sharing the good news of Jesus be because we think sharing our faith means something like the "If you died tonight, do you know where you are going?" speech? Would our attitudes change if we recognized that announcing the good news was announcing Jesus as the saving King? We have framed gospel proclamation around heaven and hell rather than centering it on Jesus himself. Our version of witnessing has become a "get out of hell" card as opposed to a "look what the Lord has done" story. The preaching of the early church, as seen in the book of Acts, offered a testimony of Jesus's lordship here and now with eternal effects that cannot be reduced to a mere transaction for a better afterlife. It is a public truth with profoundly personal implications. But if we don't start with Jesus, it won't sound like good news. And one can't be blamed for not wanting to share it.

Yet sharing the good news is not optional. Some of the pastors in my focus groups lamented the ease with which people write checks for outreach initiatives and foreign missionary support but are reluctant to serve or to share the gospel with their friends and neighbors. These pastors are trying to help them embrace the both/and of giving and telling. Announcing the good news of Jesus is every Christian's privilege and calling.

Anticipating the Kingdom

The kingdom coming in fullness must be anticipated now in the present through the mission of the church. Imagine a wide receiver in a football game running their route, anticipating where the ball is going to be. Or a soccer player timing their run past the line of defense just after the pass is made. In both sports, the player has to go to the spot ahead of the pass so that when the ball arrives there, they do too. Christians are to live now as it will be then. We are to be like signposts in the world of the coming kingdom of God. Our mission is not simply to announce but to *anticipate*. The question is *how*.

What does it look like for the church to anticipate the arriving kingdom of God? Look first at Jesus in the Gospels. The "signs" of the kingdom in the ministry of Jesus were acts of *healing* and *hospitality*. Luke is eager to show that the Spirit who anointed Jesus to preach good news to the poor and liberty for the captives (Luke 4:18) is the same Spirit who anoints the church (Acts 2). In his Gospel, Luke shows us Jesus leaving the synagogue after announcing his anointing by the Spirit and driving out demons and healing many who were sick with various kinds of illnesses (Luke 4:31–41). In Acts, the story Luke tells shortly after the outpouring of the Spirit at Pentecost is of church leaders Peter and John healing a poor crippled beggar (Acts 3). Healing follows the anointing of the Spirit as a sign of the arriving kingdom.

In his Gospel, Luke also repeatedly shows us Jesus reaching those on the margins, including Samaritans and sinners. In Acts, Luke describes the first major challenge facing the early church as a decision about how to care for Jewish and Greek widows with equal attention (Acts 6). Hospitality to the outsider is yet another marker of the mission of the Spirit through Jesus and through the church.

The last story Luke tells about Jesus in his Gospel is of Jesus as a guest in the home of some disappointed and disillusioned disciples. Jesus, breaking with tradition, takes the bread and says the blessing. In this act of eucharistic hospitality, their spiritual blindness is healed and they recognize him as the crucified and risen Messiah. In one of the last stories Luke tells in his volume 2, the book of Acts, Paul is on a prison ship in the middle of a storm (Acts 27). He is ignored until the sailors and soldiers begin to fear for their lives. Paul, having had an angelic dream, speaks a word of hope to them, telling them no one will die. Then he encourages them to eat. Paul takes bread, blesses it, breaks it, and gives it to them. In what seems like an obvious breadcrumb (I'm sorry, I couldn't resist the pun!) for the listener and reader, Luke uses the same word he had used for what Jesus did with the bread at Passover—*eucharisteo*. Paul acted *eucharistically* in a setting that was not just nonreligious but overtly hostile to the mission.

The mission of the church is the mission of Jesus. Jesus was the guest who acted like a host. Paul was the prisoner who acted like a priest. Jesus continues his priestly ministry of blessing unlikely people in unexpected places through the Spirit-anointed church.

The Mission Expressed

Healing and hospitality are still how the church anticipates the coming kingdom. The wounds of the world have come to the surface. We see the wounds of racism, the wounds of exploitation and greed, the wounds of violence and war. The best the world around us has to offer is an eye for an eye. Another wound for my wound. But Christians can carry on the mission of Jesus by being healers. N. T. Wright sees healing as a powerful picture of the vocation of all Christians in a broken and hurting world:

> We need Christian people to work as healers: as healing judges and prison staff, as healing teachers and administrators, as healing shopkeepers and bankers, as healing musicians and artists, as healing writers and scientists, as healing diplomats and politicians. We need people who will hold on to Christ firmly with one hand and reach out the other, with wit and skill and cheerfulness, with compassion and sorrow and tenderness, to the places where our world is in pain. We need people who will use all their God-given skills . . . to analyze where things have gone wrong, to come to the place of pain, and to hold over the wound the only medicine which will really heal, which is the love of Christ made incarnate once more, your smile and mine, your tears and mine, your patient analysis and mine, your frustration and mine, your joy and mine.[15]

We need to be healers.

And we need to offer hospitality. Hospitality is about much more than providing meals, but there's something about meals that helps us understand the heart of what Eugene Peterson called "eucharistic hospitality." When I was growing up in Malaysia, food was a part of everything we did. Malaysian street food is famous and is available at all hours of the day and night. Our home was always full of people coming over for feasts my mother had prepared. Holly and I have tried to carry on the tradition in our own home.

And it has spilled over into our church. Our small group model is built around tables. We worship at the Lord's Table on Sundays, and we gather around one another's tables during the week. Our main pathway for welcoming skeptics and seekers is through Alpha, whose very model is built on a kind of radical hospitality with delicious food and where no question is off-limits. One of the major outreach initiatives locally is the Dream Centers of Colorado Springs, which includes an apartment complex and several other transitional housing units for single moms and their kids. Helping people share meals together and make a home for their families is one expression of the hospitality of Jesus.

Dan, a pastor in the Dallas area who is in one of my focus groups, shared a story of how his church used a portion of their church property to start a community garden. Their land is close to the only apartment complex in their town, and they saw it as a mission field. At the urging and under the guidance of a congregant who had her own garden, they removed grass, tilled the soil and began planting a garden in the suburbs. Dan wrote to tell me that "in a few short years the church has donated over one ton of fresh vegetables to the local pantry" and that through a COVID grant they have added "an orchard of thirty trees which should produce in five years." The garden became a "living parable" for them, an act of hospitality that has seen a woman from Africa cultivate a plant from her home country that flourished in the Texas soil and heat, a lady from Southeast Asia plant a shrub for tea, and a group of high school girls taking pictures with the sunflowers.

Other pastors in my focus groups described paying attention to the neighborhood around the church, reaching out to the residents and schools and local businesses in their immediate community. Stefan in Toronto described how every Christmas, they receive an offering that goes to a mosaic partnership in the city, which includes other religious communities, to provide care for the homeless. Every Easter, they do a refugee sponsorship. For him, these are all "methods and modes" of "showing God's love first" in their community.

During the global pandemic of 2020, churches across the world learned how to facilitate house fellowships, where people could gather in small numbers outside or in homes and worship and pray together. We strengthened the forgotten muscles of what used to be called "lay ministry"—ordinary people doing holy work together.

Churches also became storehouses of groceries and meals and suppliers of masks. Our church donated and delivered tens of thousands of pounds of groceries and ready-made meals. People were sewing masks and donating them to prisons and eldercare facilities. And the stories from pastors across the country confirmed similar work. Showing up with food or cleaning supplies or masks is extending the hospitality of Jesus outward. Churches learned that hospitality is not simply being ready to welcome people *in*—it was months before we could do that—but also going *out* to where people are.

One notable picture of going to where people are is the story of the Archbishop of Canterbury, the spiritual leader of the global

NON-CHRISTIANS EXPECT A HANDS-ON LOCAL CHURCH
What is a church's role in a community?
Top three results among non-Christians

Provide hands-on help to people in need	39%
Practically assist those in need	38%
Offer counseling and care	38%

n=611 non-Christian U.S. adults, October 9–20, 2020.

Anglican communion, who went undercover as a hospital chaplain during the early weeks of the pandemic. Unable to gather in churches or even to go there for prayer, The Most Reverend and Right Honourable Justin Welby would wear his clerical shirt under PPE (personal protective equipment) and serve as a volunteer chaplain. Welby had been publicly criticized in the *London Times* for a "lackluster response" to the crisis, perhaps because he didn't give a rousing Easter sermon or push back against government guidelines or elbow his way into the limelight.[16] That is just not his style. Instead, he quietly and faithfully showed up at St. Thomas, his neighborhood hospital, to join other chaplains and pray for the sick and the dying.

Sometimes the work of announcing the kingdom comes along with the work of anticipating the kingdom through hospitality and healing. Alice, a friend who pastors in a small community in the North East of England, shared a story with me of just such a convergence. A woman in her seventies came to the church one day. She had often walked past the church, but that day a thought popped into her head that she should go in. So on that day she did. She had been widowed just a few months earlier and was now facing treatment for cancer. She was worried and fearful. Alice and some others prayed with her. The woman was having trouble with her finances because she struggled with math. And she also longed to rekindle her love for crafts now that she had time on her hands, but she didn't know where to start. Well, as it turned out, the woman who welcomed her at the church that morning was a retired math lecturer from the university who also happened to run the church craft group. That morning the woman decided it must have been God who arranged these coincidences, and she gave her life to Christ. Her family and friends commented in the following weeks that she actually *physically* looked better. Alice wrote to me, "Jesus has literally transformed her life. She turned into a natural evangelist and died 18 months later still encouraging others to trust in Jesus as she had done."

Sounds like the mission of Jesus to me.

Who Needs the Local Church?

For Christians, expectations of the local church begin with their own spiritual health. For non-Christians, they begin with the practical needs of the community. In general, however, individuals outside the faith are reluctant to turn to a church for much help in any area of their lives.

WHAT IS THE CHURCH'S ROLE IN A COMMUNITY?
Top Five Responses

● Christians ◉ Non-Christians

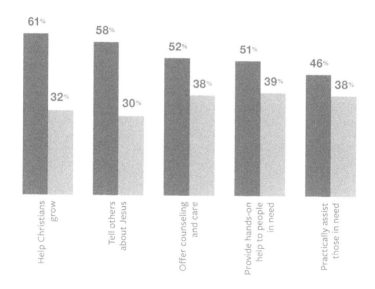

HOW LIKELY ARE YOU TO GO TO CHURCH FOR HELP WITH . . . ?*

Among Christians

● Very likely ● Somewhat likely

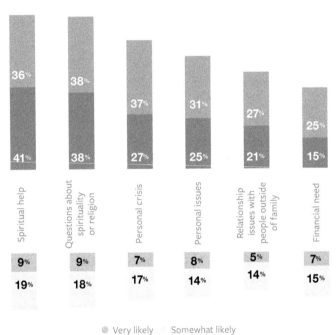

36%	38%	37%	31%	27%	25%
41%	38%	27%	25%	21%	15%

Spiritual help · Questions about spirituality or religion · Personal crisis · Personal issues · Relationship issues with people outside of family · Financial need

9%	9%	7%	8%	5%	7%
19%	18%	17%	14%	14%	15%

● Very likely · Somewhat likely

Among non-Christians

n=909 self-identified Christian U.S. adults, n=611 non-Christian U.S. adults, October 9–20, 2020.
*This data also appears on p. 222.

Reflections from Christine Caine, activist, author, speaker, and cofounder of the A21 Campaign

When I began to speak about slavery on behalf of A21 more than a decade ago, I was shocked at the initial resistance I encountered. Many people did not believe slavery still existed. In fact, I was encouraged to stick to evangelism and leave social justice to someone else. I realized there was a massive disconnect between what we were reading in our Bibles and how we were applying it in the world around us. The world was not listening to our message because we were not hearing their cries. Our good news was not reaching the trenches of pain, suffering, and injustice. We had to *be* good news before we could proclaim it.

Today, I see us more in touch than ever about the needs facing a broken and dying world. Whether it's teaching refugees a new language, sponsoring a child's education, facilitating racial reconciliation, encouraging someone recovering from addiction, initiating prison and asylum reforms, or providing fresh water where there is none—I see us engaged in cultures and communities up close and far away. We want to follow the Jesus we see in the Gospels; we want to be his hands and feet in the world.

The way forward is for us to always remember that justice and evangelism are two sides of the same coin. We do not have to throw out one to do the other, nor should we. We affirm what we say by the works that we do. The way forward is simple and not complicated: "Mankind, he has told each of you what is good and what it is the LORD requires of you: to act justly, to love faithfulness, and to walk humbly with your God" (Mic. 6:8 CSB).

WHY WE NEED RESILIENT PASTORS

Challenges facing the pastor

VOCATION
What are pastors called to do?

35 percent of pastors feel "more confident" in their calling than they did when they entered ministry—though this proportion is down from 65 percent in 2015.

35%

SPIRITUALITY
How do pastors cultivate a deeper life with God?

Just over half of pastors have a daily habit of personal Bible reading.

55%

RELATIONSHIPS
How do pastors develop meaningful relationships?

Three in five pastors have felt lonely at least sometimes in the past year.

60%

CREDIBILITY
How do pastors become trustworthy in a disillusioned world?

31 percent of Christians—and just 4 percent of non-Christians—say a pastor is "definitely" a trustworthy source of wisdom.

31%

n=408 U.S. Protestant pastors, September 16–October 8, 2020; n=415 U.S. Protestant pastors, January 22–27, 2021; n=1,520 U.S. adults, October 9–20, 2020.

Pastors and the churches they lead are up against numerous cultural shifts and pressures. Here's a picture of the challenges of ministry in a rapidly changing world and what faithful stewardship of a pastoral calling will require.

Challenges facing the church

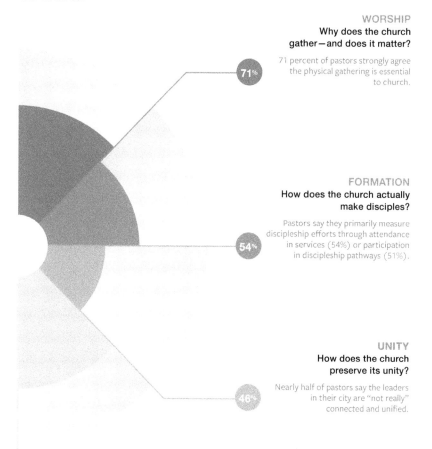

WORSHIP
Why does the church gather—and does it matter?

71 percent of pastors strongly agree the physical gathering is essential to church.

71%

FORMATION
How does the church actually make disciples?

Pastors say they primarily measure discipleship efforts through attendance in services (54%) or participation in discipleship pathways (51%).

54%

UNITY
How does the church preserve its unity?

Nearly half of pastors say the leaders in their city are "not really" connected and unified.

46%

72%

MISSION
What is the church called to do in the world?

According to pastors, missional priorities start with sharing the gospel with local non-Christians (72%) then move to addressing local poverty (57%).

PART 3

Hope for Tomorrow

the collaborative church

Between the tectonic shifts of cultural thinking, the surging waters of opposition, and the clutter of fragmented opinions, the church finds itself disoriented and disconnected. My hope for the church in a rapidly changing world is that we would become a collaborative church. I think of collaboration in layers of concentric circles, each circle smaller and more focused than the previous one.

The first layer and largest circle is what I am calling *symbiotic influence*. This is where church traditions bleed into one another. It looks like Methodists singing Hillsong music and Pentecostals following the church calendar. It looks like creative fusions of the liturgical and the contemporary. It's casual contexts with high expectations of engagement and commitment. It's expository preaching in a room with LED screens and moving lights. It might appear to be a seeker service until the worship or preaching starts. In a global village, we've all been peering over the fences into each other's yards for decades. But in an age when every church of every style is live on Facebook, the potential to influence and shape one another has been magnified.

The second layer is what might be described as *missional partnership*. This is the refusal of each church to reinvent the outreach wheel. In the business world, vertical integration that allowed megacorporations to own everything from the supply chain to the distribution channel was seen as the ideal. Today, an openness to partnerships with smaller more agile businesses that innovate at what they're best at is how behemoths like Google and Amazon rule the world. From citywide service projects to overseas missionary work, local churches are no longer starting from zero, nor are they restricted to denominational priorities and agendas.

The third layer and smallest circle is about *healthy teams*. The focus now is within churches themselves. One of the threads that runs through the crises facing pastors is the impossibility of the job. The expectations that people have of us or that we have of ourselves make us think we must be brilliant theologians, world-class preachers, visionary leaders, and compassionate counselors all at the same time. This, of course, is impossible. We know we need a team. We know it takes a team to lead the church of the future. But how do teams work in a healthy way? There is a shift away from a team model that has one dominant leader surrounded by competent followers. Just as the NBA has moved from a singular superstar putting the team on his back to the rise of so-called superteams with many stars learning to play together, organizations are embracing a collaborative approach. In this section of the chapter, I will explore two aspects of healthy teams: first, the way teams discern and decide things together, and second, the way teams operate in relation to freedom and vision.

Let's explore each circle of collaboration with a bit more detail.

Circle 1: Symbiotic Influence

I knelt with my face close to the carpet, my long white robe folding awkwardly under me. There, in a room where I had spent countless hours leading worship for prayer meetings, participating in staff chapels, officiating at weddings, and presiding over funerals, a life-changing moment was about to occur. My bishop sat on a chair in front of me, my senior pastor in the row behind me to my right. My family was gathered in the row behind me to my left. On the stage was my friend for the better part of two decades at the time—more now—Jon Egan, leading worship for the service.

The order of the service escapes my memory, but I know there were opening songs, a sermon from Pastor Brady, a recitation of vows of service to the Lord, and the laying on of hands. At some point, a priest chanted a Latin prayer inviting the Holy Spirit, with the chorus of an old Vineyard song peppered in. The circle of people who surrounded me in prayer included my family, my pastor, my closest friends, the bishop, and some other Anglican clergy. There were prayers in English and in tongues, words of knowledge and of encouragement. It was all a sacred blur, the night I became an Anglican priest at a nondenominational church.

It's a strange story that was as unexpected to me as it was to everyone else. It began five years prior, in 2009, when we started a Sunday evening service at New Life at Pastor Brady's urging. We chose to treat that service as a sort of liturgical laboratory. We had been looking for ways to integrate some of the historic worship practices of the church into a contemporary worship setting. The new Sunday evening service was the perfect place to experiment. Best of all, we had the blessing and encouragement of our senior pastor. We began with weekly communion and with a prayer of confession pulled from Psalm 51. Shortly after, we began saying the Nicene Creed as part of the worship-in-song section of the service. We discovered a hunger in people for these ancient roots. It was a tether for faith in a nondenominational context that was too often swayed by the gifts and preferences of a star leader. It was just what a church that was three years removed from the scandal of its founding senior pastor and two years removed from a tragic shooting on its campus needed.

Because it was on a Sunday evening, this was the second church service of the day for several people—a handful who had been at an Anglican church that morning. One such person was my dear friend Robert Brenner. Robert had worked for Integrity Music during my days as a songwriter and worship leader in the Desperation

Band. He has a Barnabas spirit, able to see beyond the moment, counseling with wisdom and strength. Robert had been attending an Anglican church in town on Sunday mornings—one that was covered by the Anglican Church in Rwanda after splitting from The Episcopal Church in America. He would come up to me after the Sunday evening services, saying how I should meet his pastor, Father Ken Ross, how I would love him, and how the Rwanda Anglicans were full of the Spirit and a fire for mission. He saw the elements we were incorporating and discerned a consonance with Anglican practice. I laughed and dismissed his exhortations for a few years.

Then one day his rector became a bishop, and Robert began suggesting I consider meeting with him about becoming an Anglican priest. I met with Bishop Ken over coffee one morning and had more questions than answers. But there were two pictures he gave me that struck a chord. The first was about being a bridge between two worlds—the charismatic evangelical world and the liturgical Anglican one. He showed me that there was more in common than I might have guessed. Many Anglicans around the world—particularly those in the Global South—are charismatic and evangelical. And charismatics, evangelicals, and nondenominational folks were growing in their hunger for deeper roots and historic practices. Being a bridge resonated deeply with my own sense of vocation in the kingdom.

The second picture was that of dual citizenship. I would live and function within nondenominational land but also have access and authority to go in and out of Anglican land. Since I would continue to serve at New Life, I would fully conform to the ministry norms and practices there. But the strength of Anglican ordination would be that I could borrow from the tradition while being under its authority, making me less like a liturgical thief and more like that wise steward Jesus spoke of who brings out treasures both old and new. As a first-generation immigrant to America, I understood the dual citizenship picture (though I had to renounce my Malaysian citizenship when I became an American citizen). That coffee with the bishop led to a meeting in Pastor Brady's office to explore more details of what this would mean and how it would work. The openness to the fresh work of the Spirit and the willingness to think outside the ecclesial box is something I deeply admire about both Pastor Brady and Bishop Ken. It didn't take long for all the hurdles to be cleared. But I still wasn't sure *why*.

In 2013, I traveled to England to present a paper at an academic conference on congregational music. In exchange for helping to cover part of my travel costs, Integrity Music wanted me to meet some of their U.K. worship leaders and artists. Adrian Thompson was kind enough to drive me and a friend I was traveling with to a festival called "New Wine." There, under a large white tent in the middle of the countryside, several thousand people gathered in worship. The worship leaders that night were Nick and Becky Drake, soon to become dear friends who would open their home and hearts to me and my family on multiple trips to the U.K. in the years to come. That night in worship, I sensed the presence of God deeply. There was a feeling of purity and innocence. It was not hyped up or manufactured. Then the speaker came to the stage: the Archbishop of Canterbury, Justin Welby. He spoke about the church needing a renewal through a prayer movement— communities of fellowship and fasting, prayer and service. My jaw was on the dirt floor in awe. I leaned over to ask the person next to me why such a distinguished church leader would come to such a humble setting. My new acquaintance explained that New Wine is a festival or conference for many of the charismatic Anglican churches in the U.K. The young man went on to tell me that earlier that day in one of the seminars, Welby had talked about praying in tongues daily as he read the Bible. My head was about to explode.

A couple years later, I would attend an Alpha conference where I learned more about John Wimber's influence on Anglican churches in the U.K., particularly on Holy Trinity Brompton (HTB), which would become an influential carrier of the charismatic renewal within the Church of England. It was then that I heard both Sandy Miller, the vicar of HTB when Wimber would come, and his successor, Nicky Gumbel, talk about Wimber as the second most influential figure in the Church of England in recent centuries, after only John Wesley. For now, I was overwhelmed by witnessing and experiencing the convergence of charismatic, evangelical, and liturgical streams. My heart was strangely warmed.

Ecumenism is nothing new. It has been something churches have worked on for decades with varying degrees of success. Sometimes the goal has not been all that clear. Are we all just trying to get along? Are we constructing the ecclesial version of that 80s hit "We Are the World"? Chances are, you've been in your fair share of ecumenical church gatherings or events. They are heavy on sentiment but light on substance. What really is the point?

I don't think the goal for the church in the days ahead is simply more citywide church gatherings or events. I think the goal is actual symbiosis and collaboration. In the discussion on a pastor's spiritual practices in chapter 3, I shared how the integration of practices from the contemplative and charismatic streams has enriched my life. In a similar way, when churches bleed into each other, learning from each other and borrowing from each other, the kingdom is enriched. But when we start acting like our traditions are proprietary, we've got problems. Anglicans don't own the church calendar and ought not to become fussy about "low-church" evangelicals observing Lent or Advent. Charismatics don't have the corner on contemporary worship and should not mock traditional churches for adopting contemporary worship songs in their liturgies. Examples abound. Each tradition has its gifts to offer the body of Christ. Freely we have received, freely let us give.

When I have, on several occasions, remarked to my friends who are church leaders in the U.K. about the collaboration of Church of England churches with Baptist churches, Vineyard churches, and other free church traditions, they remind me wistfully that there are not many churches eager to remain faithful to the call of the gospel and the kingdom. Those that hold to orthodoxy and remain engaged in mission are in the minority in the U.K. This is a word of warning to the church in America: *being divided is a luxury that those in less-churched countries can ill afford.* If we are going to persevere in the swirling currents of cultural change, we're going to have to learn to walk together.

Circle 2: Missional Partnership

In the research we conducted in the fall of 2020, one in three pastors (32 percent) said that during the COVID-19 pandemic, they had not—at any point during the pandemic—partnered with other churches in their area. That's why we need to talk about meaningful, missional partnerships and what that might look like. Partnership among churches and organizations takes on many different shapes. There are justice and care organizations that connect local churches in North America with churches in Africa or Central and South America. There are organizations that "franchise" local chapters in communities nationwide. New Life takes part in both of these types of partnerships. We are connected to an indigenous ministry in Guatemala that we help with financial resources and more. We mobilize teams to visit various communities that we are in relationship with, often bringing medical, educational, and theological training and care. And we help supply volunteers and leaders for local chapters of organizations that care for kids in the foster system, mentor students in local schools, and more. None of this is unique. I suspect you do many of the same things at your church.

What can be difficult, however, is not the *what* but the *why*. Why do missional partnerships matter? There is, of course, the obvious pragmatic answer: because we can't do it all! This is true enough, and not insignificant, as already noted. But there is a deeper reason worth keeping in front of our people: *serving together is one of the primary ways we give visible expression to our unity as the body of Christ.*

A few decades ago, New Life was a uniting force in our city but not around local service or justice and care. We rallied people around propositions and political agendas. The red thread that bound us together was not the blood of Christ but Republican politics. That crashed after the scandal of our founding senior

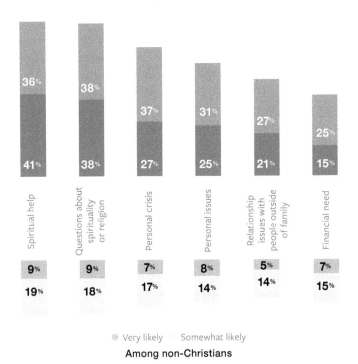

n=909 self-identified Christian U.S. adults, n=611 non-Christian U.S. adults, October 9–20, 2020.

pastor in 2006. As we have struggled to find a way to be present in our own community, we have learned a good deal about taking the posture of the listener, not the speaker. We have traded in our megaphone for a towel. We have learned that Christian unity is seen not so much in taking a stand but in bending the knee in prayer and in service.

Prayer was very much in the DNA of our church. New Life was where the "Praying-Through-the-Window" efforts of the late

1990s and early 2000s took place, informing and inspiring millions of Christians about how to pray for the most unreached parts of the world, the "10/40 window." New Life is where the World Prayer Center, the hub of that prayer movement, still stands today. In the rubble, there are always things to discard and things to preserve. We left partisanship, but we reclaimed prayer.

Service to the needy in our own community, however, was a new muscle that required practice. Ross Parsley, my first boss at New Life and the heroic interim pastor who held things together for nine long months, turned the focus of our grieving church outward. In the early summer of 2007, he called the church to a summer of serving, with hundreds of projects done by thousands of people on a series of Saturdays. It was the beginning. When Brady Boyd came a few months later, he carried us further along the trajectory. After listening to various city and organizational leaders about where the gaps in care were in our city, a team prayerfully decided to launch the Dream Centers of Colorado Springs—a series of care points for vulnerable people that began with a women's medical clinic and now includes an apartment complex for single moms and their kids, complete with career training, counseling centers, and more.

But a quantum leap in church collaboration came when the oldest church in our city, First Presbyterian, decided to open up their annual CityServe weekend to other downtown churches. We joined together for a worship night that featured team members from various churches, and then hit the streets the next day for a number of community projects. New Life Church's downtown congregation, New Life Downtown, loved being part of it. Word got out, and churches that weren't in the downtown area wanted in. It soon became a citywide effort. Eventually, some people wanted to brand it in a more striking way, and so the week—now with a dinner with city pastors and the mayor, a worship night, and the day of serving—came to be called COSILoveYou. The pun is plain. The power of COSILoveYou is not simply in the number of service hours provided for the community or in the fact that the mayor praises the churches for their good works. The

(LACK OF) LOCAL COLLABORATION DURING CRISIS

● Daily   ● Weekly   ● Monthly   ● Less often   ● Never

During the COVID-19 pandemic, how often, if ever, do you or
have you partnered with other churches in your area?

1%	8%	20%	38%	32%

n=408 U.S. Protestant Pastors, Sept 16–Oct 8, 2020.

power is in the way it gives visible expression to our unity in
Christ.

In 2015, I attended a global Alpha event in London called
"Leadership Conference," which I mentioned earlier. On one of
the evenings, the Anglican bishop of London and the Catholic
cardinal of that same diocese shared a stage together. They were
quick to remind the audience—people from about seventy different nations—that it was only a few hundred years ago that the
two denominations the two men represented would have been
literally killing one another. England's bloody history of the mon-
archy bouncing between Reformation convictions and Catholic
sympathies is well-documented, as every tourist to the Tower of
London can attest. Yet here they were affirming each other, worshiping together, and lifting up the name of Jesus. The cardinal
said something that night that has stuck with me. He said that
any discussion about doctrine and theology would quickly devolve
into a contentious debate. And even an attempt to come to the
Lord's Table together would be blocked by different views about
the Eucharist. So how is the church united? How can the world see
us as one? Simple, he said. When we bend our knees in prayer and
in service of the poor. There, on our knees, we are one.

Circle 3: Healthy Teams

To bring the lens into closer focus, we turn now to the smallest circle
of collaboration: the teams in our own churches. We will focus on

two aspects of healthy teams: the way teams make decisions together, and the way teams function with both freedom and vision.

The Most Important Church Meeting Ever

How do healthy teams make decisions together? Decision-making may seem like an overly practical thing. But you can gauge the health of a team by how they navigate crucial decisions together. In 2009, when Apple launched its Apple University to help their thousands of employees understand and integrate into their corporate culture, they hired the dean of Yale's School of Management to compile a series of case studies that analyzed important decisions the company had made, including the decisions to switch to Intel microprocessors and to open Apple stores. Decision-making at crucial moments is when the values of an organization and the health of its team are revealed.

It would not be an exaggeration to describe the Jerusalem Council in Acts 15 as the most important church staff meeting ever. At stake was the decision of how—or even if!—the Jesus-Messiah movement was going to spread beyond Jewish communities to the wider world. Paul and Barnabas had come down from Antioch. Peter was there, memories of his time with Cornelius fresh in his mind but foggy as to what that experience might mean. Also present were followers of Jesus who had been Pharisees. Think about that for a minute. I know Pharisees are often portrayed as the villains in our reading of the Gospels, the foil to Jesus the rule-breaking, grace-dealing rebel. But the Pharisees were well-respected, devout religious leaders. They were admired for their obedience, sacrifice, and devotion. In the long absence of temple worship, which had been the main way for Israel to show their covenantal fidelity to Yahweh, Torah study and Torah obedience filled the gap. I'm not sure how these Pharisee-followers-of-Jesus-as-Messiah would have understood what was going on, but reading Paul's letters gives us a clue about the kind of fresh theological reading of the Old Testament that following Jesus would have required. Did they have the depth of that insight at the time of the Jerusalem Council? We can't say. But I'm going to hazard a guess that these Pharisees would not have allowed gentiles into the church without wanting them to first become *Jewish* in some obvious way.

I'm trying to set the scene here so that the text startles you. This was not a humdrum church leadership meeting. Stakes were high, convictions ran deep, and opinions burned hot. In fact, what occasioned the meeting, according to Luke, was that "some men came down from Judea and were teaching the brothers, 'Unless you are circumcised according to the custom of Moses, you cannot be saved'" (Acts 15:1 ESV). It doesn't take a biblical scholar to guess how that went over. It makes complete sense that "Paul and Barnabas had no small dissension and debate with them" (v. 2 ESV).

In Acts 15 there are, as I see it, at least three elements of the decision-making process that are instructive for us as we reflect on collaboration among strong leaders. The first element is the *discussion*. The discussion was vigorous because the team was diverse. From Peter the fisherman to Paul the Pharisee, these leaders came from different contexts and offered different perspectives. True collaboration is not the result of homogeneity; it is the fruit of honest and open discussion among a "fellowship of differents."[1] If we're going to foster a culture of collaboration, we've got to take a good look at who is in the room. After getting the right people in the room, we then have to pay attention to the conversational dynamics. Are people sharing? Are the same one or two people dominating every discussion? What is keeping others from talking? What is keeping people from listening? It's crucial to note here that the leader of the church in Jerusalem—James—speaks last. He is the first listener and the last speaker.

When I was a younger leader, a team member told me that every time she offered a different opinion, I told her she was wrong. I confess, I was tempted to respond in the moment with reasons why she was wrong! Of course, I saw her point right away and began working on that.

One reason why our discussion is not as robust is because people don't feel safe to speak up. Another reason why people don't contribute to the conversation is that they haven't been prepared. Not everyone thinks on their feet about complex issues. Everyone who came to Jerusalem knew what the meeting was about, and they had time to prepare their thoughts in advance. Leaders are often people who ideate out loud. But if we want the best collaboration from our team, we need to give them the chance to bring their best ideas to the table.

The second element of collaborative leadership that we find in Acts 15 is the *decision*. A discussion without a decision is not collaboration. Though James was the last to speak, he was evidently a trusted decision-maker. Every team needs a leader—a quarterback, a point guard, a captain, a coach. Pick your metaphor. It may seem counterintuitive, but for collaboration to work, the team needs to know who the leader is, and the leader needs to be trustworthy. I have made too many mistakes to recount by trying to wait until there was consensus. Looking for a quorum is wise; waiting for consensus is not. Someone needs to make the call.

But it's not all on the leader. The team needs to understand that having *weighed* in on the matter, once a decision has been made, it's time to *buy* in. The time for discussion is over. An unhealthy team second-guesses or sabotages decisions that they disagree with. The rule of thumb needs to be, say what you need to say to the strength of your convictions—that is a mantra of Pastor Brady's—and then once the decision is made, be a team player. Don't go rogue. Don't talk to others about how you were the dissenting voice. Throw the full weight of your energy and gifting behind making the decision work. I'm not sure Paul was entirely happy with the decision James made. Paul would eventually write long letters wrestling with the Jew-gentile issue—letters much more nuanced and liberating than the one James wrote at the end of Acts 15. But for now, Paul was content to carry that letter.

The third element of collaboration is the *delivery*. This may seem peripheral to the actual collaboration around an issue, but the truth is many teams fracture because of how a decision is communicated. If collaboration is going to extend beyond the "room where it happens," then we must pay attention to how the decision is delivered. In Acts 15, Paul and Barnabas are sent back to Antioch not only with the decision in written form but also with companions from the church in Jerusalem. That speaks of two things: clarity and a personal touch. Having a controversial decision in writing reduces the chances of it being misinterpreted or misunderstood or even misreported. But it wasn't as if the decision was cold or impersonal—the ancient equivalent of a Facebook post or email blast. Silas and Judas went with Paul and Barnabas not only to tell them "the same things by word of mouth" (Acts 15:27 ESV) but also to encourage and strengthen the church in Antioch "with many words," for they themselves were "prophets" (v. 32 ESV). The delivery was *clear* and *personal* and *pastoral*. As well it should have been. I mean, imagine being a gentile man waiting to find out if you needed to be circumcised before you could truly be part of the church.

The more delicate the decision, the more personal the delivery. This is how trust is cultivated, nourished, and sustained.

Freedom or Vision?

How do healthy teams operate in relation to freedom and vision? When we discerned that the Lord was calling us to grow not through expansion but through multiplication, we stumbled into a different model of being a church. This was when we began thinking more deeply about how healthy teams balance the need for freedom—to create and innovate and problem-solve—and for vision—to stay in sync with each other. We tend to think of freedom and vision like a zero-sum game—the more freedom you give, the less vision you provide; the more vision you give, the less freedom you provide. We imagine the two words on either end of a continuum, and thus we need to choose which to prioritize. But as is often the case with things we think are mutually exclusive but are actually not, plotting them both on a plane can help. If the x-axis is freedom and the y-axis is vision, we might fill out the quadrants in the following way.

In the lower left quadrant are teams with low freedom and low vision in which everyone is going *crazy*. No one knows what

CLONES		COLLABORATION
Low freedom		High freedom
High vision		High vision

VISION

FREEDOM

CRAZY		CHAOS
Low freedom		High freedom
Low vision		Low vision

they're supposed to be doing or why, and no one has the power to change it or to act differently.

In the lower right quadrant are teams with high freedom but low vision, which produces *chaos*. This is what the writer of the book of Judges described in Israel, where everyone did what was right in their own eyes. There is a freedom to do as you please, but no one knows if they are working toward any particular goal or for any particular purpose. I have been in church environments like this, where every ministry area competes for resources and the praise and attention of the senior pastor, but no one is working together. The men's ministry makes a goal of drawing greater numbers at their events but takes no notice of when the high school ministry is meeting. The only people who see the chaotic pace—and the ones who pay the price for it!—are the creative teams who have to design the promo pieces and the tech and facility teams who must produce and pull off each event. It's a circus where every department vies for attention.

In the upper left quadrant are teams with high vision but low freedom. In keeping with my alliterative goals, this results in a culture of *clones*. But the truth is, there are many teams that should function this way. Collaboration does not mean every team member gets equal measures of freedom and vision. Newer staff members and services in which the stakes are higher (like Sunday morning services) are both reasons to limit the amount of freedom each team member might have. As an example, a Sunday morning service typically has a clear shape with agreed-upon expectations of who is doing what. That is a high-vision context. But it is also a low-freedom context. The worship leader is not free to take an hour in free-flowing singing, leaving no time for the preacher or for communion. The preacher is not free to end after a few minutes (not likely, I know) and ask the worship team to just wing it with thirty minutes of extra music. So high-vision/low-freedom models are not automatically the marks of an unhealthy team.

However, the highest levels of an organization should operate in the upper right quadrant: high vision and high freedom. This is where *collaboration* happens at its best. In the research we conducted, we found that only 47 percent of pastors (and furthermore, only 37 percent of leaders under the age of fifty) strongly agree that the people who lead their church "often work together in a collaborative way." There is much room to grow. Make it clear what you're trying to accomplish and why, then turn your team loose to run in that direction.

As we stumbled into our version of a multi-congregational model of being a church, we had to think about what things would be shared among the congregations and what things would be, in counseling and psychology terms, *differentiated*. New Life Downtown, the congregation I planted and lead, was the first foray into our new model. We were definitely making things up as we were going along. We decided from the first that this would not be a church plant. It would not be a separate 501c3. All financials would be shared. We didn't know it at the time, but consolidated financials is actually one of the things that makes Apple different from many other large corporations. While other companies have various divisions that all too often live up to that designation, Steve Jobs refused to "organize Apple into semiautonomous divisions." Each team was pushed to work as "one cohesive and flexible company, with one profit-and-loss bottom line."[2]

Symbiotic influence. Missional partnership. Healthy teams. These are three concentric circles of a collaborative church. I'm sure there are more, but I hope these give you a start in the right direction. Lord knows we need each other, and we need all the help we can get in learning to work well together across denominations, across churches, and across ministry areas in the same church.

Leading, Together

Collaboration—among leaders and across genders and generations—appears to be a skill strengthened with age. Pastors who are 50 or older are more likely than their younger peers to strongly agree there is trust and symbiotic relationships on their teams.

"IN OUR CHURCH'S LEADERSHIP TEAM, THE MEN AND WOMEN WORK WELL TOGETHER"

● Strongly agree ● Somewhat agree ● Somewhat disagree   Strongly disagree
● Not applicable

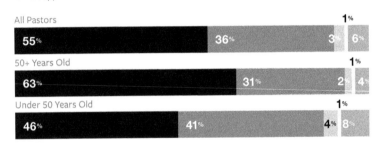

All Pastors
| 55% | 36% | 3% | 6% |

1%

50+ Years Old
| 63% | 31% | 2% | 4% |

1%

Under 50 Years Old
| 46% | 41% | 4% | 8% |

1%

"THE MEMBERS OF OUR LEADERSHIP TEAM TRUST EACH OTHER"

● Strongly agree ● Somewhat agree ● Somewhat disagree   Strongly disagree

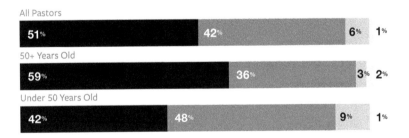

All Pastors
| 51% | 42% | 6% | 1% |

50+ Years Old
| 59% | 36% | 3% | 2% |

Under 50 Years Old
| 42% | 48% | 9% | 1% |

"THE PEOPLE WHO LEAD OUR CHURCH OFTEN WORK TOGETHER IN A COLLABORATIVE WAY"

● Strongly agree ● Somewhat agree ● Somewhat disagree   Strongly disagree

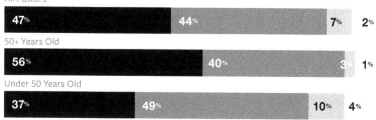

All Pastors
47% 44% 7% 2%

50+ Years Old
56% 40% 3% 1%

Under 50 Years Old
37% 49% 10% 4%

"IN OUR CHURCH'S LEADERSHIP TEAM, THE YOUNGER AND OLDER GENERATIONS WORK WELL TOGETHER"

● Strongly agree ● Somewhat agree ● Somewhat disagree   Strongly disagree
● Not applicable

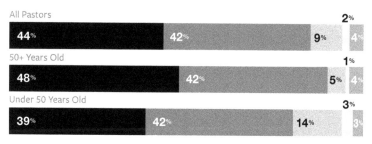

All Pastors
2%
44% 42% 9% 4%

50+ Years Old
1%
48% 42% 5% 4%

Under 50 Years Old
3%
39% 42% 14% 3%

n=408 U.S. Protestant Pastors, September 16–October 8, 2020.

Reflections from Brady Boyd, pastor, author, and speaker

Pastors of any size church share the same problem—we need people to help us and we needed them yesterday. I've never heard a pastor complain about too many volunteers or an overabundance of talented staff. There always seems to be more demand than supply. So what's the real hindrance? What's really curtailing people's involvement in local churches?

First, church leaders are notoriously insecure, and admitting our need for help is difficult for many. We're the shepherds, the one providing help and care. We're the God experts with all the answers, and we tend to find our identity in getting things done with little help. Most people are willing to serve alongside their pastor, but first the pastor must admit they need help.

Second, we must build a culture of trust and open communication. Most teams break down not because of ineptitude but an insufficiency of relationship. We all know trust is the currency of leadership. The more we trust one another, the more we move forward with strength. Trust is earned only one way—doing the right thing for the right reason for a really long time. Leaders who are willing to invest in real relationships tend to build the best teams.

Third, most people cannot identify the real reason for all the activity at church. Why are we doing this? How do we know if we're being successful? The pastors who can clearly identify the "why" and the "win" build the best teams. Both have to be repeated and reinforced constantly and consistently. Celebrate and reward your team at every opportunity. Learn to throw great parties, and be a leader who laughs and is fun to be around. People will serve well when they are celebrated well.

the presence and the power

The local church is not the hope of the world. Whoever said that might have been well-intentioned, and the statement may have come with the expected qualifiers and modifiers. But I have never liked it. It has always rubbed me the wrong way.

The local church is not the hope of the world. Jesus is, always has been, and forever will be the only hope for this world.

I know it sounds like the Sunday school answer and perhaps like I am quibbling about semantics. But any sliver of an inclination that what *we* do is what makes a difference in the world is what feeds our narcissism, our ego, our frenzied pace of work and ministry, our anxiety and depression, and more. If the local church is the hope of the world, then pastors are crucial to that hope. Our role to cultivate, grow, and expand the church becomes paramount, and the pressure becomes unbearable. Our shoulders are not broad enough for the weight of the world. And when a pastor falls or a church fails its mission, it can feel like the sky is falling. I've been there when it's happened.

No, the good news is better than that. Jesus is the hope of the world *and* the head of the church. The gates of hell itself will not prevail because Christ himself has conquered.

But what does it mean to say that Jesus is the hope of the world? What is the substance of the hope that Christians hold out to the world? The vision of Christian hope—the hope on offer to the world—comes into focus when we look at Jesus. Jesus is the *means* and the *model* of Christian hope.[1] He is the ground for our hope, and the firstfruits of it. In the early Christian centuries, the church developed a confession that came to be called "the mystery of faith." It proclaims, "Christ has died. Christ is risen. Christ will come again." In the center of this summary of Christian faith is the core of Christian hope: Christ is *risen*.

Christian hope, in a word, is resurrection.

If Christian hope is resurrection, we are saying it is something other than *progress*. Progress is incremental and gradual. Progress draws the line of human history up and to the right. Resurrection does not emerge from possibilities that are latent in a corpse. What is grievous at the funerals of young people is the lament that they had so much *potential*. At the moment of death, all potential ends and all possibilities cease. But resurrection says, "This is not the end." It is a voice calling from beyond, not from within.

If Christian hope is resurrection, it is also not an *escape*. Resurrection is not a new way of saying that at death the soul departs the body and finds its rest in an immaterial heaven. Such may have been the vision of Plato and all who revisited and revised his philosophy centuries later, both in the early centuries of church history and even in our own day. If resurrection was simply code for the soul's departure into a disembodied afterlife, that is not the defeat of death. That's like being hit by the bully on the playground and taking your ball and going home. When the disciples arrived at the tomb that first Easter morning, they did not see a vacated body; they saw an empty tomb. In raising Jesus from the dead, God had conquered death. Resurrection is not an escape from this world; it is the defeat of all the forces of decay and death that have corrupted and enslaved it.

Resurrection is the Creator God being faithful to his creation to bring it *through* death into completion and perfection. This completion and perfection are necessary not only because of the decay and death in the world but also because of the way earth is separated from heaven. Sin has created a fracture between human space and God's space. Though God keeps arriving and filling the earth with his presence, the completion and perfection of creation will be when his presence fills the earth completely. His dwelling place will be here; heaven and earth will be one (see Rev. 21–22). New creation is about *liberation* from the forces of death and *occupation* by the presence of God. It is about both a new exodus and a new temple. A *new creation* is what happens when resurrection comes to creation.

So in saying that Christian hope is resurrection, we are saying that it is not the belief in progress nor the expectation of an escape. But it is also not mere *optimism* or an empty wish. Christian hope is rooted in a *Person*—the Son of God who was born of a virgin, lived a sinless life, was crucified under Pontius Pilate, and was raised up by the Father. Because Jesus is risen from the dead, we know that our own resurrection and the renewal of creation *will* occur. Jesus is not only the *model* of what the hope of resurrection will be like; he is also the *means* by which it will occur. The great theologian of hope of the twentieth century, Jurgen Moltmann, wrote that "Christianity stands or falls with the reality of the raising of Jesus from the dead by God."[2] Or as the British missionary theologian Lesslie Newbigin famously quipped, "I'm neither an optimist nor a pessimist. Jesus Christ is risen from the dead."

Jesus the crucified and risen Lord is the hope of the world.

As long as Jesus is the head of the church, as long as Jesus is the one at work in the world building his church, there is hope not only for the world but also for the church. We are not waiting for progress, nor are we devastated by regress. We aren't passing the time, merely hanging on until we get airlifted out of here. We can invest; we can plant and cultivate and water. And none of this is just mind-over-matter wishful thinking. Jesus Christ is risen from the dead! This is why, even after a lengthy tour of the many challenges facing pastors and the church in the world today, we can lift our heads high. The God who did not abandon Jesus in the grave will not abandon us. He called us and gave us a mission to fulfill. We have something to offer—someone to point to who deserves the attention of the entire world: Christ who loves us and gave himself up for us, the Lord before whom we bow in grateful adoration and worship. Behold the Son of God, the hope of the world.

What the World Is Longing to Find

As I write this chapter, vaccines for the novel coronavirus are being delivered across the U.S. It is a history-making, record-shattering event. Never before has a vaccine been developed this quickly. Operation Warp Speed was a public-private partnership between the U.S. government and the pharmaceutical industry for the development and distribution of vaccines and therapeutics that featured unprecedented collaboration even among the major pharmaceutical companies. Though vaccines normally take years to develop, the first vaccine to be approved in the U.S., U.K., and Canada was deployed in about eleven months. Scientists and regulators insisted that no scientific corners were cut; only administrative hurdles were removed. As businesses shuttered and citizens languished under the weight of restrictions on gatherings, the vaccine offered a glimmer of hope. The nation—indeed, the world—breathed a collective sigh of relief. *Maybe this will all be over soon.*

But imagine arriving at the local hospital or vaccine administration site only to find leather couches, the warm glow of lamps, and a coffee bar. Before taking your place in line, a slim and stylish concierge asks if he could take your drink order. "No, thank you," you sheepishly reply. "I'm here for the vaccine." He smiles and presses a bit more. "But our pumpkin spice latte is *excellent*," he insists. You're tempted. But you could grab coffee anywhere. This is the only place that has the vaccine for the virus that has been plaguing the globe. As you scan the lobby, you see others sipping their mochas and lattes. Some have made themselves at home on the couches, staring at their phones in a trance or even striking up socially distant conversations with others. There's laughter and . . . wait . . . jazz music in the background? No . . . *It's a live band!* Wow. Every effort has been made to make people feel comfortable and at home.

Then something in you rises up. You want to shout it out but aren't ready to disrupt the scene. Inside your body, your soul is screaming, *We did not come for the coffee!*

This slightly absurd thought experiment is not a way of knocking churches that have coffee bars. That would be a little too on the nose. Besides, Lord knows I'm thankful for cafes and coffee shops in church lobbies when my between-services craving hits. Nor is this about the things we offer or the way we try to extend warmth and welcome to people as they come to our churches. All of that is good and right and can even be an extension of Christian hospitality. The point here is that in the end, people don't go to churches because of the couches or the coffee, the music or the vibe. Their hunger is for something much deeper and far more transcendent.

In the new survey of the general population that Barna conducted for this book, we asked people how likely they were to go to a church for help with several types of questions, issues, or needs. Sixty-three percent said they are "somewhat likely" or "very likely" to go to a church for "spiritual help," and 62 percent said the same for "questions about spirituality and religion."[3] This is what people turn to churches for. When asked more directly about the main reason for going to church, about one in three U.S. churched adults gave as their number one reason to "meet with God/experience the presence of God." This was twice as many as the second-ranked option.

Those who self-identified as non-Christians but who have attended a church within the last six months said the reasons they go to church are to "study the Bible," to "keep/observe traditions," and to "meet with God/experience the presence of God." Think about that. Even among non-Christians, if they're going to go to church, they want to learn more about the Bible, keep traditions, and meet with God. They aren't looking for TED Talks with a little Jesus-y inspiration peppered in. They aren't all that intrigued by the whole "this isn't your grandmother's church" angle. It might just be helpful if they heard the congregation praying the Lord's Prayer or reciting a creed or receiving communion. They expect a church to be a *church*. And they aren't there for cool vibes. They want to meet with God. *They did not come for the coffee.*[4]

In an indicting essay following the public moral failure of Carl Lentz, a prominent pastor in New York City, Ben Sixsmith wrote about Christians who add a "twist of Christianity" to their pre-existing cultural commitments.[5] An astute observer of the most influential if also the most problematic sectors of American Christianity, Sixsmith sees this tendency in Jerry Falwell Jr., who was "representative of the right-wing, business-oriented evangelicals who offer capitalist self-enrichment and hubristic jingoism . . . with a twist of Christianity." And in Nadia Bolz-Weber, Sixsmith found a progressive Christianity that promotes "the usual left-wing causes . . . with a twist of Christianity." That's quite the spread. And yet, there is a common thread: "The former believe secular individualists mysteriously share God's wishes for what should be done with money while the latter think that secular progressives mysteriously share God's wishes for what should be done with bodies." In the end, he articulates a question that perhaps gives voice to our post-Christian yet Christ-haunted age: "So, if Christianity is such an inessential add-on, why become a Christian?" The final paragraph made me put down my phone and pray for mercy.

> I am not religious, so it is not my place to dictate to Christians what they should and should not believe. Still, if someone has a faith worth following, I feel that their beliefs should make me feel uncomfortable for not doing so. If they share 90 percent of my lifestyle and values, then there is nothing especially inspiring about them. Instead of making me want to become more like them, it looks very much as if they want to become more like me.[6]

Cracks in the Canopy

In chapter 1, we talked about how this post-Christian, neo-pagan, neo-pluralistic world may have closed off earth to the heavens. Like the retractable roof of a sporting arena, we are so captivated by life in the "immanent frame"—the here and now—that we have become largely indifferent to the transcendent. But there are cracks in the canopy. The seal of the secular is fraying at the seams. As James

K. A. Smith puts it, "The secularist's doubt is faith; what counts as 'temptation' for the nonbeliever is belief. If the believer is haunted by an echoing emptiness, the unbeliever can be equally haunted by a hounding transcendence."[7] The church, then, is to punch "skylights in our brass heavens."[8] We let the light from the stars fall downward and pray it raises people's eyes of longing higher.

There are many ways of doing this. I will highlight three of them.

1. Tell the Whole Story of God

"That was a bit too much Bible and theology." That's what I sometimes think after I'm done preaching. And sometimes my wife—a pastor and counselor often more in tune with the needs of our congregation than I am—agrees with me. I'm not sure when the shift occurred or how widespread it really is, but sometime in the past fifteen years or so, it became normative and even trendy for pastors to preach long sermons from books of the Bible—preferably difficult ones. Maybe it was Rob Bell humble-bragging about the naivete of launching his church with a series on Leviticus, or Mark Driscoll saying that he had to preach for an hour because nobody knew anything about the Bible. Forty-five-minute sermons became a badge of honor, a way to separate newer megachurches from the seeker variety that might preach topically or do a series on movies.

The truth is there are merits to the various approaches. But it is perhaps more urgent today that pastors preach in a way that tells the whole story of God. This is different from expository preaching, where each verse is broken down and words are analyzed in the original language. That is an important and necessary element of preaching. But preaching that tells the whole story of God lifts our eyes from the words and sentences to the themes and motifs. It is the kind of preaching that helps people see the invisible structure in Scripture, the kinds of sermons that sweep the congregation up into the movements of the symphony and help them hear the echoes and variations on major themes that show up on every page.

It's also important to preach with the people in mind, to be close to their questions and fears, longings and hopes. We've become more aware that there are prodigals and skeptics and seekers sitting in our sanctuaries. We can't assume much Bible knowledge or interest. Odds are they aren't coming wondering if Paul should be understood in a "new perspective" or not. The world of the congregation must be ever before us even as we immerse ourselves in the world of the text.

Holding both the story of Scripture and the world of the congregant together is an exercise in spiritual discernment. I once heard Miroslav Volf share the advice that Jurgen Moltmann gave him about being a theologian: "Find out what moves people and shine the light of the gospel on it." That guides my thinking about preaching. We discover what moves people by naming the questions they can't shake, the longings they can't name, the fears they can't face, or the sadness they can't escape. And then we shine the light of the gospel by showing how the Scriptures confront, affirm, redirect, or comfort us. In the end, we want people to see the originating work of the Father, the finished work of the Son, and the ongoing work of the Spirit. The gospel is good news about who God is and what he has done, not good advice for us and what we need to do. If we are only in touch with our congregation's felt needs, we fail to give them the medicine they sorely need. But if we only expound on the text without connecting it to their questions and longings, desires and fears, we are explaining the science of how the medicine works but not yet dropping it on their tongues.

When Barna asked the general population about their reasons for going to church, more than one in five who called themselves non-Christians said it was to learn more about the Bible. Tell them the good news. Tell them the whole marvelous story with a good beginning and a glorious ending. They aren't there for the coffee.

2. Embrace the Presence of God

It was my first time leading an Alpha "weekend away." Actually, it was my first time leading Alpha, the course developed by Nicky Gumbel, vicar at Holy Trinity Brompton in London, to help people explore their questions about the Christian faith. Launched in 1990 as a course for seekers,[9] it has exploded around the world with millions of people who have gone through it in 112 different languages. I had been introduced to it in 2015 on a trip to London and was struck by the hundreds of people who streamed into the old church building on a weeknight to have a meal at a table and hear a talk about faith and the meaning of life. When we began introducing Alpha at our New Life Downtown congregation, there were two things I was most nervous about: including a worship song each week and taking a day or a weekend away to talk about the Holy Spirit. It felt like exactly the wrong thing to do with seekers. Wouldn't they mock the songs? Wouldn't the "retreat" feel too churchy? But in one of the training videos, my friend Tim Hughes—British worship leader, songwriter, and now vicar of Gas Street Church in Birmingham—explains that it's not really about the song or even about getting people to sing along. It's simply about creating an atmosphere for the Holy Spirit to work in.

We took the risk. We included a song each week. It seemed to go well. But then came the real test: the "Holy Spirit Weekend," as it is called among Alpha insiders. After teaching on the gifts of the Spirit, our worship leader began to lead a few songs. I felt a nudge in my heart to go over and talk to Nate, an unbeliever who had only ever been to church on the occasional Easter or Christmas. He told me that he felt like he was dipping his toe in the water of faith but still felt on the outside. I thanked him for sharing and walked back to my seat. Later that day, we had one final time of worship in song. This time I looked over at Nate, and he had his face in his hands. I walked over to check on him. With tears streaming down his face, he told me that he felt the love of God washing all over him, that somehow he believed, and that he *knew* he was a child of God. I prayed for him with feeble words and trembling voice. *Surely the Lord was in this place.*

"Alpha," as Nicky Gumbel is fond of saying, "is all about the Holy Spirit!"

One of the unintended consequences of the Reformation was that in trying to discard medieval superstition with its gargoyles and chants and incense, the Reformers inadvertently paved the way for an anti-supernaturalism. Deism—the belief that God is just up there somewhere and may pop down occasionally—is one of the unfortunate branches that grew up during the Enlightenment, which ostensibly sprang from Reformation roots. But one of the gifts of the Pentecostal movements in the early 1900s and the charismatic renewals in the 1960s and '70s—despite some of the excess or misplaced emphasis on tongues as the only evidence of being filled with the Spirit—was its insistence that God has never left the building. God is still here. When the Holy Spirit was poured out on Pentecost, he didn't have an expiration date.

In a culture that wants to live within an immanent frame, the presence of God here with us becomes a crucial Christian claim. We open the cracks in the canopy when we welcome the presence of God. We remember that Christians don't live in a closed universe with a text and a tradition of rituals. We serve a living God who speaks and breathes and moves among us in a myriad of ways. Which leads us to the third and final piece.

3. Make Room for the Power of God

As I mentioned in chapter 6, my doctoral research a few years ago was about how hope is encoded and experienced in contemporary worship songs and services. You might recall that when I analyzed the songs that were said to be songs of hope, I found them to be overly focused on the present tense, the proximate space, and the personal case. They seemed to lack key dimensions of a robust Christian eschatology, such as the anticipation of the believer's bodily resurrection and the renewal of creation. Yet when I did my fieldwork with two churches—one in Denver and one in Dallas, one a Presbyterian church, and one a charismatic church—I found that the experience of hope in both churches was consistent and resilient. People talked about a hope that helped them make it through divorce proceedings and strained relationships with adult children, cancer and the fear of death, and more. Their worship in church did not create ease in their circumstances, but it gave them the strength to make it through another week.

One of the reasons for this is the way hope, from the perspective of cognitive psychology, is about the confluence of agency and pathway.[10] It has to do with feeling that you have the power and the path to achieve a particular desired outcome. To take a simple example, if a person was hoping to take a vacation this year but lost their job, they might feel despair because they no longer have the power to earn money for necessities, let alone a vacation. If their job search remains fruitless after months, they might really begin to spiral because it may feel like every path is a dead end.

I discovered that for the Christian, hope intuitively is not simply about *our* agency but God's. One of the things that can happen in church is that we remember *divine agency*—God is powerful!—and *divine pathway*—God can make a way where there is no way! When the people in my focus groups would go to church carrying their burdens and feeling despair, they would begin to sing, "Great are you, Lord!" and *feel* hope—even if they did not fully understand why. They were transferring agency upward to the God for whom nothing is impossible.

But there is another dimension for the Christian. Not only is God powerful and able, but the Holy Spirit, in Gordon Fee's marvelous phrase, is "God's empowering presence."[11] The Holy Spirit is how we can, like Paul, do all things through Christ. We can endure hardship and enjoy abundance. We can make it because the Holy Spirit imparts the very power of God to us. Hope is possible because of God's powerful and empowering presence with us. And God is with us in a special way when we gather as the church.

Healings may not happen every day. A prophetic word or a word of knowledge may not drop into our hearts on many Sundays. And yet, we serve a living God who loves to surprise us. He hears our prayers. Pray with the confidence that he not only hears but also answers our prayers. The power of God does not mean that God works in ways that are fast and obvious. Sometimes he does. But power is no less powerful for its pervasive and persistent work to change, heal, and restore.

The Glory and the Ordinary

When I met Easton, he had just called off his wedding. It was a destructive relationship built on toxic habits and a dysfunctional codependency. It had begun in the trauma of military deployment and was fueled by alcohol and sex. He knew it was better to end the relationship, but he could not see beyond the pain of the moment. As we kept meeting regularly, we talked—mostly he would talk and I would listen—and prayed together. We kept believing for resurrection. I told him that this relationship needed to die, that the old Easton needed to die, and that God was bringing a new life out of the old. He believed it. He had gotten saved during Alpha a year prior, but it had not reformed his life or his relationship. Now he was ready to surrender in earnest. I asked him if he would pray about getting baptized. That Wednesday night service when I stepped into the baptismal tank with him was one of the most meaningful pastoral experiences I've had. But the next day he called me to ask why he didn't feel all that different. I explained to him that transformation takes time, that the Holy Spirit was inviting him to participate in the work of forming new habits, wiring new neuropathways, and more. Resurrection had occurred; living like a new man would take time.

Several months later, Easton reached out to tell me some unbelievably good news. He had met a girl, a pastor's daughter, and he asked if I would do their premarital counseling. I admit, I was skeptical, but I of course agreed. In the course of meeting with him and his fiancée, I kept saying, "Easton, you're a different man!" He grinned and agreed. During the pandemic, he texted me updates and pictures. We marveled at the power of God to transform a life, and we rejoiced together.

Jesus is the hope of the world, and the hope that he brings looks like resurrection.

The invitation for pastors is to never lose sight or lose heart even in the mundane and the messy. Most of our work and many of our services are ordinary. Yet God, with his presence and his power, is on the scene. My friend and Pentecostal theologian Chris Green said to me in a Twitter conversation that pastors ought to be like the shepherds in Luke 2. We tend the flock faithfully but remain alert to activity in the heavens. He writes that "we must not let the habits necessary for slow, painstaking work dull our expectation of the 'suddenlies' of the Spirit." We ought to be "going about [our] daily work faithfully, but always ready to drop everything and run to Jesus when the glory of the Lord breaks into their lives!"[12] I love this image. Pastors, like those shepherds, understand that most of our work is not glamorous or spectacular; it is ordinary and hard, dirty and messy. And yet, we do not give up expecting the Lord to break through.

You see, in the end, it is not we who pierce the canopy. It is God. God who spoke in the beginning, God who came in human flesh, God who comes by his Spirit.

This is why I quibble a bit with James K. A. Smith's claim that the future of the church will be ancient, "drawing on the wells of historic, 'incarnate' Christian worship with its smells and bells and all its Gothic peculiarity, embodying a spirituality that carries whiffs of transcendence." Smith has no illusions of these being massive or influential movements, but "they will grow precisely because their ancient incarnational practice is an answer to the diminishing returns of excarnate spirituality." In this way, "historic Christian worship is not only the heart of discipleship" but "might also be the heart of our evangelism."[13]

He's not wrong. The retrieval of historic Christian worship practices is enriching, and these practices are rooting the evangelical church, particularly the nondenominational stream. We can testify to this at New Life, a nondenominational charismatic megachurch that practices weekly communion as the climactic moment of the service, embraces the Nicene Creed as our statement of faith, and gently marks the seasons of the church calendar.

And yet, this is not the full answer. The future of the church is sacramental *and* Pentecostal, historic *and* charismatic. If we fail to let church be a place where the presence and the power of God can be experienced or even expected, we are foreclosing on the possibility of hope. When we tell the whole story of God, embrace the presence of God, and make room for the power of God, we are holding out the hope of resurrection to a dying world.

Reflections from Tim Hughes, pastor, songwriter, worship leader, and speaker

The Knepp Estate is a thirty-five-hundred-acre estate in West Sussex, U.K. In 2001 after years of the land being intensively farmed, a decision was made to let the land run wild in a pioneering project known as *rewilding*. Here the driving principle was to establish a thriving ecosystem in which nature was given as much freedom as possible. A natural process was encouraged rather than the historic obsessing over goals and outcomes. The project has seen remarkable increases in wildlife and the return of extremely rare species alongside the land exploding into life. The results have been so stunning that many other estates have followed suit.

I believe there is a rewilding process that needs to take place in our churches. At times our worship services and ministries have become so carefully organized, curated, and controlled, much like the intensively farmed land of the Knepp Estate, that we've lost any sense of being surprised by God's Spirit, his empowering presence. I am convinced the great need for the church today is to see the Spirit of the living God being given freedom to lead and move. It is essential that our worship be marked by a continual openness to the Holy Spirit's inspiration. We need more disruption. More mess. More risk.

The words of Canadian pastor and author Carey Nieuwhof offer us a great challenge: "It's a shame when people come to church looking for God and only find us!" As Glenn has beautifully reminded us, we are not the hope of the world. Jesus is!

epilogue

No Labor in Vain

We began in the prologue with a few assumptions: you're tired, you don't need predictions about the future of the church, and you don't need some self-proclaimed expert telling you what to do. My hope is that as you have read this, you have found you are not alone. Not only are there others facing the same challenges you are in this moment in history, but the church has been here before as well. I hope that my choice to frame the challenges in ways that are not exclusive to this cultural moment have helped make that plain. Pastors in every age have had to wrestle with the nature of their vocation, the rootedness of their spirituality, the complexity of their relationships, and the basis for their credibility. And church leaders have always had to think theologically about why the church gathers in worship, how we are formed in the image of Christ, how we preserve church unity, and what our mission is in the world and how we might best go about it. These are challenges to be revisited repeatedly, with fresh situational analysis and rich theological reflection. So even as we stand in this moment in time and space, there is a great cloud of witnesses, others who have gone before who offer their wisdom. It is possible to last, to be faithful, to be *resilient*—not by might, not by power, but by the same Holy Spirit who sustained the church throughout the centuries.

But perhaps your discouragement persists. After surveying the data and assessing the task ahead, you might find yourself slumping deeper in your chair, wondering if you're really up for the task. Maybe it all just feels too overwhelming, and your candle in the darkness doesn't seem to be quite enough.

Does our work really matter? Can we actually make a difference? Can we rebuild after the earthquake and the surge amid the clutter of the debris?

These questions must have been swirling around the heads of the first church planters, the apostles and their protégés in the early centuries of Christianity. When Paul wrote to the Corinthian church, who no doubt dealt with challenges like those facing the church today (and then some!), he painted a soaring picture of Christian hope, centering it on the resurrection of Jesus: "And if Christ has not been raised, then our preaching is in vain and your faith is in vain. We are even found to be misrepresenting God, because we testified about God that he raised Christ, whom he did not raise if it is true that the dead are not raised" (1 Cor. 15:14–15 ESV).

The only thing that could make our preaching and our faith in vain is if Jesus Christ is not risen from the dead. If Christ is not risen, our "faith is futile," we are still in our sins, and we "are of all people most to be pitied" (vv. 17–19). Our hope would be "in this life only" (v. 19). We would be speaking of the good of a church and of pastors *only* in terms of material benefit and present gain. We would measure our worth and our significance by social goods alone. But Christ *has* been raised! The existence of your church is not weighed in ways that can *only* be seen in this life. The difference that your faithfulness makes is eternal.

Paul reminds the Corinthian church: "In fact Christ has been raised from the dead, the firstfruits of those who have fallen asleep" (v. 20). And this means that one day the bodies of all who "belong to Christ" will be brought through death and raised up in new life (v. 23). Christ will come again in glory and "reign until he has put all his enemies under his feet," destroying the final enemy of death itself (vv. 25–26).

Then after this glorious vision of the end and the most detailed attempt in the New Testament to sketch what resurrected bodies will be like, Paul turns to the pastoral. The implications of this future hope reverberate in the present: "The sting of death is sin, and the power of sin is the law. But thanks be to God, who gives us the victory through our Lord Jesus Christ" (vv. 56–57).

God *gives* us the victory. We are receiving it even now. It is coming, and it is here.

As he closes, Paul returns once more to the notion that without the resurrection our preaching and our faith would be in vain. This time he says it in the affirmative. Having said all that he has about resurrection—Christ's and ours—he summons us to our mission: "Therefore, my beloved brothers, be steadfast, immovable, always abounding in the work of the Lord, knowing that in the Lord your labor is not in vain" (v. 58).

Your labor is not in vain. By God's grace and by the power of the Holy Spirit, you can be steadfast and immovable, you can abound—excel, flourish, thrive!—in the work of the Lord. Why? Because Jesus Christ is risen from the dead! The Greek word we translate as "resurrection" means to stand up. Because Jesus has been made to stand up, we too can stand. Because God is the God who raises the dead, no labor in the Lord is ever in vain.

When I was a younger pastor, I was overly concerned with the impact of our ministry. I wanted to be a "history maker," a "world changer," and all the other phrases that had inspired me in my college years. I stepped into the church world ready to make my mark.

But after more than twenty years in pastoral ministry, I am keenly aware of the reality that we are not in charge of our legacy and impact. Nor should we be. Jeremiah the prophet was called to preach though no one would heed his words. Jonah was sent with a message and an entire city repented. The results are not for us to obsess over. Neither Jeremiah nor Jonah wanted the tasks they were given. And yet the difference between the two prophets is not their results but their response. Jeremiah yields and becomes an obedient, weeping prophet. Jonah resists and becomes the prodigal, whining prophet. Faithfulness—the very goal of resilience for the Christian—is not in the outcome but in the obedience.

J. R. R. Tolkien captured the idea of being faithful to the task we've been given in the Lord of the Rings trilogy when Frodo, in anguish about the inescapable task ahead of him, laments, "I wish it need not have happened in my time." Gandalf, the wise wizard responsible for getting him into it in the first place, replies, "So do I, and so do all who live to see such times. But that is not for them to decide. All we have to decide is what to do with the time that is given us."[1]

Decide what to do with the time you have been given.

Pray for the grace to steward your moment faithfully.

My friend Dominic Black posted a picture recently from the wall of his church in the North East of England. He and I were at Durham University together doing our doctoral research, and he now serves as the vicar, or senior pastor, at Hull Minster, formerly called Holy Trinity, in the diocese of York.[2] The picture is of a plaque on the wall that lists the names of all the vicars who have served that congregation. The first name begins in 1326, Robert de Marton. It goes all the way to 2010. That church has been there for seven hundred years. When I shared the picture on social media, my friends at St. Aldates Church in Oxford commented that they have a similar wall in their church, going back a thousand years. I suspect many churches in the U.K. and Europe have commemorative walls like these.

It is at once a sobering and inspiring picture. Whether you're a church planter or the latest in a long line of pastors at a historic church, the lesson holds true. The church was here before us, and the church will be here long after we're gone. We may not be the first and, by the grace of God, we will not be the last. As my senior pastor, Brady Boyd, is fond of saying, "We are all interim pastors."

You don't have to make your mark or leave a legacy. Just steward your season faithfully. No labor in the Lord is ever in vain. Jesus Christ is risen from the dead. This is the conviction of the resilient pastor.

May the God of peace,
> who brought back the great shepherd of the sheep,
> our Lord Jesus,
> from the dead by the blood of the eternal covenant,

equip you with every good thing to do his will,
> by developing in us what pleases him through Jesus
> Christ.

To him be the glory forever and always. Amen. (Heb.
13:20–21)

And may the blessing of God almighty, Father, Son, and Holy Spirit, rest on you and remain with you, now and forever, amen.

FOUR CHALLENGES FOR PASTORS

The Challenge of Vocation
Challenge: What are we called to do?
Resilient Response: To love Jesus and to feed his sheep.

The Challenge of Spirituality
Challenge: How do we renew our relationship with God?
Resilient Response: Dig new wells.

The Challenge of Relationships
Challenge: How do we cultivate meaningful relationships?
Resilient Response: Invest diversely, intentionally, and consistently.

The Challenge of Credibility
Challenge: How can we regain credibility and trust?
Resilient Response: Use power rightly.

FOUR CHALLENGES FOR THE CHURCH

The Challenge of Worship
Challenge: Why do we gather in worship?
Resilient Response: To encounter the presence of God, to be formed in the image of Christ, and to be sent on mission into the world.

The Challenge of Formation
Challenge: How do we make disciples?
Resilient Response: Through teaching, practices, and community apprenticeship.

The Challenge of Unity
Challenge: How do we preserve unity in the church?
Resilient Response: Offer radical hospitality, engage in courageous solidarity, and participate in genuine mutuality.

The Challenge of Mission
Challenge: What is our mission in the world?
Resilient Response: To announce Jesus as King and to live in anticipation of his kingdom coming in fullness.

acknowledgments

When Barna president David Kinnaman reached out inviting me to partner with him and their world-class team on a book about the challenges facing church leaders in a changing world, I was honored but unsure. I would never have presumed to write a book like this. I care deeply for pastors. My parents were pastors, and I have been a pastor for over twenty years. I hold the vocation in high enough esteem to be hesitant about offering advice to pastors, many of whom are already weary and weighed down. Furthermore, this was a major project that would require countless hours of research design, reading widely, and listening to other pastors recount their experiences. Could I really do this?

Despite my initial trepidation at David's invitation, there was a deep excitement that sprang from the awareness of the need for such a project. But more than that, I feel a fire in my bones that because Jesus Christ is risen from the dead and because he is the head of the church, the gates of hell cannot prevail against the church and the arriving kingdom of God. There is hope, there is good news, and there is grace in Jesus's name. So with a sober mind, I agreed to collaborate with Barna on this research and this book.

Gratefully, a team surrounded me throughout the process. And, as I reflect on it, there have been people who have shaped and prepared me for this undertaking throughout my life. Here are a few of them, past and present, who have made this book possible and have made me the person and pastor that I am:

To David Kinnaman for your belief in me from the beginning and for your feedback and insight along the way. You have been serving and resourcing the church for a long time, and it was an honor for me to contribute.

To my friend and literary agent, Alex Field, for championing this idea from day one. Your advice and advocacy mean the world to me.

To the team at Barna—Joe, Alyce, Savannah, Aly, Brenda—for being a joy to work with every step of the way. From brainstorming the research design to helping me correctly interpret the data, you were excited, patient, encouraging, and brilliant.

To the incredible team at Baker, from editors to designers to marketing mavens, for your enthusiasm, creativity, and belief in this project. You brought your best to this, and the book is better for it.

To the brilliant leaders and thinkers who agreed to write reflections at the end of each chapter, thank you for carving out time to engage with this content and to invest in church leaders. You are bright and shining lights in our generation.

To Pete Ward, David Wilkinson, and Mathew Guest at Durham University, who trained me to engage in the kind of practical theology that blends robust situational analysis with rich theological reflection. You've given me tools for a lifetime of thinking and practice.

To all the pastors in the US, Canada, and the UK who said yes to my focus group invitation. First of all, thank you for your faithful ministry to the Lord and to his people. Thank you for giving up hours of your time to talk with me. You allowed me to be a witness to your life and godliness. You are good shepherds.

To the many pastors who have shepherded me, from my childhood and youth in Malaysia—Michael Raj, Rockie Siew, Beram Kumar, Dennis Balan, Koh Chu Soon, to name a few—to my time in college—Bill and Lisa Shuler. From early days in local church ministry—Ross Parsley—to my current role—Brady Boyd. For all these and many more who showed me what a pastor looks like by the way they cared for me and cultivated God's call on my life.

To the sages who have gone before, who took time to speak into my life. To Eugene Peterson for opening up his home to me in a crucial season of life and ministry and helping to shape my imagination of what a pastor is and how I could attempt such a life in my own context. And to Tom Wright for being a trustworthy guide, first in his writing and now in his friendship. You've been generous with your time, gracious in your replies, wise in your counsel.

To New Life Church for welcoming me into your family twenty-two years ago. I could say you've watched me grow up, but the truth is you've *helped* me grow up. I am grateful to be rooted here.

To my friends and colleagues who have journeyed with me in the pastoral vocation for more than two decades—too many to name, but you know who you are. You are my constellation of stars in the night. You consistently challenge me and confront me, sharpen me and shape me. I love laughing with you, working with you, learning from you, and thinking out loud with you. You lighten the load and light the way. I am honored to be named among you.

To my parents for raising me to love the local church. You have faithfully followed Jesus at great cost to yourselves; you have loved sacrificially and consistently, served in hidden ways, and given yourself away for others. Someday, I hope to be a pastor like you.

To our kids for being patient and forgiving when a book project like this eats away at my margin. You listen to my excitement and remind me of what's actually important. You're such radiant lights. Being your dad is one of the greatest honors and holiest vocations I have.

Finally, to my wife, Holly, for being the best partner in life and in ministry I could have ever dreamed of. You are the love of my life, the joy of each morning, and the peace that steadies me in the darkest night. I love you with all my heart.

notes

Prologue

1. C. S. Lewis, *Reflections on the Psalms* (New York: Harcourt, 1958), 1–2.

2. Methodology: Barna conducted 408 online interviews with Protestant senior pastors from September 16 to October 8, 2020. Sample error plus or minus 4.8 percentage points at the 95 percent confidence level.

Adults: GenPop conducted an online survey of 1,520 U.S. adults ages 18+ from October 9 to 20, 2020. Sample error plus or minus 2.3 percentage points at the 95 percent confidence level.

Chapter 1 The Shift, the Surge, and the Aftermath

1. Harriet Sherwood, "Churches Tally Up Their Value to Society—at £12.4bn," *The Guardian*, October 17, 2020, https://www.theguardian.com/world/2020/oct/18/churches-tally-up-their-value-to-society-at-124bn.

2. Barna Group, "One in Three Practicing Christians Has Stopped Attending Church During COVID-19," July 8, 2020, https://www.barna.com/research/new-sunday-morning/.

3. Barna Group, "One in Three Practicing Christians."

4. Dave Roos, "The 2004 Tsunami Wiped Away Towns with 'Mind-Boggling' Destruction," The History Channel, September 18, 2020, https://www.history.com/news/deadliest-tsunami-2004-indian-ocean.

5. Charles Taylor, *A Secular Age* (Cambridge, MA: Harvard University Press, 2018), 221–69.

6. This metaphor appears in James K. A. Smith's summary of Taylor's work in *How (Not) to be Secular* (Grand Rapids: Eerdmans, 2014), 51.

7. The phrase "cross-pressured" shows up in Smith's *How (Not) to Be Secular*, 4.

8. David Kinnaman and Gabe Lyons, *Good Faith: Being a Christian When Society Thinks You're Irrelevant and Extreme* (Grand Rapids: Baker Books, 2016).

9. Gene Edward Veith, *Post-Christian: A Guide to Contemporary Thought and Culture* (Wheaton: Crossway, 2020), 15.

10. Veith, *Post-Christian*, 15.

11. See Ross Douthat, "The Return of Paganism," *New York Times*, December 12, 2018, https://www.nytimes.com/2018/12/12/opinion/christianity-paganism-america.html, in which he summarizes and reviews Steven D. Smith's "Pagans and Christians in the City: Culture Wars from the Tiber to the Potomac," where the same point is made.

12. Veith makes this observation in *Post-Christian*, 296–97.

13. Andrew Root, *The Pastor in a Secular Age: Ministry to People Who No Longer Need a God* (Grand Rapids: Baker Academic, 2019), 17.

14. Taylor, *A Secular Age*, 27.

15. Taylor, *A Secular Age*, 27.

16. Taylor, *A Secular Age*, 38–39.

17. "Once individuals become the locus of meaning, the social atomism that results means that disbelief no longer has social consequences." Smith, *How (Not) to be Secular*, 31.

18. Smith, *How (Not) to Be Secular*, 55, emphasis in original.

19. Veith, *Post-Christian*, 241.

20. Veith, *Post-Christian*, 241.

21. N. T. Wright, *History and Eschatology: Jesus and the Promise of Natural Theology* (Waco: Baylor University Press, 2019), 35.

22. N. T. Wright, *History and Eschatology*, 35.

23. Quoted in Smith, *How (Not) to Be Secular*, 5.

24. Barna study with 2,007 U.S. adults, conducted January 28 to February 20, 2021.

25. Pew Research Center, "In U.S., Decline of Christianity Continues at Rapid Pace," October 17, 2019, https://www.pewforum.org/2019/10/17/in-u-s-decline-of-christianity-continues-at-rapid-pace/.

26. It's higher for evangelicals—98 percent—and churchgoers—79 percent.

27. Thirty-two percent of unchurched and 31 percent of non-Christians marked "unsure" in response.

28. Ed Stetzer, "Nominals to Nones: 3 Key Takeaways from Pew's Religious Landscape Survey," *Christianity Today*, May 12, 2015, https://www.christianitytoday.com/edstetzer/2015/may/nominals-to-nones-3-key-takeaways-from-pews-religious-lands.html.

29. Barna study with 2,007 U.S. adults, conducted January 28 to February 10, 2021.

30. Frank Newport, "Milliennials' Religiosity Amidst the Rise of the Nones," Gallup, October 29, 2019, https://news.gallup.com/opinion/polling-matters/267920/millennials-religiosity-amidst-rise-nones.aspx.

31. The findings were published in David Kinnaman, *You Lost Me* (Grand Rapids: Baker Books, 2011); see Barna Group, "Church Dropouts Have Risen to 64%—But What About Those Who Stay?," September 4, 2019, https://www.barna.com/research/resilient-disciples/.

32. Barna Group, "Church Dropouts Have Risen to 64%."

33. Barna Group, "Only 10% of Christian Twentysomethings Have Resilient Faith," September 24, 2019, https://www.barna.com/research/of-the-four-exile -groups-only-10-are-resilient-disciples/.

34. Smith, *How (Not) To Be Secular*, 4.

35. Smith, *How (Not) to Be Secular*, 63.

36. "I think it is safe to say that while the South is hardly Christ-centered, it is most certainly Christ-haunted." Flannery O'Connor, *Mystery and Manners* (New York: Farrar, Straus and Giroux, 1970), 44.

37. Tom Holland, "The Way of the Cross," *The Spectator*, April 20, 2019, https://www.spectator.co.uk/article/the-way-of-the-cross.

38. Tom Holland, *Dominion: The Making of the Western Mind* (New York: Basic Books, 2019), 239.

39. Holland, *Dominion*, 239.

40. Holland, *Dominion*, 346–47.

41. Holland, *Dominion*, 347.

42. John Updike, "Fine Point," *The New Yorker*, March 9, 2009, lines 1–2, https://www.newyorker.com/magazine/2009/03/16/fine-point-3.

43. Updike, "Fine Point," lines 11–14.

Chapter 2 Vocation

1. Eugene H. Peterson, *Under the Unpredictable Plant: An Exploration in Vocational Holiness* (Grand Rapids: Eerdmans, 1992), 1.

2. Peterson, *Under the Unpredictable Plant*, 4.

3. Peterson, *Under the Unpredictable Plant*, 4.

4. Peterson, *Under the Unpredictable Plant*, 5.

5. Peterson, *Under the Unpredictable Plant*, 5.

6. Peterson, *Under the Unpredictable Plant*, 22.

7. Peterson, *Under the Unpredictable Plant*, 22.

8. Eugene H. Peterson, *Working the Angles: The Shape of Pastoral Integrity* (Grand Rapids: Eerdmans, 1987), 1.

9. Peterson, *Working the Angles*, 1.

10. Pete Greig (@PeteGreig), Twitter post, February 10, 2020, https://twitter .com/PeteGreig/status/1226841105242738688.

11. Barna, *The State of Pastors* (2017), 72.

12. Barna, *State of Pastors*, 72.

13. Barna, *State of Pastors*, 72.

14. Barna, *State of Pastors*, 72.

15. Barna, *State of Pastors*, 63.

16. Barna, *State of Pastors*, 63.

17. Barna, *State of Pastors*, 102.

18. Barna, *State of Pastors*, 103.

19. Barna, *State of Pastors*, 102–3.

20. Daniel's remarkable story of friendship with Eugene Peterson is written about beautifully in his book *Chasing Wisdom: The Lifelong Pursuit of Living Well* (Nashville: Thomas Nelson, 2020).

21. "St. Cuthbert's Life," Durham World Heritage Site, https://www.durham worldheritagesite.com/history/st-cuthbert/life.

22. "History of Lindisfarne Priory," English Heritage, https://www.english -heritage.org.uk/visit/places/lindisfarne-priory/History/.

23. "History of Lindisfarne Priory."

24. "History of Lindisfarne Priory."

25. "Lindisfarne Gospels," British Library, https://www.bl.uk/collection-items /lindisfarne-gospels.

26. Bev Stephenson, "Heritage: The Cradle of English Christianity," *The Guardian*, n.d., https://www.theguardian.com/business/onenortheast/story/0,,206 9819,00.html.

27. Barna, *State of Pastors*, 57.

28. Barna, *State of Pastors*, 58.

29. Barna, *State of Pastors*, 58–59.

30. Barna, "COVID-19 Conversations: Many Pastors Are Tired, Overwhelmed, and Lonely," May 20, 2020, https://www.barna.com/research/covid-19-pastor -emotions/.

31. https://careynieuwhof.com/29-of-pastors-want-to-quit-how-to-keep-going -when-youve-lost-confidence-in-yourself/.

Chapter 3 Spirituality

1. Quoted in Glenn Packiam, *Worship and the World to Come: Exploring Christian Hope in Contemporary Worship* (Downers Grove, IL: IVP Academic, 2020), 149.

2. Henri J. M. Nouwen, *In the Name of Jesus: Reflections on Christian Leadership* (New York: Crossroad, 2002), 20.

3. Barna, *State of Pastors*, 27.

4. Barna, *State of Pastors*, 27.

5. Peter Scazzero, *Emotionally Healthy Spirituality* (Grand Rapids: Zondervan, 2014), 22 (emphasis in original).

6. Ruth Haley Barton, *Strengthening the Soul of Your Leadership: Seeking God in the Crucible of Ministry* (Downers Grove, IL: InterVarsity, 2018), 104–6.

7. Gordon D. Fee, *Paul, the Spirit, and the People of God* (Grand Rapids: Baker Academic, 2011), 202.

8. Barna, *State of Pastors*, 30.

9. Barna, *State of Pastors*, 30.

10. Barton, *Strengthening the Soul of Your Leadership*, 28.

11. James Martin, *The Jesuit Guide to (Almost) Everything: A Spirituality for Real Life* (New York: HarperCollins, 2012), 11.

12. "Saint Ignatius of Loyola," Franciscan Media, July 31, 2020, https://www .franciscanmedia.org/saint-ignatius-of-loyola/.

13. Martin, *Jesuit Guide*, 15.

14. Martin, *Jesuit Guide*, 15.

15. The Society of Jesus, "About Us," https://jesuits.org/about-us/global -community/.

Chapter 4 Relationships

1. Barna, *State of Pastors*, 39.
2. Barna, *State of Pastors*, 38.
3. Barna, *State of Pastors*, 40.
4. Nouwen, *In the Name of Jesus*, 60.
5. From the song "Nature Boy," written by Eden Ahbez and recorded by Nat King Cole (Capitol Records, 1948).
6. Barna, *State of Pastors*, 39.
7. Rick Hellman, "How to Make Friends? Study Reveals It Takes Time," University of Kansas News Service, March 28, 2018, https://news.ku.edu/2018/03/06/study-reveals-number-hours-it-takes-make-friend.
8. Paul D. Stanley and J. Robert Clinton, *Connecting: The Mentoring Relationships You Need to Succeed in Life* (Colorado Springs: NavPress, 1992).
9. Barna, *State of Pastors*, 42.
10. Grothe, *Chasing Wisdom*, 26–28.
11. J.R.R. Tolkien, *The Return of the King* (Boston: Houghton Mifflin, 1991), 976.
12. Peterson, *Under the Unpredictable Plant*, 35.
13. Quoted in Winn Collier, *A Burning in My Bones: The Authorized Biography of Eugene H. Peterson* (Colorado Springs: WaterBrook, 2021), 199.
14. Barna, *State of Pastors*, 34.
15. Barna, *State of Pastors*, 34.
16. Barna, *State of Pastors*, 34.
17. Barna, *State of Pastors*, 35.
18. Barna, *State of Pastors*, 36.
19. Barna, *State of Pastors*, 37.
20. Barna, *State of Pastors*, 37.
21. Barna, *State of Pastors*, 37.
22. Holly and I have written a book about this, explaining more of what we do on these retreats. It releases with NavPress in fall 2022.

Chapter 5 Credibility

1. Barna, *State of Pastors*, 115.
2. Barna, *State of Pastors*, 115.
3. Barna, *State of Pastors*, 116.
4. Barna, *State of Pastors*, 116.
5. Barna, *State of Pastors*, 116.
6. Barna, *State of Pastors*, 119.
7. 29 percent of Millennials vs. 60 percent of Elders; Barna, *State of Pastors*, 119–20.
8. 12 percent vs. 5 percent; Barna, *State of Pastors*, 120.
9. Barna, *State of Pastors*, 122.
10. Barna phrased it as "how the church can help people live according to God's will." *State of Pastors*, 123.
11. Cf. Barna, *State of Pastors*, 125.

12. Ferguson makes this argument in his book *The Square and the Tower* (New York: Penguin, 2017).

13. Pauline Cheong, "Authority," in *Digital Religion: Understanding Religious Practice in New Media Worlds*, ed. Heidi Campbell (New York: Routledge, 2013), 4, www.drpaulinecheong.com/uploads/5/5/9/8/55989981/cheong-authority_review_chapter.pdf.

14. Cheong, "Authority," 6.

15. Cheong, "Authority," 5.

16. Cheong, "Authority," 8.

17. Cheong, "Authority," 13.

18. Root, *Pastor in a Secular Age*, 50–51.

19. Root, *Pastor in a Secular Age*, 52.

20. Root, *Pastor in a Secular Age*, 54.

Chapter 6 Worship

1. Barna, "What Research Has Revealed about the New Sunday Morning," June 3, 2020, https://www.barna.com/research/new-sunday-morning/.

2. Barna, "What Research Has Revealed."

3. Barna, "One in Three Practicing Christians."

4. Packiam, *Worship and the World to Come*, 29.

5. Packiam, *Worship and the World to Come*, 31.

6. Packiam, *Worship and the World to Come*, 31.

7. Alan Rathe, *Evangelicals, Worship, and Participation: Taking a Twenty-First Century Reading* (New York: Ashgate, 2014), 130.

8. Robert Webber, *Ancient-Future Worship: Proclaiming and Enacting God's Narrative* (Grand Rapids: Baker Books, 2008), 168.

9. Quoted in Packiam, *Worship and the World to Come*, 32.

10. Rathe, *Evangelicals, Worship, and Participation*, 247.

11. Packiam, *Worship and the World to Come*, 42.

12. See Swee-Hong Lim and Lester Ruth, *Lovin' on Jesus: A Concise History of Contemporary Worship* (Nashville: Abingdon, 2017), 132–38.

13. Martin Buber, *I and Thou: A New Translation*, trans. Walter Kaufmann (New York: Simon & Schuster, 1996).

14. Packiam, *Worship and the World to Come*, 45.

15. Note how Barna defines this term as those "who typically attend a church service at least once a month."

16. The last line of the Nicene Creed.

17. This, of course, doesn't let songwriters, worship leaders, and preachers off the hook. God's kindness is not an excuse for our sloppiness. We should make it our aim to paint a more vibrant picture of our hope. For more, see Packiam, *Worship and the World to Come*.

18. Cited in Packiam, *Worship and the World to Come*, 37–38.

19. For a fuller picture of what this looks like in the Christian life, see *Blessed Broken Given* (Colorado Springs: Waterbrook, 2019).

Chapter 7 Formation

1. Thirty-five percent of pastors say a lack of commitment is the most frustrating part of the job, while 27 percent say it's the low level of spiritual maturity. Barna, *State of Pastors*, 100.

2. Barna, *State of Pastors*, 20.

3. "Pastors at high risk of burnout are three times more likely than those at low risk to say church politics is among their top frustrations." Barna, *State of Pastors*, 100.

4. Barna, *State of Pastors*, 63.

5. Barna, *The State of Discipleship* (2015), 27.

6. Barna, *State of Discipleship*, 23.

7. Sixty-six percent of practicing Christians chose this option; Barna, *State of Pastors*, 27.

8. Stanley Hauerwas, *The Hauerwas Reader*, ed. John Berkman and Michael Cartwright (Durham, NC: Duke University Press, 2005), 148.

9. This retelling is by Hauerwas in *The Hauerwas Reader*, 257–58.

10. Hauerwas and Berkman, *The Hauerwas Reader*, 133.

11. Martin Luther King Jr., *Strength to Love* (Minneapolis: Fortress, 2010), 12.

12. Martin Luther King Jr., *A Testament of Hope*, ed. James Melvin Washington (New York: HarperCollins, 1986), 334.

13. King, *Testament of Hope*, 336.

14. King, *Testament of Hope*, 337.

15. King, *Testament of Hope*, 337.

16. Barna, *State of Discipleship*, 51.

17. Barna, *State of Discipleship*, 53.

18. Barna, *State of Discipleship*, 52.

19. Barna, *State of Discipleship*, 11.

20. Barna, *State of Discipleship*, 59.

21. Barna, *State of Discipleship*, 59.

22. Alan Kreider, *The Patient Ferment of the Early Church: The Improbable Rise of Christianity in the Roman Empire* (Grand Rapids: Baker Academic, 2016), 169.

23. Kreider, *Patient Ferment*, 133.

24. Kreider, *Patient Ferment*, 135.

25. See Larry Hurtado, *Destroyer of the Gods: Early Christian Distinctiveness in the Roman World* (Waco: Baylor University Press, 2016), 154.

26. *Epistle to Diognetus*, cited in Hurtado, *Destroyer of the Gods*, 153.

27. Kreider, *Patient Ferment*, 143.

28. Kreider, *Patient Ferment*, 156.

29. Kreider, *Patient Ferment*, 152.

30. Kreider, *Patient Ferment*, 169.

31. Kreider, *Patient Ferment*, 193.

32. Kreider, *Patient Ferment*, 193.

33. Kreider, *Patient Ferment*, 115.

34. Kreider, *Patient Ferment*, 116.

Chapter 8 Unity

1. Hurtado, *Destroyer of the Gods*, 47.
2. Hurtado, *Destroyer of the Gods*, 47.
3. Hurtado, *Destroyer of the Gods*, 48.
4. Hurtado, *Destroyer of the Gods*, 58.
5. Holland, *Dominion*, 87.
6. Holland, *Dominion*, 92.
7. J. Russell Hawkins and Phillip Luke Sinitiere, "Introduction," in *Christians and the Color Line: Race and Religion after* Divided By Faith, ed. J. Russell Hawkins and Phillip Luke Sinitiere (New York: Oxford University Press, 2014), 4.
8. Hawkins and Sinitiere, "Introduction," 4.
9. Michael O. Emerson and Christian Smith, *Divided by Faith: Evangelical Religion and the Problem of Race in America* (New York: Oxford University Press, 2000), 90–91.
10. Ryan J. Cobb, "Still Divided by Faith? Evangelical Religion and the Problem of Race in America, 1977–2010," in *Christians and the Color Line*, 129.
11. Cobb, "Still Divided by Faith?," 132–33.
12. Barna, "White Christians Have Become Even Less Motivated to Address Racial Injustice," September 15, 2020, https://www.barna.com/research/american -christians-race-problem/.
13. Barna, "White Christians Have Become Even Less Motivated."
14. Barna, "White Christians Have Become Even Less Motivated."
15. Erica Rya Wong, "Knotted Together: Identity and Community in a Multiracial Church," in *Christians and the Color Line*, 205.
16. Warren Bird and Scott Thumma, "Megachurch 2020: The Changing Reality in America's Largest Churches," Hartford Institute for Religion and Research, 4, http://hirr.hartsem.edu/megachurch/2020_Megachurch_Report.pdf.
17. Bird and Thumma, "Megachurch 2020," 4.
18. Korie L. Edwards, "Much Ado About Nothing?," in *Christians and the Color Line*, 241.
19. Edwards, "Much Ado About Nothing?," 250.
20. Andrew L. Whitehead and Samuel L. Perry, *Taking America Back for God: Christian Nationalism in the United States* (New York: Oxford University Press, 2020), 16.
21. Whitehead and Perry, *Taking America Back for God*, 16.
22. Whitehead and Perry, *Taking America Back for God*, ix–x.
23. Whitehead and Perry, *Taking America Back for God*, 164.
24. Whitehead and Perry, *Taking America Back for God*, 164.
25. Whitehead and Perry, *Taking America Back for God*, 23.
26. Whitehead and Perry, *Taking America Back for God*, 20, emphasis in original.
27. Whitehead and Perry, *Taking America Back for God*, 21.
28. Jonathan Sacks, *Morality* (New York: Basic Books, 2020), 262.
29. Compiled by Matthew Gordley, *New Testament Christological Hymns: Exploring Texts, Contexts, and Significance* (Downers Grove, IL: IVP Academic, 2018), 134.

30. Quoted in Gordley, *New Testament Christological Hymns*, 135.

31. The phrase is used by N. T. Wright in an interview, "God and the Pandemic: An Interview with N. T. Wright," Bible Gateway, June 3, 2020, https://www.biblegateway.com/blog/2020/06/god-and-the-pandemic-an-interview-with-n-t-wright/.

32. Sandra Maria Van Opstal, *The Next Worship: Glorifying God in a Diverse World* (Downers Grove, IL: InterVarsity, 2016), 74.

33. Rich Villodas, *The Deeply Formed Life: Five Transformative Values to Root Us in the Way of Jesus* (Colorado Springs: Waterbrook, 2020), 74.

34. Sourced from Jeffrey Kranz, "All the 'One Another' Commands in the NT [infographic]," March 9, 2014, OverviewBible, https://overviewbible.com/one-another-infographic/.

Chapter 9 Mission

1. PBS, "Interview: Mark Noll," *Frontline*, April 29, 2004, https://www.pbs.org/wgbh/pages/frontline/shows/jesus/interviews/noll.html.

2. Christopher J. H. Wright, *The Mission of God: Unlocking the Bible's Grand Narrative* (Downers Grove, IL: InterVarsity, 2018), 275.

3. Wright, *Mission of God*, 287.

4. Wright, *Mission of God*, 288.

5. Matthew W. Bates, *Gospel Allegiance: What Faith in Jesus Misses for Salvation in Christ* (Grand Rapids: Brazos, 2019), 228 (emphasis in original).

6. Bates, *Gospel Allegiance*, 228–29.

7. Holland, *Dominion*, 80.

8. Holland, *Dominion*, 81.

9. Holland, *Dominion*, 82.

10. Barna, *Spiritual Conversations in the Digital Age* (2018), 12.

11. Barna, *Spiritual Conversations*, 12.

12. Barna, *Spiritual Conversations*, 12.

13. Barna, *Reviving Evangelism* (2019), 10.

14. Barna, *Reviving Evangelism*, 10.

15. N. T. Wright, *For All God's Worth: True Worship and the Calling of the Church* (Grand Rapids: Eerdmans, 1997), 110.

16. Harriet Sherwood, "Archbishop of Canterbury Secretly Volunteering as Hospital Chaplain," *The Guardian*, May 13, 2020, https://www.theguardian.com/world/2020/may/13/archbishop-of-canterbury-justin-welby-secretly-volunteering-as-hospital-chaplain.

Chapter 10 The Collaborative Church

1. The phrase comes from the title of Scot McKnight's book on the church, *A Fellowship of Differents: Showing the World God's Design for Life Together* (Grand Rapids: Zondervan, 2014).

2. Walter Isaacson, *Steve Jobs: A Biography* (New York: Simon & Schuster, 2011), 408.

Chapter 11 The Presence and the Power

1. N. T. Wright uses this language of means and model in his book *Surprised by Hope: Rethinking Heaven, the Resurrection, and the Mission of the Church* (New York: HarperCollins, 2008), 149.

2. Jurgen Moltmann, *Theology of Hope*, trans. James W. Leitch (Minneapolis: Augsburg Fortress, 1993), 165.

3. See Prologue note 2.

4. Again, "coffee" is a metaphor here for all the good but secondary things we include in a church service. They are ornamental but not essential.

5. Ben Sixsmith, "The Sad Irony of Christian Celebrity," *The Spectator*, December 6, 2020, https://spectator.us/life/sad-irony-celebrity-pastors-carl-lentz-hillsong/.

6. Sixsmith, "The Sad Irony of Christian Celebrity."

7. James K. A. Smith, "Cracks in the Secular: Longing for 'Something More' in the Secular," *Comment*, September 1, 2014, https://www.cardus.ca/comment/article/cracks-in-the-secular/.

8. James K. A. Smith, *You Are What You Love: The Spiritual Power of Habit* (Grand Rapids: Brazos, 2016), 102.

9. It was created in 1977 as a course for new believers, but when Nicky Gumbel took it over in 1990, he reshaped it for the unchurched and the unbeliever.

10. The work of psychologist Charles Synder on the cognitive model of hope was a key part of my research.

11. Gordon D. Fee, *God's Empowering Presence: The Holy Spirit in the Letter's of Paul* (Grand Rapids: Baker Academic, 2012).

12. Chris Green (@cewgreen), Twitter thread, December 28, 2020, https://twitter.com/cewgreen/status/1343722515550646272.

13. Smith, *You Are What You Love*, 102.

Epilogue

1. Tolkien, *The Fellowship of the Ring* (Boston: Houghton Mifflin, 1991), 64.

2. Wikipedia, s.v. "Hull Minster," last modified May 10, 2021, https://en.wikipedia.org/wiki/Hull_Minster.

Glenn Packiam (DThM, Durham University) is associate senior pastor at New Life Church in Colorado Springs and lead pastor of one of its eight congregations, New Life Downtown. A senior fellow at Barna Group, a visiting fellow at St. John's College at Durham University, and an adjunct professor at Denver Seminary, Glenn is the author of several books, including *Blessed Broken Given* and *Worship and the World to Come*. He is also an ordained priest with the Anglican Church of North America, speaks regularly at conferences, and has appeared on numerous podcasts and radio shows. As one of the founding leaders and songwriters for the popular Desperation Band, he has also released three solo albums with Integrity Music and has written or cowritten nearly seventy worship songs. Glenn and his wife, Holly, live in the shadow of the Rocky Mountains with their four children. Learn more at glennpackiam.com.

Connect with Glenn

GLENNPACKIAM.COM

Returning to
What Matters Most

What is essential to your ministry? Follow along as we rediscover the things that every local church ministry needs to thrive.

Podcast
An ongoing conversation about the most important issues facing the local church today.

Learning Community
Visit Colorado each spring and fall and take part in the conversation.

Resources
Blogs, articles, and resources that will provide practical help for your ministry.

Coaching Network
For pastors looking for more focused help on either their own leadership or congregational issues.

Learn more at **THEESSENTIAL.CHURCH**

Connect with
BakerBooks
Relevant. Intelligent. Engaging.

Sign up for announcements about new and upcoming titles at

BakerBooks.com/SignUp

@ReadBakerBooks

Lightning Source UK Ltd.
Milton Keynes UK
UKHW022323170222
398852UK00006B/215